For my pal Tom Carson

Acknowledgements

I would like to thank my editors at Peachpit—Becky Morgan, Kristin Kalning, Judy Ziajka, and Liz Welch—and the rest of the super editorial and development team. Thanks to my family for their support, and to my agent, Matt Wagner, for keeping me on track.

A special thanks to Adobe for their input in my projects, and the opportunity to delve into the depths of my favorite piece of software. And finally, thanks as always to my musical muse, Tom Waits.

Adobe® Acrobat® 7
PS and TRICKS
E 150 BEST

Donna L. Baker

Adobe Press

Adobe Acrobat 7 Tips and Tricks
The 150 Best

Donna L. Baker

Adobe Press books are published by Peachpit
Peachpit
1249 Eighth Street
Berkeley, CA 94710
510/524-2178
800/283-9444
510/524-2221 (fax)

Peachpit is a division of Pearson Education

To report errors, please send a note to errata@peachpit.com

For the latest on Adobe books, go to www.adobepress.com

Editors: Kristin Kalning, Becky Morgan, Judy Ziajka
Production Editor: Becky Winter
Copyeditor: Liz Welch
Compositor: Danielle Foster
Indexer: Rebecca Plunkett
Cover design: Maureen Forys
Interior design: Maureen Forys

This book was designed and laid out in Adobe InDesign.

ISBN 0-321-30530-2

9 8 7 6 5 4 3 2 1

Printed and bound in the United States of America

Contents

CHAPTER ONE

Getting Started

Adobe Acrobat has become a workhorse program. Whether you are a graphic designer or a Web designer, whether you work with business systems or run a small office, Acrobat can assist you in a wide range of tasks, and it handles information and content in mind-boggling ways.

Acrobat isn't like "ordinary" software in that you can't define its purpose in a single word as you can with a spreadsheet, word processing, or image-manipulation program. It's not that simple.

Successful users of Acrobat understand both the program's capabilities and what Acrobat can do for them. For example, did you know that with Acrobat 7 Professional you can create a multimedia presentation? Or create a complex document that incorporates a range of other types of material such as spreadsheets or Web pages along with PDF files? Or test and evaluate the output of a document before sending it to your print provider? Or set up and monitor a system of reviewing your shared documents? Or add security to a document to control access and changes to the work? Or...?

Clearly the program's scope is wide, which is probably why Adobe describes it as a "tool for the new work."

In this book, I have assembled a collection of tips that will show you what Acrobat can do, and how you can integrate the power of the program into your daily work life. As you read the tips, consider how the information can help you do your job smarter and faster.

In this first chapter, you'll see what makes up the program's interface, learn how to look at your document, and find out some ways to make the program work for you.

What's Your Status?

You can navigate between pages using the navigation controls, or change the viewing layout. You can also choose a viewing method, such as full-screen. Special features of the document, such as layers or security, are indicated by icons at the left of the Status bar.

Getting Around the Interface

When you open Acrobat 7 Professional, the default program includes several elements (**Figure 1**). You can configure the Acrobat layout in a variety of ways by adjusting the panel groupings and settings.

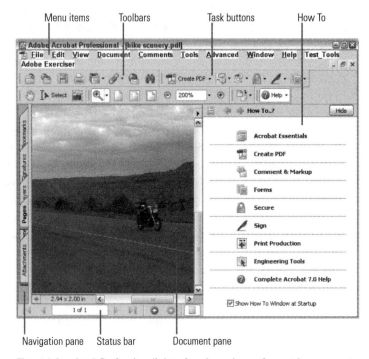

Figure 1 Acrobat 7 Professional's interface is made up of several components.

- **The Main menu.** The Main menu across the top of the program contains common headings like File and Edit, as well as Acrobat 7 Professional headings such as Advanced and Document.

- **Toolbars.** Acrobat contains a wide variety of toolbars; most items found in toolbars are available as menu commands as well. An icon with a pull-down arrow to the right indicates that a subtoolbar is available.

- **Task buttons.** You can access a variety of tasks and functions for a specific type of work such as creating a PDF or signing a document using the task buttons.

- **Navigation pane.** The tabs along the left side of the program window make up the Navigation pane. The options on these tabs let you manage and control the content of your PDF document.

- **Document pane.** An open PDF document displays in the Document pane. The document's page size and scroll bars frame the bottom and right side of the Document pane.

- **Status bar.** Below the Document pane you see the number of the visible page as well as the total page count and controls for moving between pages.

- **How To.** The How To pane, displayed at the right of the screen, contains links to common tasks as well as the program's complete Help files. You can increase the width of the pane from its default size, but you can't decrease it.

Look Before You Touch

You can modify the screen display—toolbars, Navigation pane tabs, and so on. But before you do, familiarize yourself with the contents. Click the pull-down arrows to see what's in a subtoolbar, for example. Click a tab in the Navigation pane to see its contents and click its Options menu to learn what you can do in the pane. Checking out Acrobat's default offerings may help you as you learn to work with the program.

TIP 2 Assistance, Please

The How To pane contains a list of the most common tasks you are likely to perform in Acrobat 7 (**Figure 2a**) and includes specific groupings of tools for special purposes such as examining and measuring engineering drawings and preparing a document for print production. For example, click Create PDF to open a list of topics. Follow these pointers to make your way through the How To topics:

Figure 2a Click one of the main topic areas in the How To pane to open a list of topics.

- A list of the main topics appears in the How To pane (**Figure 2b**). Click a link to the particular task you are trying to accomplish.

Figure 2b Each major task lists a number of topic choices. Click a link for more information or to open the complete Help file.

- Use the navigation buttons at the top of the How To pane to control your view. Clicking the active arrow (it is blue in the program) moves you back and forth through pages you have viewed.

- Instructions for performing the task or activity appear in the How To pane. Scroll down to read the entire list.

How To How To...

If you modify the toolbar layout, you probably won't include the How To toolbar. You can still access the contents using the Help menu. Click Help > How To and choose a topic title. The How To pane reopens, displaying the main topic area.

TIP 2: Assistance, Please

3 Helping Yourself

The How To pane is fine for step-by-step instructions on basic program functions and tasks. If you need more in-depth information, use the main Help feature:

- Choose Help > Complete Acrobat 7.0 Help or press the F1 key. The Help program opens in a separate window.

- Use the navigation options at the top left of the window to make your way through the file (**Figure 3a**). The blue left- and right-facing arrows take you back and forth between pages you've visited. Click the Printer icon to print the topic displayed in the main pane of the Help window. The plus (+) and minus (-) icons let you zoom in or zoom out of the document window.

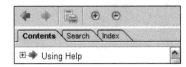

Figure 3a Use the navigation controls to make your way through the Help files.

- You can choose from three types of search options—Contents, Search, or Index—depending on what you are looking for and on your preferred method of working. You can choose from the Contents, Index, or Search tabs to locate information.

Help Is Close at Hand

Sometimes you need to refer to a page in the Help file over and over. Instead of closing the window and then reopening and finding the page again, minimize the window. The content stays as you last viewed it. If you need step-by-step direction, arrange both the program and Help windows on your screen.

The Help menu shows the Contents tab (**Figure 3b**) when it opens. The content is arranged in a hierarchy. Each + next to a topic means subtopics are available. Click + to open a nested item list. When a topic name displays a - sign, that means it has nested content that is already displayed. Click an item to display its contents in the main pane of the Help window.

Help Using Help

Pay attention to the way you work. If you are a very systematic person, the Contents tab will guide you from general to specific topics. Use the Search tab if you are familiar with the program and want to locate a specific topic. If you aren't sure what you are looking for, type a related term in the Index tab and watch the headings that display—you may find a heading triggers a mental connection to the precise topic you need.

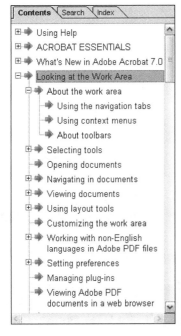

Figure 3b Specific topics are nested within larger topics in the left pane.

(Continued)

TIP 3: Helping Yourself

Click Search to open the Search tab. Type the search word and then click Search. The topics that contain the search term appear in the left pane of the Help window (**Figure 3c**) and the first entry containing the search term displays in the main pane of the Help window. Click a topic to display the content in the main pane; each instance of the search term is highlighted. If the highlighting is distracting, click the main pane of the Help window to deselect the highlights.

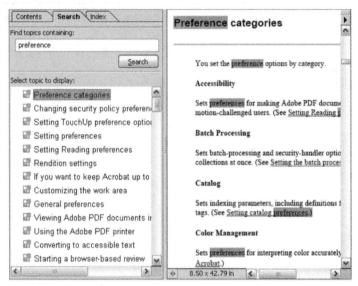

Figure 3c Searching for Help topics shows a list of matches as well as highlighted search terms.

Use the Index tab to access information by either entering a term in the field, which moves the topic list in the left pane to the matching topic title, or by scrolling through the list in the left pane to find a topic heading. Again, the content is listed in nested topics; click to display the topic's contents. Clicking a topic in the Index displays its contents in the main pane of the Help window.

TIP 4 Making Room on the Screen

One of the best ways to save space, and your eyesight, is to control what tools you display on the screen. It is possible to open enough toolbars to fill a good portion of the screen, leaving very little room for the actual document. These tips help you "unclutter" your screen:

- If you have opened a number of toolbars and want to return to the default set, choose View > Toolbars > Reset Toolbars. Acrobat closes the extras and the layout reverts to the default toolbars in the default locations.

- Even using only the default toolbars and task buttons, you may find it confusing to figure out what you have to work with. Move your pointer over the hatched vertical line at the left edge of a toolbar to display the toolbar's name (**Figure 4a**).

Figure 4a Display the name of a toolbar in a tip.

- Tool tips can show you task button names. If the button is large enough to display both the icon and text, you don't learn anything new. However, if you move your pointer over the icon, you see the task button's name (**Figure 4b**).

Figure 4b Display the name of a button in a tip.

- Move your pointer over the hatched vertical line and drag to pull a toolbar from its docked position. When you release the mouse, the toolbar is floating on the screen. Drag the toolbar back to the toolbar area and release the mouse to dock it again.

(Continued)

Button It Up

You can further control your use of screen real estate by setting how the labels are displayed. Choose View > Toolbars > Show Button Labels and then select the Default, All, or No button label options.

Locking Toolbars

When you close and reopen a program, the arrangement of toolbars and task buttons is maintained. If you like a particular arrangement of toolbars, you can lock it. When you get to the point when you are "one with the program," you can select tools and keep working without searching for a tool. Choose View > Toolbars > Lock Toolbars. The separator bars between the individual toolbars disappear. Floating toolbars don't lock, and they can't be docked with a locked toolbar.

- Task buttons work slightly differently. You can't drag an individual task button off the Task Bar (as you can with individual tools on toolbars); if you try, you'll remove the entire Task Button toolbar. Choose View > Task Buttons, and select or deselect the buttons as you require.

- Rather than using the Main menu, save one step when changing toolbars. Right-click or Control-click the toolbar to display the same options available from the Toolbars submenu (**Figure 4c**).

Figure 4c Use the shortcut menu to display many of the commands available from the View menu.

TIP 5   See What You Want to See

Acrobat offers the same sort of Zoom In and Zoom Out tool functionality as that in other Adobe products that you have grown to know and love; you can switch from one tool to the other by pressing the Control (Command) key with either the Zoom In or Zoom Out tools active.

Acrobat 7 offers more than that. You can use the Dynamic Zoom or Pan & Zoom feature (which works much like the Navigator feature in other Adobe programs), or you can use the Loupe tool to zero in on important information on a page.

Click the pull-down arrow to the right of the Zoom tool displayed on the Zoom toolbar to open the menu shown in **Figure 5a**. Select the tool you want to use for viewing the document. The selected tool is displayed on the Zoom toolbar.

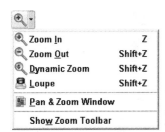

Figure 5a Choose from several specialized viewing tools from the Zoom submenu.

Tip
The Zoom tools are also available on the shortcut menu. Right-click or Control-click the document with the Hand tool to open the shortcut menu. Choose Zoom and select a tool.

Use the Dynamic Zoom tool 🔍 to quickly move the magnification higher and lower without having to use any keys or choose alternate zoom tools.

(Continued)

Outline Your Overlay

Change the color for both the Loupe and Pan & Zoom tools' outline rectangles to see the overlay on the document more clearly. In both windows, click the colored rectangle to open a Color Picker and select a different color.

Double Vision

You can use both the Pan & Zoom window and the Loupe tool at the same time. From the Zoom tool dropdown list, click the Pan & Zoom Window option to open the window, and use the Pan & Zoom controls to move around the window. If you want to see something close up, click the Loupe tool on the menu to select it and click the window with the tool for a closeup view.

Use the Loupe tool  to zero in on a specific region of the document without losing sight of the overall image or page. Click the document with the Loupe tool to activate a small window; this window shows the area identified by the rectangle on the Document pane (**Figure 5b**). You can drag the edges of the rectangle to change the content and magnification of the display; you can also click the + and - buttons or drag the slider below the magnified image shown in the Loupe tool's window.

Figure 5b Zoom in or out of a page to view content close up with the Loupe tool.

For a quick scan of a document's contents close up, click the Pan & Zoom Window option on the Zoom tool's pull-down menu. A small secondary window displays over the main program window (**Figure 5c**). Drag the Pan & Zoom box around the page to show you sections close up. Use the + and - buttons to change the magnification, type a value in the field, or drag the handles on the rectangle overlaying the image that identifies the area displayed in the Document pane. Use Pan & Zoom when you want to check several items in a multipage document; click the navigation control arrows below the thumbnail image to move forward and backward through your document.

Figure 5c The Pan & Zoom tool lets you check out different details on different pages in a document.

TIP
6 Work Those Windows

Acrobat provides several options for working with windows; some are used for specific purposes, while others are options you can choose depending on your preferred method of working.

Open several copies of the same document if you want to see multiple pages at the same time. Choose Window > New Window. Acrobat adds a number to the original document's name, e.g., MyDog is renamed MyDog:1; each time you add a new window a number is appended incrementally, such as MyDog:2 and MyDog:3. For each copy of the document, use the controls at the bottom of the Document pane to show a different page of the document. The Window > Tile options let you arrange the windows for easy viewing. When you close copies, the remaining copies are renumbered; when only the original remains, the document's name loses its appended number (I wonder if that would hurt?) and the name is restored.

Choose Window > Split to divide the program window into two equal displays, both of which show the active document. You can use the Zoom tools on each individual display, giving you different views of the same content.

Choose Window > Spreadsheet View. The window is automatically split into four sections (**Figure 6**). You can drag the content in each view in any direction with the Hand tool. This view is handy for comparing multiple columns of information.

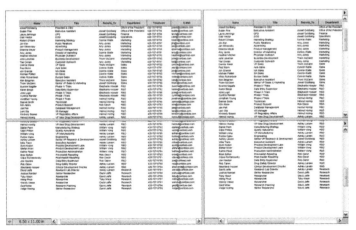

Figure 6 Use the Spreadsheet view to display segments of a page that can be moved independently.

Choose Window > Remove Split to restore the single Document pane.

Laying Tile

When you use the Add Window command each copy is sized the same as the original. Then you can use the Tile commands to arrange the windows in the Acrobat program window. Depending on the size of the original window, use either Horizontal or Vertical tiles.

If you decrease the size of the Acrobat program window, the tiled copies along the edges you resized are cut off. Choose Window > Tile and the vertical or horizontal tiling option again to resize the windows to fit the new program window's size.

TIP 7 What Do You Prefer?

You can define a number of preferences that help you get to work faster. Some preferences get you into the program faster; others show you what you are working with more quickly.

Choose Edit > Preferences (Acrobat > Preferences) to open the Preferences dialog. You see a long list of options in the left pane of the dialog; clicking an option displays a range of settings in the right pane of the dialog. Click Startup in the list at the left of the Preferences dialog to display the Startup options in the right pane of the dialog (**Figure 7a**). The Opening Documents preferences are listed at the top of the window.

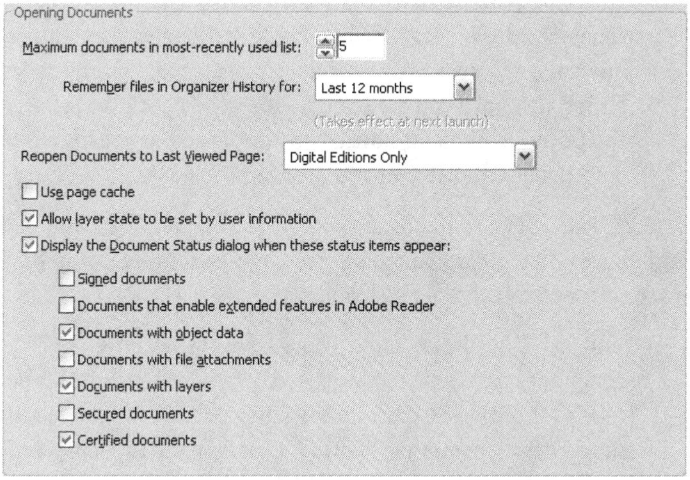

Figure 7a Customize the Startup preferences to change how the program starts and runs.

- If you work with more than five documents on a regular basis, change the value shown in the Maximum documents in most-recently used list from its default of 5. When you click the File menu heading, you see the list at the bottom of the menu and can quickly select the document you want to open.

(Continued)

Settings for All Seasons

The settings you choose are not specific to a particular document but apply to the program in general. Each time you open Acrobat 7, the program uses your preferences until you change them again.

Settings you choose in the program can also apply to the Help menu. For example, if you deselect text smoothing in the program preferences, the text in the Help menu is also affected.

- See the control Reopen Documents to Last Viewed Page. The default setting is Digital Editions, which means that only digital media (formerly known as eBooks) reopens at the page last displayed in the document. Click the pull-down arrow and choose the Marked Files and Digital Editions Only option when working with a number of documents containing comments; select All Files when you are working in long sessions with multiple files. As you open closed documents, you are automatically shown the last location you viewed in the open document.

Tip
The display feature works only during a single session; if you close and then reopen Acrobat 7, and then the document, it displays according to its document settings, usually showing the top of the first page.

- Click Use page cache (it is deselected by default). The page cache is a buffer area. If you cache the pages, as you display one page the next page in a document is read and placed in a buffer area until you are ready to view it. Pages load faster, and the faster load time is particularly noticeable if you are working with image-intensive or interactive documents.

Click Page Display in the options listed in the left pane of the Preferences dialog. You can set some page preferences to get up to working speed faster:

- Deselect the Display large images option (**Figure 7b**) if your computer has a slow redraw speed. On older computers, images take a lot of time to draw on the screen. Each time you move the image means more time waiting for the image to redraw again.

Page Display

Default Page Layout: Automatic

☐ Display art, trim, bleed boxes
☑ Display large images
☐ Display page to edge
☐ Display transparency grid
☑ Use logical page numbers
☐ Use CoolType (Recommended for laptop/LCD screens)
☐ Overprint Preview
☑ Smooth text ☑ Smooth line art ☑ Smooth images
☑ Use greek text below 6 pixels

Resolution

◉ Use system setting Current Display: 96 Pixels/Inch
○ Custom resolution: 72 Pixels/Inch

Figure 7b Changing some Page Display settings can change how quickly your documents are displayed.

- Deselect the smoothing preferences—text, line art, and images—if your computer is particularly slow. Deselecting the smoothing may save some time in displaying your documents, although you sacrifice some of the clarity and crispness of the content for display speed.

- Click the Use greek text below xx pixels option to make the text on a page smaller than the value specified (the default value is 8 pixels) appear as gray lines (**Figure 7c**). Selecting this option speeds up redraw time as well.

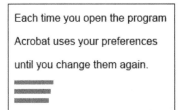

Each time you open the program
Acrobat uses your preferences
until you change them again.

Figure 7c Substitute gray lines for very small text to display pages more quickly.

(Continued)

TIP 7: What Do You Prefer?

Set Your Autosave

Click the automatically save document changes to temporary file field to set the autosave time. By default, Acrobat saves document changes every five minutes. If you are working on a very large document, the autosave can take some time away from your work; you may want to increase the duration between autosaves.

• Click General in the Preferences dialog's left pane to show the General preferences (**Figure 7d**). Look for these settings in the miscellaneous section of the dialog's pane.

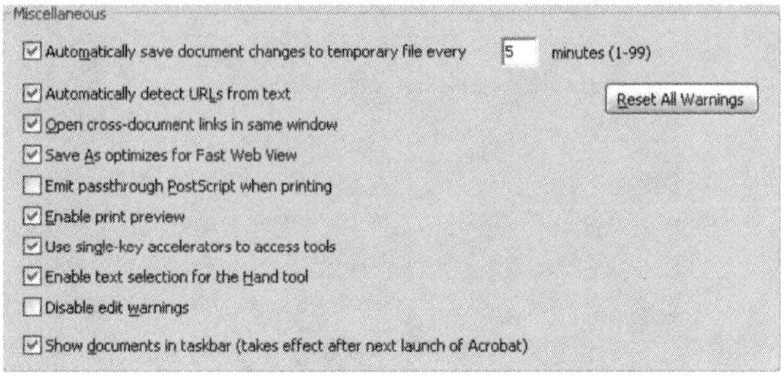

Figure 8d Change how often Acrobat saves your document, and how you access open documents using General preferences.

• Click Show documents in taskbar to display a button for each open document on the Windows taskbar. This way you don't have to open Acrobat's Window menu to select an open document.

When you have completed setting and changing preferences, click OK to close the Preferences dialog and apply your settings.

CHAPTER TWO

Organizing, Searching, and Cataloging

One of Acrobat's strongest features is its ability to help you manage your documents. New in Acrobat 7 is the Organizer, a separate window used to organize, sort, and filter the PDF files in your computer. You can organize the files in a number of ways based on date, location, and other characteristics. You can also define a number of characteristics for the files that you can in turn use for searching and organizing.

As if organizing weren't enough, you can also assemble collections of your PDF documents. You'll learn some tips about collections in this chapter.

Searching PDF documents is an amazing way to draw common concepts and terms from a broad range of documents. See how to save time and zero in on what you need to find. You can use different tools of varying complexity for your searching, ranging from a simple toolbar to a full-blown index.

Aside from the generic searching you can do with any sorts of PDF documents, you can also assemble a collection and index it to create a formal catalog. Cataloging is the best way to control large quantities of information across collections of documents. You can make document collections comply with a global standard called PDF/A, which defines how images, fonts, and other characteristics must be used in documents for long-term storage.

TIP 8 Getting Organized

Acrobat 7 contains a nifty new feature called the Organizer. Use the Organizer to—you guessed it—organize your PDF files. Click the Organizer button on the File toolbar or choose File > Organizer > Open Organizer.

The Organizer opens in a separate window and displays three frames (**Figure 8**). You can drag the splitter bars between the frames to resize each frame as you are working. Click an option in the Categories pane to display its list of PDF files in the Files pane; click a file in the Files pane to display its content in the Pages pane.

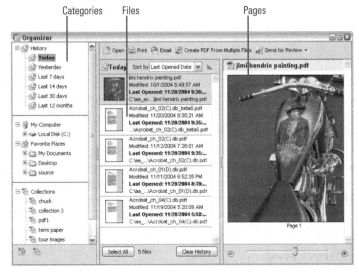

Figure 8 Organize and control your PDF files using the Organizer.

The Categories pane uses a hierarchy of folders. There are three types of categories: History, your computer's folders (to which you can add favorites), and Collections.

- History works like the History function on your Web browser. Select a time frame from the History listing to show the PDF files you have opened during that time frame in the Files pane. To clear the history, select the item in the History listing and click the Clear History button at the bottom of the Files pane.

- To add a Favorite Place ⊞, click Add a Favorite Place at the bottom of the Organizer Window. Locate the folder you want to add in the resulting dialog, and click OK. You'll see that your selected folder has been added to the Favorite Places list.

- To add a collection, right-click/Control-click the Collections label ⊞ and follow the prompts to name the collection and add files. Right-click/Control-click an existing collection to add or delete files.

In the Files pane, information displayed about each listed document includes basic information. An unprotected document shows a thumbnail; a document containing security shows only a PDF document icon. The default listing is by filename; you can click the pull-down arrow to choose other sorting options such as keywords, the document's title, or the author.

The file selected in the Files pane is shown in the Pages pane. Use the - and + buttons to change the magnification of the view, or drag the slider to show the file's content. Scroll bars display when the view is magnified if the document contains several pages, or if you have selected more than one document in the Files pane.

TIP 9 Staying Organized

When you have organized your files, you can access your documents from the program's interface rather than reopening the window.

Regardless of where you access the Organizer's information, here are a few tips to help you stay organized:

- Take care when clearing the History. If you choose a History setting such as Last 12 Months or Last Week, all history listings of shorter duration, such as Today or Yesterday, are also cleared.

- Name your collections to keep track of your work.

- Delete a collection when you have finished working on a project. You can always rebuild a collection if need be.

- Organizing content into collections makes it easier to access your working documents from the main program window. Click the pull-down arrow to the right of the Organizer button on the File menu to open a menu; click Collections, then the name of the collection, and the file you want to use (**Figure 9**).

Figure 9 Select files from your collections from the pull-down menus.

- Ditto for the History, also available from the Organizer button's pull-down menu. The History listing uses the same set of time frames as listed in the Organizer window.

- Choose File > Organizer > Collections to access your collections' contents from the main program menu.

- The History contents are also available in the File menu. Choose File > History and one of the date options. The History command is conveniently listed above the last documents opened in the File menu.

TIP 10 Finding Words

One feature we all use at one time or another is the dependable Search function. Acrobat 7 offers two ways to do a search—either through a Find toolbar or using the Search pane.

New in Acrobat 7 is the Find toolbar (**Figure 10**). Use it to quickly search an open document. To access the toolbar, use the Ctrl+F/Command+F shortcut keys; choose View > Toolbars > Find; or choose Edit > Find.

Widening Your Search

If you need to expand the search to additional documents or want to use more complex search terms, select Open Full Acrobat Search from the pull-down menu.

Figure 10 Use the Find toolbar to locate words or phrases in an open document.

Type in the field the word or phrase you want to search for, and then click Find Next to show the first match on the visible page. Each time you click the button, the next match is highlighted in the document. Use the Find Next or Find Previous button to move back and forth among matches.

Here are some hints for using the Find toolbar:

- The hits include hyphenated returns—for example a search for the term "book-mark" is returned as a hit for the term "bookmark."

- Use the scroll bars or the navigation controls at the bottom of the Document pane to move to another location in a document. When you click the Previous or Next button on the Find toolbar, the search starts at the visible page.

- Click the pull-down arrow next to the Find label to open a menu that allows you to choose search parameters. For example, if you are looking for a term such as Bookmarks, if you choose the case sensitive option, only those matches using the same capitalization are identified.

- Click to select any combination of the search criteria from the pull-down menu.

TIP 10: Finding Words

TIP 11 Conducting Searches

The Find toolbar works well for searching a single document, but if you need to track down words or phrases through all the PDF files in a folder, another drive, or even on the Internet, use the Search function. Click the Search button on the File toolbar  choose Edit > Search or use the Shift+Ctrl+ F/Shift+Command+F shortcut keys to open the Search pane at the right of the Document pane (**Figure 11a**).

Zeroing In on Your Searches

Use the customization options when possible to cut down on the number of search hits. The Case-Sensitive option can be used with a string of text. For example, "Rock and Roll" returns only those files containing the exact words in that exact sequence with the same capitalization. Searching for "rock" returns the text, but can also return hits for "rockabilly."

Just a warning, though—searching for "Rock And Roll" (with an uppercase A in "And") provides no returns if your document uses a lowercase "and."

Figure 11a The Search pane offers a number of ways to search for documents.

Type the word or words you want to find in the first field. You can't search using wildcards such as (*) or (?). Next select the file or folder you want to search. Click the first radio button to search the currently active file; click the second radio button to search in multiple files. Then, click the pull-down arrow and select the folder and drive location.

Choose search options by clicking the check boxes. Click to select whole words, or case-sensitive results, and to search in bookmarks and comments as well as document text.

Click Search. When the search is finished, the results and their locations appear by filename in the Search PDF Results pane (**Figure 11b**).

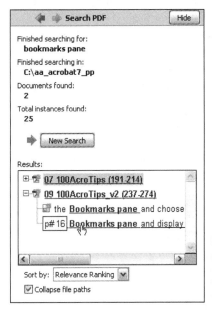

Figure 11b Acrobat displays the results of your search in a list. Choose an entry from the list to load the document and view the highlighted terms.

Taking a Shortcut

Shortcut keys allow you to work quickly through a long list of search results. In Windows, open the first document, and then press F3 to jump to the next and subsequent hits. Press Ctrl+] to go to the next document; press Ctrl+[to go to the previous document. In a document, press Ctrl+G to go to the next result; press Ctrl+Shift+G to go to the previous result.

You can see the number of instances of the word occurring in the set of files you searched, along with the number of documents containing the word. Click the box to the left of the file path to open a list of the results' locations and then mouse over a result listing to display the document page number.

Click a result in the Search PDF Results pane. Acrobat obligingly loads the document you selected (if it is not already displayed in the Document pane) and highlights the term on the document for you.

Sorting by filename isn't the only way to view results. To reorder the results, click the pull-down arrow below the Search PDF Results area and choose a Sort by method. You can choose from modification date, location, and relevance ranking.

TIP 11: Conducting Searches

Searching for PDF Files on the Internet

With one mouse click, Acrobat can take the hassle out of searching for a PDF file on the Internet. Click Search the internet using Yahoo (or Google, depending on the preference you choose) from the Search pane's list of options shown in Figure 11a.

If you don't have the Search pane displayed, click Search the Internet [YM] on the Search the Internet toolbar to open the Search pane, ready for an Internet search. Right-click/Control-click the toolbar well to display the toolbar list, and click Search the Internet to open the toolbar. Type the terms you wish to search, and define how precise you want the search to be (**Figure 12**). Click the pull-down arrow and specify whether you want to search for all the words, for the exact phrase, or for any of the words. You can narrow your search to only PDF documents by clicking Search only in PDF Files.

Figure 12 Use the Internet search feature to save lots of time searching for PDF files online.

Click Search the Internet to start your search. Your browser opens to Yahoo (or Google if you've changed your default search engine) with the results displayed in a list. When you click a result, the PDF document opens in Adobe Reader within your Web browser. Close the browser to terminate the search.

If you want to search locally, click Search Across Local PDF documents to return to the basic Search pane. You have to close the Web browser window manually.

Start Your Engine

The default search engine in Acrobat is Yahoo. If you are a Google person, you can choose Google as your default search engine in Acrobat. Choose Edit > Preferences or Acrobat > Preferences, and click Search in the left pane of the dialog to display the Search preferences. Click the Search provider for searching PDFs on the Internet pull-down arrow and choose Google. Click OK to close the preferences. The Search toolbar displays the Google icon [Google], and it is shown as the search engine on the Search pane.

Multiple Searches

When you are on a quest for information, you might need to do several searches in a row. After you have done more than one search, notice that the blue left and right arrows at the top of the Search pane are activated; click an arrow to move backward and forward through the searches you have carried out. You can hide the Search pane, but as long as you haven't closed and reopened Acrobat, the searches are still available.

Organizing, Searching, and Cataloging

TIP 13 Advanced Search Techniques

You can fine-tune a search using the Advanced Search options, or search for content such as keywords or metadata. Click the Use Advanced Search Options link at the bottom of the basic Search pane (shown earlier in Figure 11a) to display additional searching parameters.

To search the text in the document, you can choose from matching the exact phrase, or some of the words, or you can use a Boolean query.

Fewer search options are available if you are searching one document than if you are searching multiple documents. **Figure 13** shows the Search pane for a search done on a folder, and the search is based on keywords rather than text in the document. You can use up to three additional search parameters.

Figure 13 Use Advanced Search features for pinpointing precise results or searching for content other than text.

Use the pull-down menus below the "Use these additional criteria" label. Click the left pull-down menu to display a list of options, as shown in the figure. Select the search option you desire, and then click the right pull-down arrow and select a modifier. Finally, type the search term in the field, such as the keyword you wish to search for. A green checkmark displays in the check box to the left of the criteria's fields.

Click the Search button to search the document properties for the files in the selected folder. Acrobat returns results that contain *all* additional search criteria only. You can remove criteria by clicking the green checkmark to deselect it.

(Continued)

TIP 13: Advanced Search Techniques

Saving Searching Time Using Preferences

You can spend a lot of time sifting through documents, and in some cases, such as building an annual report, you may have to repeat searches several times. Save yourself time and headaches by setting Search Preferences:

- If your documents contain diacritics or accents, be sure to check the Ignore Diacritics and Accents option. That way if your work includes both premiere and première, for example, you can find both terms.

- Select the Always use advanced search option if you are likely to do only complex searches to save a couple of mouse clicks expanding the options in the Search pane.

- When searching enormous collections, set the preference for the Maximum number of returned documents. The default is 100; set it higher if necessary, but remember that searching so many documents will require more processing time.

- If you use Proximity searching a lot, modify the preference. The range of words for Proximity searches is 900; tinker with the value according to the contents of your documents. Proximity searching is an advanced search technique used with multiple documents or indexes, and needs the Match Exact word or phrase option selected from the Return results containing pull-down arrow on the Advanced Search pane. Type two or more words to search for in the documents. Any occurrence of the search terms within 900 words of each other are returned.

- Use the Fast Find preference to cache the returns from your searches. You can specify the size of the cache, which defaults at 20 MB. Be sure to clear the cache when you have finished a big project to save processing time.

TIP 14 Using Custom Search and Category Options

Beyond regular text searches, Acrobat offers other ways for you to organize, search, and catalog the PDF documents you work with. For example, in an enterprise environment, searching for a document author's name may be useful. Searching PDF photos using metadata, the data stored within the images such as camera settings or edit history, may get you results quicker (**Figure 14a**).

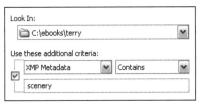

Figure 14a You can search using metadata added to the source files, such as Photoshop XMP data.

When you create a PDF, technical data that is part of the source document is converted along with the text and images you see on the page. You can also add many types of data from within Acrobat by modifying the Document Properties.

(Continued)

Properties in Windows

If you are working in Windows, you can right-click the name of the file from the desktop or Windows Explorer and select Properties from the shortcut menu. Add properties and custom values as desired. When you open the PDF in Acrobat, the properties are included.

Develop a System

If you are working with hundreds of documents or PDF images, developing a system before embarking on a document properties adventure is the smart thing to do. Decide if a term is used as a subject or a keyword, not both. If you search using a subject term and have used it as a keyword in some documents, your search results are limited.

If you want to use an author's name, decide beforehand if the first name, first name and initial, or full name of the author is to be used. This way, anyone working with the files understands your properties system. Unless you create a naming and description system that is understandable to all using the documents, it's a waste of time to make the effort to include additional descriptions.

Open the document you want to alter, and then choose File > Document Properties, or use the shortcut Ctrl+D (Command+D) (**Figure 14b**).

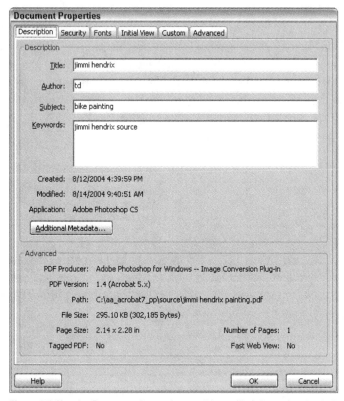

Figure 14b Use the Document Properties to add specific information that helps you organize large numbers of files.

Enter the additional information you want to use for searching and organizing in the appropriate fields. If you are working with images, clicking the Additional Metadata button opens the Document Metadata for [filename] dialog to add further information about the image.

Click OK to close the Document Properties dialog. Save the document to save the information you added in the dialog.

Now you can search, organize, and catalog using the additional terms.

TIP 15 Designing an Index

The Acrobat Search function is a highly developed tool and very useful for general searches. However, if you are working with hundreds of documents, building an index and including it with the documents it indexes will make searching much quicker. You can build indexes in Acrobat that work in much the same way as a book's index, although their functions are much more advanced than a paper index.

Here are some tips for preparing documents for indexing:

- Move or copy the files you want to use into a separate folder. Acrobat adds indexing files and folders (**Figure 15**). Keeping everything all in one place prevents indexing errors.

Name ▲	Size	Type
tips1_5		File Folder
01_tips.pdf	1,683 KB	Adobe Acrobat 7.0 Document
02_tips.pdf	4,438 KB	Adobe Acrobat 7.0 Document
03_tips.pdf	2,520 KB	Adobe Acrobat 7.0 Document
04_tips.pdf	2,079 KB	Adobe Acrobat 7.0 Document
05_tips.pdf	3,458 KB	Adobe Acrobat 7.0 Document
tips1_5.log	0 KB	Text Document
tips1_5.pdx	1 KB	Adobe Acrobat Catalog Index

Figure 15 Move the documents used in an index into a separate folder for safekeeping.

- Make sure all the information required in the individual documents is complete. This includes bookmarks, links, special document properties such as keywords, and so on. If you later add additional information to a document, it won't be included in the index.

- Break a large document into chunks. For example, create PDF files from individual chapters of a manual. The indexed searches will be faster.

- Be careful with the filenames if you intend the information to be used cross-platform. There are numerous naming issues and conventions to consider based on naming conventions—Mac versus PC naming, networking, and the like. The simplest solution is to use short names with no spaces.

Add a Helping Hand

If you are designing a number of document collections, include a Readme text file so your users understand what they can search for and how to use the index.

The PDF/A Standard

PDF/A, a standard for archiving documents in Acrobat, is designed to ensure the content in multipage documents is preserved and available.

To comply with the PDF/A standard, the document:

- Can include only text, raster images, and vector objects
- Can't include scripts
- Must have all fonts embedded
- Can't contain security options such as passwords or other types of encryption

TIP 16
Building and Applying an Index

Assembling material for an index takes more time than generating the index itself. Assemble and prepare the documents you want to use (see Tip 15), and then choose Advanced > Catalog to open the Catalog dialog.

Click New Index and add information to the dialog box to name and describe the index, and define the folders you want to include (as well as any subfolders you want to exclude).

Click Options to display ways to either add or remove content from the index in the Options dialog (**Figure 16a**). Consider using stop words—words that are excluded from the index, such as *and*, *if*, *or*, and so on by clicking Stop Words on the Options dialog to open a Stop Words dialog, also shown in Figure 16a. You can exclude up to 500 case-sensitive words, which can result in faster search returns. In the Options dialog you can click Do not include numbers to exclude numbers from your index.

If you use stop words in an index, or any other sort of custom option, include details in the index's Readme file so your index users can work with the index more effectively. When you use stop words, the index user can't search for "around the house", for example, if "the" has been excluded.

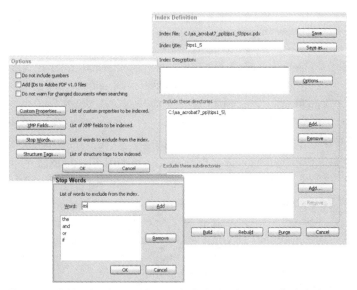

Figure 16a Add optional parameters to the index; make sure to include these options in your index's Readme file.

When you have finished making your selections, click Close to dismiss the Options dialog and then click the Build button in the Index Definition dialog. The Index Definition dialog closes, and results appear in the Build dialog. Click Close to dismiss the Build dialog. Several files are added to the index's folder, including a log file and the index.pdx file, which is the index's database file. There is also an additional folder containing two more indexing files. Don't delete or move any of the indexing folders or files, or you will corrupt the index.

To see your index in action, click Search to open the Search pane. Click Use Advanced Search Options and choose Select Index from the Look in pull-down list. The Index selection dialog opens (**Figure 16b**). Select the index from the list. Click Add if you want to use other indexes from your computer as well. Click OK to close the dialog and attach the index or indexes to your PDF.

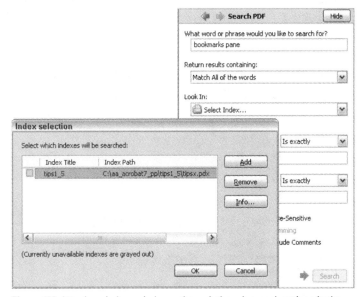

Figure 16b Attach an index or indexes through the advanced settings in the Search pane.

TIP 16: Building and Applying an Index

TIP 17 Archiving Outlook Messages

Acrobat 7 lets you archive your Outlook email messages, which you can then index and search or add to other PDF documents. There are two ways to archive your email messages. You can create a PDF file from a single email message and add to it, or you can select a folder of messages and create a PDF document from its contents.

To start an archive, select the first email in Outlook list and then click Create PDF From Selected Messages ![icon]. The Save Adobe PDF File As dialog opens. Browse to the location where you want to save the file. Type a name for the file, and click Save. You can add a file to an existing archived message as well. Select the file you want to add from the Outlook messages and then click Convert and append selected messages to an existing Adobe PDF. ![icon] Again the Save Adobe PDF File As dialog opens. Select the file you want to add the additional document to. Click Open to close the Save As dialog box; the file is processed and added to the selected PDF file.

Finally, you can create a PDF document from an existing Outlook folder. Select the folder and then click Convert selected folder to Adobe PDF. Type a name and choose a location for the archive PDF in the Save Adobe PDF File As dialog. Click Save to save the file.

In Acrobat, a number of bookmarks are added to the file (**Figure 17**). You can locate the contents of the archive based on sender, date, or subject.

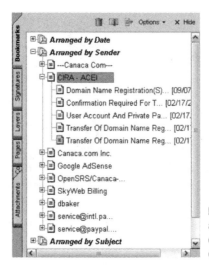

Figure 17 The default email archive process includes a set of bookmarks to locate individual emails quickly.

Organizing, Searching, and Cataloging

CHAPTER THREE

Creating PDF Files Outside Acrobat

There are many ways you can create a PDF file from within other applications, and these capabilities have expanded with each revision of Acrobat. After you install Acrobat, you find new menus and toolbars in most Microsoft Office programs, such as Word, Excel, PowerPoint, and Outlook. The menus and toolbar make up PDFMaker 7, which you use to configure settings and create PDF content right from your Office program. Other programs, such as those in Adobe Creative Suite, contain internal commands and settings for generating PDF files.

Acrobat also installs the Adobe PDF printer driver, which lets you print PDF documents from many programs, as well as Adobe Distiller, a program that converts PostScript or Encapsulated PostScript (EPS) files, such as those created in Illustrator, to PDF format.

Conversions can be controlled by PDFMaker settings, by Acrobat Distiller, and by source programs that export PDF-formatted files directly. You'll learn how to configure conversion settings according to the material you are working with—and according to what you intend to do with it. You prepare information for print use, for example, differently than you prepare information for online use. You have a lot of choices!

TIP 18 Creating PDF Files from Source Programs

PDFMaker is a set of tools that Acrobat installs into Microsoft Office programs in addition to a main menu item called Adobe PDF. The contents of the Adobe PDF menu vary according to the program, but typically the menu offers the commands Convert to Adobe PDF, Convert to Adobe PDF and Email, Convert to Adobe PDF and Send for Review, and Change Conversion Settings (**Figure 18**). Installation of PDFMaker in Office XP for Mac doesn't include the Convert to Adobe PDF or Send for Review options.

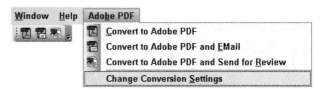

Figure 18 The PDFMaker 7.0 toolbar and menu heading are installed into Microsoft Office programs automatically.

The four basic types of PDF conversion that you use for most circumstances can be chosen through Acrobat Distiller or from a PDFMaker's Conversion Settings dialog:

- Standard—The default set used for basic business document conversion and viewing. Standard settings use a printing resolution of 600 dpi.

- High Quality Print—Used for high-quality output; prints to a higher image resolution but includes only a limited amount of coded information about the document's fonts. High Quality Print sets the printing resolution to 2400 dpi.

- Press—Used for high-end print production, such as image setters, and prints at a high resolution. All the information possible is added to the file. This setting includes all coded information about the fonts used in the document.

- Smallest File Size—Creates the smallest file size possible; used for distributing content for the Web, email, or onscreen viewing. Images are compressed and their resolution is decreased. Fonts are not embedded.

Easy Loading

In earlier versions of Acrobat, if you installed an Office program that used PDFMaker after Acrobat was already installed, you had to reinstall Acrobat to add PDF-Maker to the Office program. The sequence in which you load programs doesn't matter in Acrobat 7. If you install an Office program after Acrobat has already been installed in your system, choose Help > Detect and Repair from the Acrobat menu. Acrobat finds the Office program sans PDFMaker and automatically installs it for you.

Before you convert a document to PDF format, be sure to:

- Check spelling and grammar, and make sure the finished content is how you want it to appear in the PDF format. Although you can certainly edit content in Acrobat, it is much simpler to ensure that the original document is complete.

- Decide how the document is to be used. You choose different conversion settings for an online document, for example, than for one intended for high-quality printing.

- Check links and other hidden content such as comments if you plan to convert them for PDF use.

- Check the conversion option's settings. For example, you may choose a Standard conversion option but require changes in the graphic conversion settings.

Several other options are available for converting documents according to PDF standards both for printing and archiving:

- PDF/A archival standard—Used for documents intended for long-term storage and use. (See Tip 15 in Chapter 2 for information on the PDF/A standard).

- PDF/X standard—The PDF conversion settings include four PDF/X standards versions. These files are intended for high-resolution print production. You can't produce a standards-compliant PDF/X document using PDFMaker. (Read Tips 52 and 53 in Chapter 6 for more on these standards.)

Converting a Group of Documents

If you are converting a large number of documents, convert one and check that it meets your needs before converting the others. This will save you valuable error-checking time.

TIP 18: Creating PDF Files from Source Programs

TIP
19 Printing with the Adobe PDF Printer

If you can print a file in a program, you can usually generate a PDF file. The key is the printer driver called Adobe PDF, named Adobe PDF 7.0 in Mac OS. You don't have to install the driver independently; it is included as part of the Acrobat 7 installation process.

To create a PDF file from a source program, open your program and the document you want to convert to a PDF. Choose File > Print to open the Print dialog box. Click the pull-down arrow and choose Adobe PDF from the printer list (**Figure 19a**).

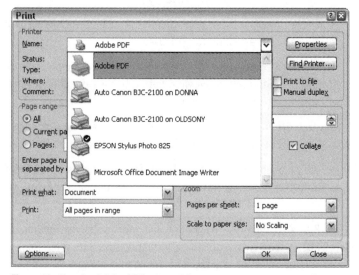

Figure 19a Use the Adobe PDF printer driver to convert many types of documents to PDF format.

You can select from a number of options for printing from the Print what pull-down list at the lower left of the dialog. Printing choices include the entire document, of course, or you can specify components such as document properties, markups (for reviewing), or styles.

Click OK to process the file, choose a name and storage location depending on the program's print command process, and click Save. The file saves to PDF, rather than to your printer, and you have a PDF version of the source file.

Click Options at the bottom of the Print dialog to open a secondary Print dialog. Here you can choose additional print options, such as draft printing or printing PostScript over text. You can choose to include content such as document properties or XML tags. If your document is a form, you can even select an option to print the form content only. Click OK to dismiss the secondary Print dialog; you return to the main Print dialog.

You can modify preferences and settings for the Adobe PDF printer driver. In the Print dialog, click Properties to open the Adobe PDF Document Properties dialog. Choose default conversion settings (**Figure 19b** shows the Standard selection), security, an output folder, and a page size.

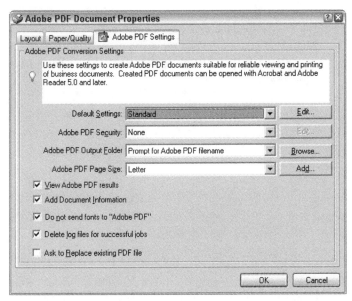

Figure 19b You can configure settings for the Adobe PDF printer driver in the dialog accessed from the main Print dialog.

(Continued)

TIP 19: Printing with the Adobe PDF Printer

Save yourself some time and future problems by reviewing the check boxes at the lower part of the dialog:

- If you are printing to save the document for future use, deselect View Adobe PDF results to prevent the file from opening in Acrobat.

- Leave the Add Document Information option selected; the information can be later used in Acrobat for searching, indexing, and identification.

- Deselect the Do not send fonts to "Adobe PDF" if you are planning to use the document later in Acrobat or in Acrobat Distiller. Distiller requires embedded fonts, and you often use font embedding to prepare a document for distribution.

- Leave the Delete log files for successful jobs option selected. You don't need to troubleshoot a document that converts successfully.

- The Ask to Replace existing PDF file option is deselected by default. If you are indeed replacing an existing file, the Save As dialog asks you about replacement, so you don't have to duplicate the function.

TIP 20 Using PDFMaker in Word

One of the most common programs used in conjunction with Acrobat is Microsoft Word. You can use the PDFMaker that Acrobat automatically installs into Word to quickly generate a PDF version of the document.

The Standard conversion setting, the default used by PDFMaker, produces a PDF file that is both suitable for printing and small enough for easy distribution. Once you specify the settings, they remain until you adjust them again. Converting a Word document to a PDF is a one-click process.

When your document is ready for conversion, save it and then click Convert to PDF on the PDFMaker 7.0 toolbar 📷 or choose Adobe PDF > Convert to Adobe PDF. Using the default PDFMaker settings, a Save As dialog opens displaying the same name as your Word document; change the file's name and location if necessary and then click Save to close the dialog and convert the file.

To view the settings, choose Adobe PDF > Change Conversion Settings to open the dialog (**Figure 20**).

Figure 20 Choose the basic conversion settings from the Conversion dialog.

(Continued)

Converting Word Files Using Mac OS X

When you install Acrobat 7 on a Mac on which Microsoft Office with SR1, SR2, or SR3 is running, you'll find a two-button toolbar added to Word, consisting of the Convert to PDF and Convert to PDF and Email icons.

The Convert to PDF icons launch Distiller and let you define conversion settings, unlike when you're working in Windows, where PDF-Maker maintains the settings within the Office program.

Choose the conversion settings you want to use; the options include Standard, Press Quality, High Quality Print, and Smallest File Size in addition to the options used for standards-compliant versions.

What's the Use?

Select or deselect the Application Settings depending on the intended use of the document. If your document contains links that you would like to convert with the document, for example, make sure the Add Links to Adobe PDF option is selected. You can also attach the original document to the converted PDF version. Click the option to select it; it is included in the Attachments pane in Acrobat. (Learn more about attachments in Chapter 9.)

The dialog displays four tabs: Settings, Security, Word, and Bookmarks. The default settings for PDFMaker are shown in Figure 20. Click the Conversion Settings pull-down arrow and choose an alternate group of settings. Regardless of the options you select, the basic Settings tab selections remain the same.

Here are some tips for working with the basic conversion options:

- The Settings tab of the Conversion Settings dialog is divided into two sections. The PDFMaker Settings are common throughout the PDFMaker tools in different programs; the Application Settings change depending on the program you are working in.

- Deselect View Adobe PDF result if you want to convert the file but don't need to work with it in Acrobat immediately. By default, a converted document is automatically displayed in Acrobat. If you are converting a very large document or using a slow computer, deselecting this option can prevent some processing errors.

- If you consistently convert documents using the same name as the source Word document, deselect the Prompt for Adobe PDF file name option. Deselecting this option saves a step.

- Leave the Convert Document Information option selected because you may need to use the information in Acrobat. It doesn't affect the processing time or file size appreciably and can save you time later.

- If you make changes to PDFMaker settings and want to revert, click Restore Defaults.

TIP 21 Choosing PDFMaker Conversion Settings in Word

Each PDFMaker installed into the various Microsoft Office programs includes different settings that vary according to the program's features. In Word you can convert content such as bookmarks and comments, as well as text.

Choose Adobe PDF > Change Conversion Settings to open the dialog. Click the Word tab to display Word-specific options (**Figure 21a**):

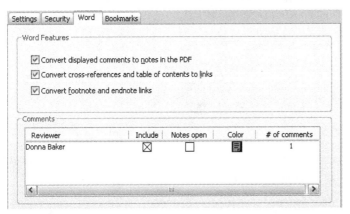

Figure 21a Convert comments in your document to notes in the Adobe PDF document.

- To preserve comments in your converted Word documents, click Convert displayed comments to notes in the PDF. (See Chapter 14 for information on using comments.) Comments in the source document are listed in the Word tab, as shown in Figure 21a. Click the X to select or deselect comments you want to convert with the document. Click Notes open to display the comments' contents in the PDF, select the color icon to choose your note color. After conversion, the Word comment displays as a note comment in the PDF document at the same page location.

(Continued)

What About Security?

The Conversion Settings dialog contains the Security tab, used to add password protection to a file. If your document is being converted for further use in Acrobat, don't add security at this point. Wait until the document is processed in Acrobat and then apply security settings. Otherwise, each time you open the converted PDF document you have to input passwords. Chapter 18 discusses using passwords and other forms of security.

- If your document contains cross-references or a table of contents, you can preserve your work and transfer it to the PDF document by choosing Convert cross-references and table of contents to links. You can also preserve footnotes and endnotes in a converted Word document by selecting Convert footnote and endnote links.

The Word PDFMaker gives you two choices for generating bookmarks, depending on your document's structure. Bookmarks are created from document styles or from headings you select from the default template. Open the Conversion Settings dialog and click the Bookmarks tab (**Figure 21b**).

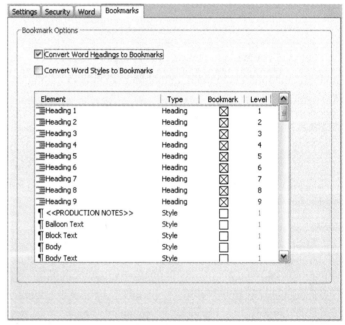

Figure 21b Use either styles or headings as the source for bookmarks in your PDF document.

Click either headings or styles, and then click to select or deselect specific levels or styles to use for conversion.

Creating PDF Files Outside Acrobat

TIP 22 Producing PDF Files in Excel, Access, and Project

Earlier versions of Acrobat included a PDFMaker for Microsoft Excel; version 7 also includes a PDFMaker for both Access and Project. For all three programs, the PDFMaker's Conversion Settings dialog includes only two tabs: Settings and Security.

The Adobe PDF menu in Excel contains a workbook command. Choose Adobe PDF > Convert Entire Workbook to convert the contents of an .xls file to a single PDF document.

Choose Adobe PDF > Change Conversion Settings in Excel to open the Conversion Settings dialog. The Settings tab includes the options described in Tip 20 for converting a Word document.

Figure 22a shows the Application settings on the Settings tab of Excel's Conversion Settings dialog. Choose the Fit Worksheet to a single page option to rescale the contents of your Excel worksheet to fit one page. Converting an Excel spreadsheet also converts bookmarks and notes, if you select those options.

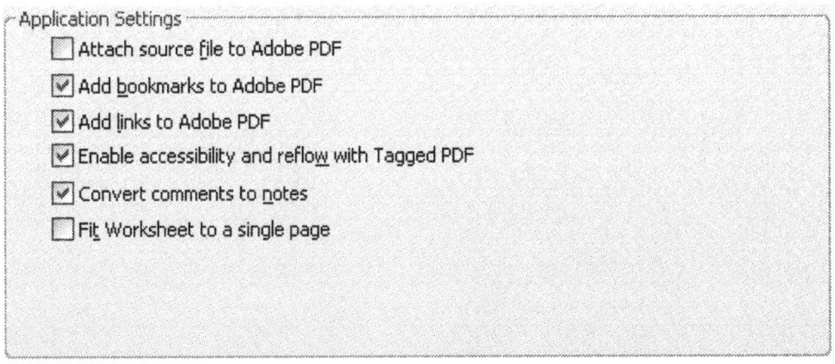

```
Application Settings
  [ ] Attach source file to Adobe PDF
  [x] Add bookmarks to Adobe PDF
  [x] Add links to Adobe PDF
  [x] Enable accessibility and reflow with Tagged PDF
  [x] Convert comments to notes
  [ ] Fit Worksheet to a single page
```

Figure 22a Choose comment and worksheet conversion options in the Excel PDFMaker Conversion Settings dialog.

(Continued)

Check the View

When you convert a Microsoft Project file, only the currently selected view is converted. Make sure you are in the correct view—calendar, Gantt chart, task usage, and so on—before running the conversion process. Test the export file; some views may not be compressed to a single page.

Taking a Shortcut

Most often you use the default settings in PDFMaker, or repeatedly use your modified settings as you work. If you use the same settings all the time, you don't even have to open the file to convert it to a PDF. Locate the file in Windows Explorer and then right-click the file's name to display the shortcut menu. After PDFMaker is installed, the Convert to Adobe PDF, Convert to Adobe PDF and EMail, and Convert to Adobe PDF and Send for Review options (Windows) are included in the shortcut menu.

The Adobe PDF menu in Access includes one report option. (**Figure 22b**). Choose Adobe PDF > Convert Multiple Reports to Single PDF to combine an Access project's reports into a single PDF document.

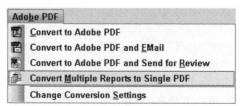

Figure 22b You can combine reports in a single PDF file exported from Access.

The Access PDFMaker has a limited number of options. In the Application settings on the Settings tab, you can choose to include bookmarks or attach the source file to the PDF.

The Adobe PDF menu in Microsoft Project includes the three basic conversion options available in Windows: converting to PDF, converting and emailing, and converting and sending for review. In the Conversion Settings dialog, the Application settings include only one option for attaching the source file to the PDF and making the project fit on one page.

TIP 23 Generating PDF Documents in PowerPoint and Publisher

How would you like to distribute a PowerPoint slideshow—complete with slide transitions and animation— without having to pack the files and add a player? Or convert your spectacular Publisher projects to PDF without first having to create a Word document? You can do both quickly and easily with PDFMakers.

PowerPoint's PDFMaker has several options you can configure for converting a presentation to a PDF document. You can choose options for exporting slide transitions and text animations as well as defining the page's layout using the PowerPoint presentation's print settings (**Figure 23a**).

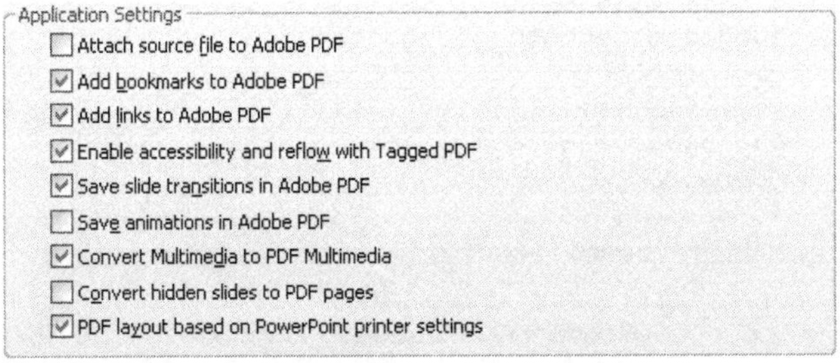

Figure 23a Select specific multimedia and animation conversion options in the PowerPoint PDFMaker's conversion settings.

Like a Word document, a PowerPoint document allows for comment, tag, and bookmark conversions.

(Continued)

Using Print Settings

If you want your slides to be used as part of a larger PDF file that uses standard-sized pages, use the PDF layout based on PowerPoint print settings in the Application Settings of the PDFMaker Settings dialog. The default layout for a presentation uses Landscape orientation and often a full-color background; printing a presentation as part of a larger document can take a lot of time and consume a lot of ink if you simply convert the presentation itself. Of course, using the print settings option depends on the content of your presentation. Bullet lists, for example, will display properly in a Portrait orientation; images or charts may not.

Acrobat 7 installs PDFMakers in many more programs than it did in earlier versions, including a PDFMaker in Microsoft Publisher. In Publisher, choose Adobe PDF > Change Conversion Settings to open the dialog (**Figure 23b**). Most programs' PDFMakers use the Standard settings as the default conversion option; Publisher's default is the Press Quality settings default.

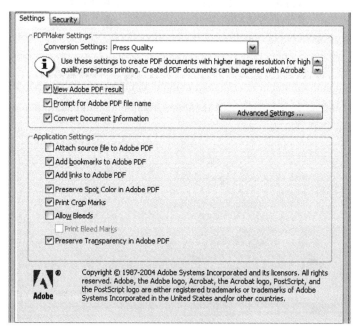

Figure 23b The Microsoft Publisher PDFMaker uses the Press Quality settings by default.

For a Publisher document, often used for high-end printing, you can select print-specific options such as bleeds, spot color, crop marks, and transparency options. PDF documents generated from Publisher files can also contain comments, tags, and bookmarks.

TIP 24 Converting Layered Visio Documents

Visio gives you the power to use one document structure and add many layers of information. For example, in a single Visio document, you can show the layout of your office on the background, and overlay drawings of network cables, telephone connections, and electrical circuits, each on its own layer. You can toggle layers on and off to view one layer or a combination of layers against the background.

You can preserve the layers and their visibility using Visio's PDFMaker. Layers can be converted intact, or the document can be flattened, which is PDFMaker's default. If the layers are flattened, the PDF document looks like the original Visio drawing, but all the content is on a single layer.

Layers are converted using the settings you choose in Visio's Layer Properties dialog, such as visibility, locks, and names. (Please see Tip 94 in Chapter 11 for information on using layers in Acrobat.)

As with the other PDFMaker 7 options, you can select from basic conversion options in the Adobe PDF program menu. You can also choose Adobe PDF > Convert all Pages in Drawing. In addition, you can choose options to support searchable text, links, comments, and bookmarks.

Choose Adobe PDF > Change Conversion Settings to open the Conversion Settings dialog. The Application Settings are shown in **Figure 24a**.

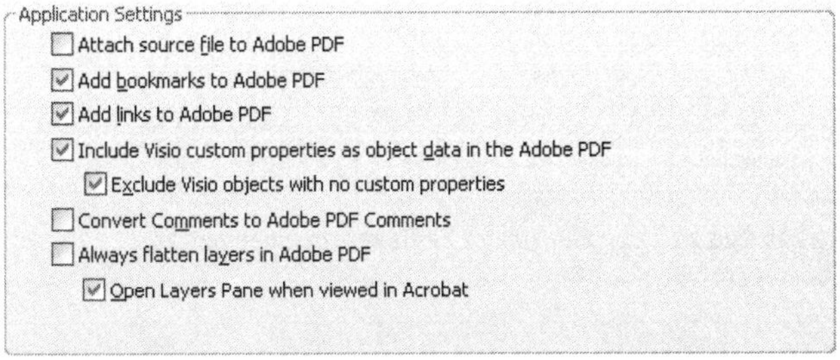

Figure 24a Choose layer and object options in the Application Settings area of the Conversion Settings dialog in Visio.

(Continued)

Data About the Objects

You can embed *object data* in a Visio file. Object data consists of custom information about aspects of the drawing or its elements. This data can then be viewed in Acrobat. (See the sidebar in Tip 92 in Chapter 11.)

Why Bother with Layers?

In some cases, you should always flatten a document to preserve its integrity, such as drawings that are certified by an engineer. In other cases, feel free to layer away. A layered PDF document can be a terrific advertising tool. Instead of showing your customer one product image and some color swatches, put the alternate colors on different layers and let your client click through bookmarked layers, viewing the product in its varying colors. The example used in Tip 94 in Chapter 11 shows three different color schemes for kitchen tile; clicking the colors' layers shows the customer how the tile would actually appear.

The conversion process in Visio uses a number of dialogs. Click the Convert to Adobe PDF icon on the PDFMaker toolbar, or choose Adobe PDF > Convert to PDF to start the process. The first pane of the dialog deals with the drawing's object data; click the check box to select whether or not object data is included. Include the object data if you think you may want to use it for searching—a useful option in a large or complex project. Click Continue to proceed to the next pane of the dialog.

Choose the layering option for the selected page or the document if you chose Adobe PDF > Convert all Pages in Drawing from the Adobe PDF program menu (**Figure 24b**). Click the appropriate radio button to flatten all layers, retain all layers, or retain only some layers. Unless you intend your users to work with different combinations of layers in the PDF document, leave the default Flatten all layers option selected (see the sidebar for examples). Click Continue.

Figure 24b Choose how you want to use layers in the exported PDF document.

If you choose to preserve some layers, the next pane of the dialog shows lists of the layers in the document (**Figure 24c**). The layers in the drawing are listed in the left column. Click a layer in the Layers in Visio Drawing column and then click Add Layer(s) to add that layer to the Layers in PDF column.

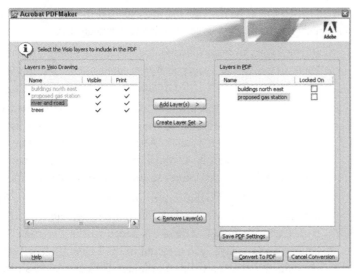

Figure 24c Choose and organize the layers for export.

Regardless of the layer option you choose, the final pane describes your layering choice. To save a step, click Don't show this step again, which then bypasses the layer conversion confirmation and converts the document automatically.

Click Convert to PDF to create the output. A Save Adobe PDF File As dialog opens; locate the folder and name the file if you wish; by default the file is named according to the Visio file and stored in the source file's folder on your hard drive. Click Save to process the file and create the PDF.

Layer Guidance

If you are unsure which layering option to select, click Help at the bottom left of the dialog to show a pop-up window that describes the layering options.

TIP
25 Organizing Layers

If you choose to preserve some layers, you use one pane of the Convert to PDF dialog to define the layers for conversion. Only those layers selected and added to the Layers in PDF list are exported to the finished PDF document. Here are some tips for working with the layer selections:

- In the Layers in Visio Drawing column, those layers that have been added to the Layers in PDF column are grayed out and can't be selected and added again.

- Click the name of the layer in the Layers in PDF column to activate the text and change the name. The layers are listed by name in the Layers panel in Acrobat, and in a large drawing technical names can be confusing; use descriptive names to make it easier for your viewer to understand the document.

- Create subfolders in the Layers in PDF column to organize groups of layers. Select a layer in the left column, and then click Create Layer Set. A folder is added to the Layers in PDF column and the layer you selected in the Layers in Visio Drawing column is nested within the folder. Click the folder's name and type a name for the set. Use sets to keep track of groups of layers if you are exporting several versions of the drawing.

- Drag the layers in the Layers in PDF column up or down to rearrange their order.

- Click a layer in the Layers in PDF column to select it and click Remove Layer to delete it from the column; its name then is reactivated in the Layers in Visio Drawing column.

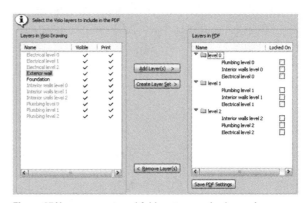

Figure 25 You can create subfolders to organize layers in groups.

TIP 26 Using Photoshop PDF

The Adobe Creative Suite products contain internal PDF file creation processes. In Photoshop CS, choose File > Save As to open the Save As dialog. Click the Format pull-down arrow and choose Photoshop PDF. In the dialog, the name and folder location of the original document is shown by default; choose an alternate name and storage location if you want. Although you work in layers in Photoshop, Acrobat 7 doesn't support the layers in the converted PDF document.

Depending on the contents of the file and its original format, a number of options appear in the Save Options area from which you can choose (**Figure 26a**). Features that are present in the original document are available, such as layers or annotations. Click to deselect options you don't want converted. Annotations added to a Photoshop document are converted to note comments in the exported PDF document.

Using Version Cue

If you are working with Adobe Creative Suite and using Version Cue, click the Version Cue button on the standard Save As dialog to open its Save As dialog. You can choose the same PDF settings options as those available from the Photoshop Save As dialog.

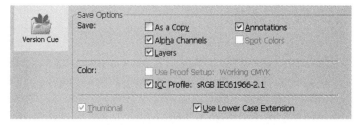

Figure 26a Select PDF file options in the Photoshop Save As dialog.

Next, choose a color option. The document's color profile is selected by default.

(Continued)

PDF Formats

Photoshop PDFs are a single image, regardless of whether the source file contains a combination of image and text. Other programs, such as Microsoft Word, Microsoft Visio, and Adobe InDesign, export the PDF document as both text and image, which is important if you want to search the document's text. Chapter 17 describes converting an image of text into actual searchable text.

Click Save to open the PDF Options dialog (**Figure 26b**). Select options according to how you intend to use the PDF as well as its content:

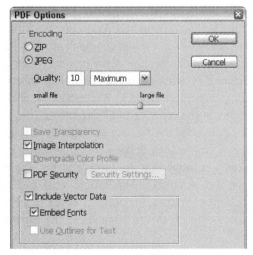

Figure 26b Configure PDF export options according to the document's contents.

- Choose from either ZIP or JPEG compression. ZIP is lossless compression, and best used for images containing large areas of single colors. JPEG compression is lossy—you can create a smaller file size than ZIP compression, but its quality is not as high. Set the quality by using the sliders, clicking the pull-down arrow, or typing a value in the field.

- Select Save Transparency to create white areas where the image is transparent. If your document doesn't contain transparency, this option is grayed out.

- Choose Image Interpolation to use antialiasing for lower-resolution images; at higher compression levels, interpolation can improve the image's appearance.

- Select the Downgrade Color Profile option to use the PDF in a program that doesn't support higher color profile versions: This option is only active if your chosen Color Profile can be downgraded. This option downgrades an ICC (International Color Consortium) Profile (Windows) or Embed Color Profile (Macintosh) to a version 4 color profile.

- Click PDF Security to add protection to the file. When you click the check box the Security Settings button becomes active; click this button to open a dialog that lets you set passwords and specify file rights (such as whether you'll allow other users to print the document or change its content).

- The Include Vector Data option is active if your document contains vector objects or type. Choose this option to preserve vector objects and type. Deselecting the option causes the objects and type to be rasterized.

- Click Embed Fonts to embed the fonts used in the Photoshop document; this allows others to use and view the file using your original fonts.

- Click Use Outlines for Text to convert the text to paths. You have to uncheck Embed Fonts to activate this option.

TIP 27 Exporting a PDF from InDesign CS

Save Your Settings

For reference purposes, you can save the contents of an export setting by clicking Save Summary at the bottom of the Summary panel. A dialog opens where you can name and save the file, which is stored on your computer as a text file.

PDF documents are often exported from InDesign CS for proofing, editing, or sending to a print shop. In InDesign CS, you can design both PDF styles and export styles.

To choose an export style, choose File > PDF Export Presets and select an option from the list (**Figure 27a**). InDesign uses the same naming as that seen in Acrobat 5, that is, eBook, Screen, Print, and Press. In addition, you can choose PDF/X standards and an Acrobat 6-compatible layered PDF option.

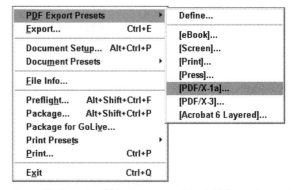

Figure 27a InDesign CS includes a number of PDF export presets.

Choose File > Export and choose PDF from the Save As type pull-down list. Click Save to save the PDF using the source file's name and folder.

The Export PDF dialog opens and shows the last selected preset in the Preset field at the top of the dialog. When you choose a preset, it remains the selected preset in the PDF Export settings until you select another option from the pull-down list. Click a heading in the column at the left of the dialog to show the preset's settings:

- **General.** The General panel contains selections for basic settings such as version compatibility, as well as items you want to include, such as bookmarks and layers. If you choose Create Acrobat Layers on the General panel, the exported PDF document will contain the layers used in the original document.

- **Compression.** Choose settings for monochrome, grayscale, and color images.

- **Marks and Bleeds.** Define and specify inclusion of printer's marks and bleed settings.

- **Advanced.** Select options for color, fonts, and OPI (Open Prepress Interface).

- **Security.** Set document passwords and permissions from the Security panel.

- **Summary.** The options under different classifications and headings chosen for the preset are listed in the Summary panel (**Figure 27b**).

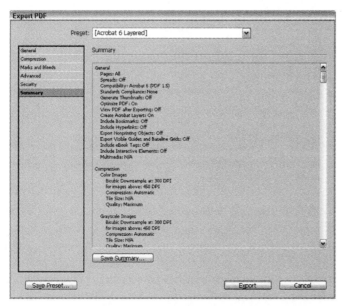

Figure 27b Modify existing presets or configure your own PDF export presets.

Creating a New Preset

To create custom preset options in InDesign CS, choose File > PDF Export Presets > Define to open the Preset PDF Exports dialog and then click New to open the New PDF Export Preset dialog. The dialog offers the same panels as those used in the Export PDF dialog. Name the preset and choose the settings from the different panels; click a panel name in the listing at the left of the dialog. Click OK when you have finished configuring the settings. The dialog closes and your custom preset is added to the PDF Export Presets list.

TIP 27: Exporting a PDF from InDesign CS

Making PDF Documents from Web Pages

Quick Conversions

If you convert a fair number of Web pages to PDF documents, save yourself some mouse clicks and time with easy preference changes. Click the pull-down arrow on the Adobe PDF toolbar and choose Preferences to open a small dialog. Select or deselect the options shown in the dialog:

- Open PDF files in Acrobat after conversion
- Ask for confirmation before deleting PDF files
- Ask for confirmation before adding pages to PDF files
- Warn before adding pages if the PDF file has been modified

A PDFMaker is installed in Internet Explorer when you install Acrobat 7. To create a PDF file from a Web page displayed in Internet Explorer, click the pull-down arrow on the Adobe PDF toolbar to display the menu and choose Convert Web Page to PDF (**Figure 28**). If the page includes frames, all the content is flattened into one PDF document page.

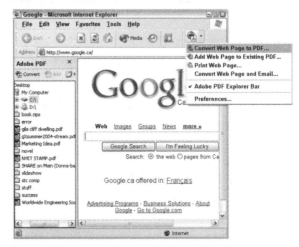

Figure 28 The Internet Explorer PDFMaker includes an option that displays a document list.

To attach the displayed Web page to an existing PDF document, click Add Web Page to Existing PDF. A dialog opens that lets you select the document to use for the attached page. Click Save to convert the Web page and append it to the end of the selected document. You can also right-click the page to display the shortcut menu, which includes both the Convert to PDF and Add to Existing PDF commands.

To search for PDF documents online or on your computer, click the pull-down arrow to the right of the Convert to PDF icon on the Adobe PDF toolbar and choose Adobe PDF Explorer Bar. A pane opens at the left of the Web browser window, as seen in Figure 28. You can select documents from the pane that you want to attach to the converted Web pages, or you can select files to open from the Explorer. A PDF document you open from the Adobe PDF Explorer Bar is displayed in Adobe Reader in the Web browser. If the Adobe PDF Explorer Bar is displayed when you close your Web browser, it is open the next time you open your Web browser.

TIP 29 Working with Acrobat Distiller

Only a limited number of programs have a PDFMaker installed with Acrobat 7, and not all programs have internal PDF-generating options for export. In many applications—illustration programs, for example—you can generate other file formats that can then be processed as PDF documents using Acrobat Distiller 7. You'll also use Distiller to create PDF documents that are press standard-compliant.

Distiller is a separate program installed with the Acrobat 7 installation process. Access the program from the desktop through the Start menu, or in Acrobat 7 by choosing Advanced > Acrobat Distiller. On a Mac, if you choose Adobe PDF > Create Adobe PDF from PDFMaker, Distiller opens automatically.

Distiller's interface looks and works like a dialog, and includes the prebuilt default settings you have seen elsewhere in this chapter.

To distill a file, choose File > Open. In the Open dialog, locate the file you want to convert, select it, and click Open. The dialog closes and the file is opened; as the file is processed, Distiller shows you details and a progress bar (**Figure 29a**).

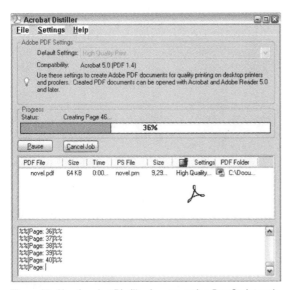

Figure 29a Use Acrobat Distiller for converting PostScript and other similar types of files generated from a range of programs.

(Continued)

Formats for Distiller

You can use either .ps or .prn files in Distiller. The .ps file format uses the PostScript language. Some programs produce .prn files instead of .ps files; other programs generate .prn files if you choose Print to File as a printing option. Both file formats are based on the printer drivers installed on your computer.

What Do You Prefer?

Choose File > Preferences to open a small dialog. If you are working on a Mac, choose Distiller > Preferences. You have several options, such as viewing generated files in Acrobat and managing log files.

Continue converting other files as required or close Distiller. You can manage the files in your Distiller session from the program's dialog (**Figure 29b**). Right-click or Control-click a distilled file from the list to display the shortcut menu and choose from the options on the list. The History is maintained for each Distiller session; when you close and reopen the program again, the list is cleared.

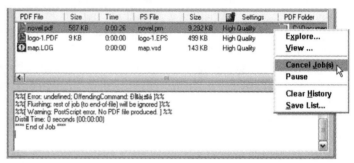

Figure 29b Manage the files distilled during a session from the Distiller dialog.

Creating Custom Conversion Settings in Distiller

You can create custom conversion settings for your own work, start from scratch, or modify one of the default options. Many variations on the defaults are available. You can create new job options through the PDF-Maker and Distiller dialogs. This tip shows the process using Distiller:

1. In Distiller, choose one of the default settings to serve as the basis for your custom settings. You can start from scratch, but modifying the option closest to what you need is a much simpler approach. The example in this tip uses the High Quality default setting as the basis for custom settings.

2. Choose Settings > Edit Adobe PDF Settings.

3. The High Quality Print-Adobe PDF Settings dialog opens (**Figure 30a**). The dialog has a list of headings in the left column; click a heading to display the settings in the right pane of the dialog. If you select either the General heading or the default setting's heading (High Quality in the figure), the same General options display in the dialog.

Working the Default Settings

The setting you select from the Default Settings heads the left column of the Custom Settings dialog. If you want to create custom settings using a different default option, don't close the Adobe PDF Settings dialog; instead, click the Show All Settings check box at the lower left of the dialog to display the list of Default Settings; double-click another default settings option to reveal the set of headings. Click the Show All Settings check box again to deselect it, and only the active default setting and its headings remain in the column.

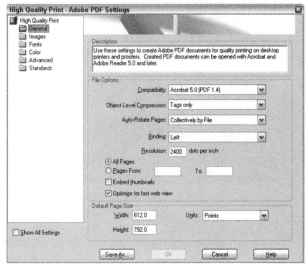

Figure 30a Modify conversion options for any default group of settings or create your own.

(Continued)

TIP 30: Creating Custom Conversion Settings in Distiller

Don't Use Page Ranges

The General tab includes an option for selecting a specific range of pages. Don't enable this option unless you are sure the custom settings are for onetime use. If you specify a range of pages when you create the job options and then reuse the settings another time, you convert only those pages specified on the General tab. This can lead to time-consuming trouble-shooting when you use your custom settings and can't figure out where your pages have gone!

4. On the General tab, you may want to modify these settings:

- Compatibility—The default is Acrobat 5.0 (PDF 1.4). Depending on your users, you can choose an option as far back as Acrobat 3. Older versions of the program have fewer options for settings such as security, font embedding, and color management. For example, Acrobat 7's security settings aren't functional in Acrobat 4.

- Object Level Compression—Choose from Off or Tags options. Compression of objects combines small objects into compressible content. Off leaves the document's structure as is; the Tags Only option compresses structural information in the PDF document. If you compress tag information, your document's features such as bookmarks are viewable only in Acrobat 6 and 7; leaving the option set to Off allows structure and tagging information to be usable in Acrobat 5 as well.

- Resolution—You can set this option to emulate the resolution of a printer for PostScript files. A higher resolution usually produces higher quality but larger files. Resolution determines the number of steps in a gradient or blend. The gradient at the left of **Figure 30b** is the same as that on the right; the only difference is resolution.

Figure 30b
Resolution determines the number of steps in a gradient or blend.

- Embed thumbnails—Thumbnail previews are used for navigation. Prior to Acrobat 5, you had to specify thumbnail generation rather than having them generated dynamically. Unless you are planning to use the output with older versions of Acrobat and Acrobat Reader, don't enable this option; it adds to the file size unnecessarily.

5. On the Images tab (**Figure 30c**), you may need to adjust and test setting changes several times for converting files with complex images. Consider these options:

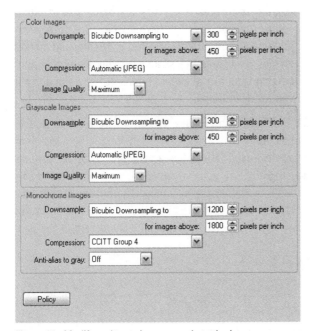

Figure 30c Modify and test changes made to the Images tab settings.

- Downsample—You can combine pixels in a sample area to make a larger pixel. Pixels in images with a resolution above a specified amount are combined to reduce the resolution. Depending on what your users are required to do with your file, you may want to increase or decrease the downsampling level. For images such as maps (where the user zooms in to a high magnification), a high resolution is much more legible.

- Compression/Image Quality—Select options depending on the file's color, grayscale, and monochromatic images. You can use different compression settings depending on the type of image.

(Continued)

Naming Job Options Files

You may create a number of custom .joboptions files over time. To keep track of their use or purpose, name them according to client name, project name, or anything else that is meaningful. For example, highquality(1). joboptions doesn't mean as much as northern_foods.joboptions.

TIP 30: Creating Custom Conversion Settings in Distiller

Error-Handling

Click the When embedding fails pull-down arrow and choose a policy from the list; as with the policy options for images, you can save time processing files if you specify how to handle embedding errors.

- Smooth jagged edges in monochrome images by turning on antialiasing.

- Click the Policy button to open a dialog used to specify how to process images when they are below the resolution you define. You can specify whether to ignore, warn, or cancel a job based on resolution of color, grayscale, and monochrome images. Setting policies can save you processing and reprocessing time in the event the images in a file don't use the correct resolutions.

6. On the Fonts tab (**Figure 30d**), specify whether you want to embed fonts or subset embedded fonts when the percent of characters used falls below a value you enter. If you are using unusual fonts, or your layout is highly dependent on the fonts, be sure to embed them. Choose the Subset option when you want to embed a portion of a font's characters. Don't use a low value if you expect to change any characters in the page.

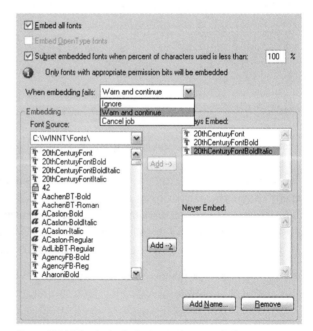

Figure 30d Maintain the look of your document using font embedding.

7. On the Color tab (**Figure 30e**), choose settings that correspond with files used in your source applications, such as Adobe Photoshop or Illustrator. The options available depend on the color settings you choose. If you are sending files to a press, you often get settings from the printer.

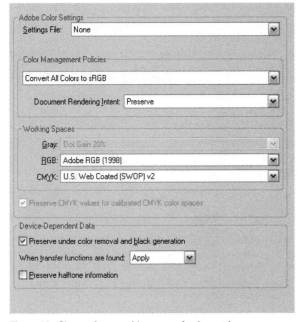

Figure 30e Choose from a wide range of color settings.

(Continued)

Sharing Job Options Files

You can share settings with others. Email the .joboptions file as you would any other type of file. Your recipients add the file to the storage folder. The next time they access the custom settings dialog from a PDFMaker, Acrobat, or Distiller, the shared settings are ready to use.

TIP 30: Creating Custom Conversion Settings in Distiller

Faster Conversions

If you are building files for online use, make sure RGB (not CMYK) is selected. RGB is the native color space for monitors and doesn't require any conversion, making viewing faster.

8. Unless you are familiar with Document Structuring Conventions and the like, you won't have to change many options on the Advanced tab (**Figure 30f**). The settings on this tab describe how the conversion from PostScript to PDF is performed. Let's look at two default options:

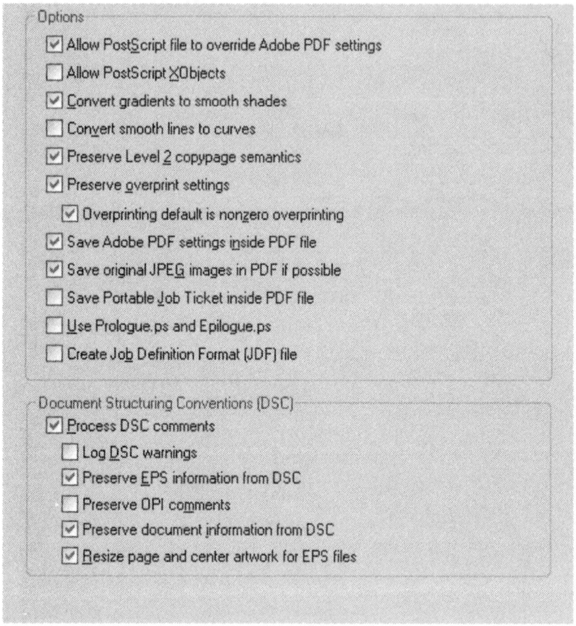

Figure 30f Most settings on the Advanced tab work fine using the default options.

- The Convert gradients to smooth shades option converts gradients from a range of programs, including FreeHand, QuarkXPress, Adobe Illustrator, and Microsoft PowerPoint. This option produces a smaller PDF file size, and often results in improved output.
- The other option of note, Save original JPEG images in PDF if possible, processes JPEG images (which are compressed) without compressing them again, resulting in faster file processing.

9. If you are constructing settings that comply with standards, you can choose options on the Standards tab that check document contents against standards before creating the PDF document (**Figure 30g**). The options displayed on the tab vary according to the standard you select from the Compliance Standard pull-down menu.

Figure 30g When you need to process a PDF according to standards, choose and configure the options on the Standards tab.

(Continued)

TIP 30: Creating Custom Conversion Settings in Distiller

10. Choose Save As to open the Save Adobe PFD Settings As dialog. Name the file and click Save (**Figure 30h**). The custom conversion settings file is saved with the extension .joboptions.

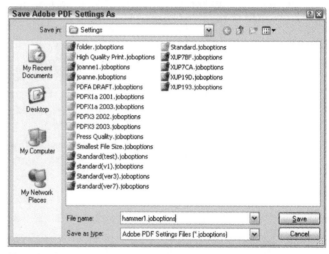

Figure 30h Save your custom settings as a named .joboptions file for reuse.

Custom .joboptions files are saved with other default conversion settings. Once you have created and saved custom settings, they are listed in Acrobat Distiller as well as PDFMakers throughout your computer.

CHAPTER FOUR

Creating PDF Files in Acrobat

Earlier versions of Acrobat allowed you primarily to export PDF files from various source programs or imported Web pages. Beginning with Acrobat 6, and now with Acrobat 7, you can work functionally—that is, according to the processes you are attempting to apply to a document—rather than manipulating a massive collection of toolbars and menu items (although they certainly do exist!). The Create PDF task assembles a collection of processes inside the program, giving you one-click access to material.

You can convert files in Acrobat 7 in numerous ways, including single or multiple documents, from a Web page, from a scan, or from a snapshot, which is content captured from the program window. The Attachments pane is new in Acrobat 7, and lets you attach source documents to a PDF either before conversion or in Acrobat using two different methods.

Creating a PDF from a File in Acrobat

Conversion Clues

Should you convert a document in the source program or in Acrobat? The short answer is: it depends. If you are working in a program and know you will need a PDF version of a file, generate the file then. If you are working in Acrobat and realize you need another file, generate the file from Acrobat.

Even if you are working in Acrobat, if you plan to generate files from PDFMaker-governed programs and either can't remember the settings you last left for the PDFMaker or know you need to change the settings, you should work through the program instead of Acrobat. That approach is preferable to generating a file that is converted using the incorrect settings and then having to redo it.

In Acrobat 7 you can generate PDF files from within the program using the Create PDF task button. You can also select File > Create PDF and choose an option from the submenu. If you use the File > Create PDF menu path, the How To ... Create PDF option isn't available. From the task button's menu, click the How To option to display a list of topic headings in the Search pane at the right of the program window.

Unless you have content placed on the system clipboard, the option From Clipboard Image is grayed out; see Tip 35 on using a clipboard image as a document source. Click the Create PDF task button to display the menu (**Figure 31a**). Click the first option, From File. In the resulting Open dialog box, locate the file you want to convert to PDF and click Open.

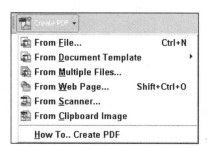

Figure 31a Acrobat's Create PDF menu offers several ways to convert files.

You'll see a progress bar window as Acrobat executes a macro that opens the file in the native program and converts it to a PDF (**Figure 31b**).

Figure 31b A progress bar shows the conversion process.

If the file is in a program that offers a PDFMaker, Acrobat uses the PDFMaker with the last conversion options you set in the program. If the file is in a program without a PDFMaker, Acrobat opens the program and converts the file using the Adobe PDF Converter.

The converted file opens in Acrobat. When converted, the file is named according to the source file's name but isn't yet saved in its PDF format. Choose File > Save to save the file as a PDF.

Not all files can be converted to a PDF from within Acrobat. The formats you can use are listed below:

- AutoDesk AutoCAD
- AutoDesk Inventor
- BMP
- GIF
- HTML
- JDF Job Definition
- JPEG 2000
- Microsoft Access
- Microsoft Word
- Microsoft Excel
- Microsoft PowerPoint
- RTF (Rich Text Format)
- Microsoft Project
- Microsoft Publisher
- Microsoft Visio
- PCX
- PNG
- PostScript
- EPS
- Text
- TIFF
- XML PDF

TIP 31: Creating a PDF from a File in Acrobat

Creating a PDF from Multiple Files in Acrobat

Use the Create PDF File from Multiple Documents window in Acrobat 7 to quickly assemble documents and files (PDF and otherwise) in a collection called a *binder* before building the file. It's a true timesaver!

Click the Create PDF task button to display the menu options and then click From Multiple Files to open the Create PDF File from Multiple Documents dialog (**Figure 32a**).

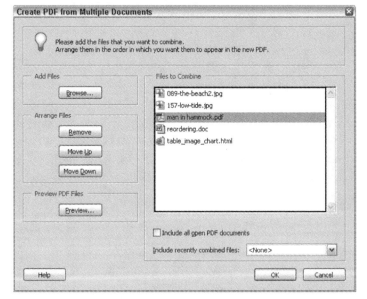

Figure 32a Use the Create PDF from Multiple Documents dialog to assemble a group of files.

Click Browse to open an Open dialog box, locate the first file you want to add to the collection, and click Add. The browse window closes and Acrobat adds the file. Repeat the selection process until you have assembled all the files you want in the binder list. You can also include the same file more than once in a binder.

To reorganize the files you add in the dialog, click a file in the Files to Combine pane and then click the named buttons to move a file up or down in the stacking order, or delete it from the collection.

Document Source Programs

When you're converting the content to a consolidated document, Acrobat opens the source programs for all non-Acrobat files in the list. So, you can't add a non-Acrobat file that was created in an application you don't have on your computer.

If you are including PDF files in the binder, when you click the name of a PDF file in the Files to Combine pane, click Preview to open a previewing dialog (**Figure 32b**). In a multipage PDF, click the up and down arrows to preview the pages, or type a number in the Page field to display its preview. Click OK to close the Preview dialog.

Figure 32b You can preview PDF files that you add to the binder list.

When your files are assembled to your satisfaction, click OK. The window closes and the content is processed as required, and then combined into one PDF document. Each file is processed separately, and any files in the list that are not PDFs are converted to PDFs. When the conversion is complete, a Save As dialog opens, and the file is named Binder1.pdf by default. Type a filename, choose a location, and then click Save. Your composite file is complete.

TIP 32: Creating a PDF from Multiple Files in Acrobat

Creating a PDF from Web Pages in Acrobat

Although you can easily download a page from a Web site using the PDFMaker that installs in Internet Explorer, you can also download a Web site from within Acrobat and control its content and how it is displayed in the resulting PDF file.

Click the Create PDF task button to display the menu and click From Web Page or choose File > Create PDF > From Web Page to open the Create PDF from Web Page dialog (**Figure 33a**).

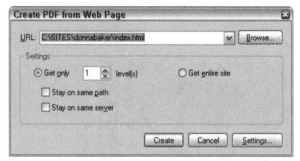

Figure 33a Choose a Web site, page levels, and other settings from this dialog.

Access the file you want to convert in one of three ways, depending on the location and type of file. You can type the URL for the file if it's on the Internet, click the arrow to the right of the URL field to work with Web files that have been opened previously in Acrobat, or click Browse to open the Select File to Open dialog to locate a file that's on a local disk.

Click Create to start the conversion process. The Download Status dialog shows you the number of connections active in the downloaded material, as well as the names, sizes, and locations of the files. When the download is complete, Acrobat displays the new PDF file in the Document pane and adds a document structure to the Bookmarks tab. Choose File > Save to save the converted Web pages.

As you scroll through the document, notice that both a header and footer are added to the pages (**Figure 33b**). The header is the Web page's name; the footer contains the URL for the page, the number of pages, and the download date and time.

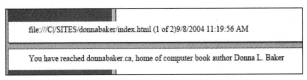

file:///C|/SITES/donnabaker/index.html (1 of 2)9/8/2004 11:19:56 AM

You have reached donnabaker.ca, home of computer book author Donna L. Baker

Figure 33b Headers and footers are added to the pages by default.

Acrobat captures Web pages using default settings for both file formats and page layouts. You can configure some formats and modify the page to your requirements. Click Settings on the Create PDF from Web Page dialog to open the Web Page Conversion Settings dialog. The General tab offers file type and PDF settings (**Figure 33c**).

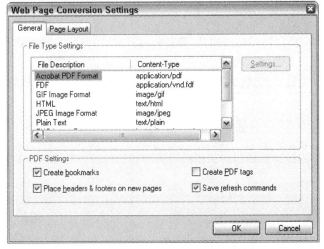

Figure 33c Configure the settings for different file and image types used in a Web page conversion process.

(Continued)

TIP 33: Creating a PDF from Web Pages in Acrobat

At the bottom of the dialog, you'll see the PDF options used by default, including bookmarks and the header and footer options. Select or deselect the options as desired. If you click the HTML or Plain Text formats in the list, the Settings button at the right of the dialog activates; click it to open the Conversion Settings dialog. You can specify file formats, fonts, and encoding. Make modifications as desired, click OK, and then click OK again to close the Conversion Settings dialog and return to the Web Page Conversion Settings dialog.

The second tab of the Web Page Conversion Settings dialog contains page layout options. You can specify standard page layout settings such as the page size, orientation, and margins. Changing the page settings to coincide with other documents you may later use in a binder document provides consistency throughout the document. Click OK to close the Web Page Conversion Settings dialog and return to the Create PDF from Web Page dialog; then click Create to process the Web page and create the PDF document.

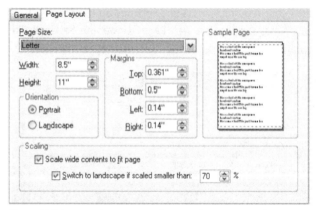

Figure 33d You can change page size, margins, and other features before converting to a Web page.

TIP 34: Creating a PDF from a Scan in Acrobat

Sometimes you don't have a soft copy of a document. If you have a printed copy, you can create a PDF version using your scanner.

Click the Create PDF task button to display the menu and click From Scanner to open the Create PDF From Scanner dialog (**Figure 34a**). Select your scanner from the Scanner pull-down list, and then choose Front Sides or Both Sides from the Scan pull-down list.

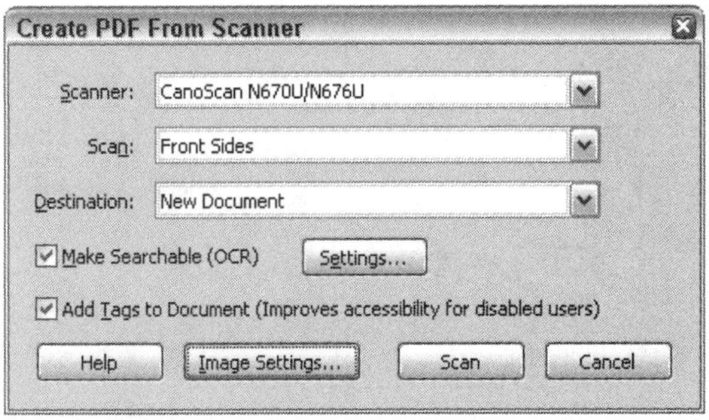

Figure 34a Choose settings for converting a scan to a PDF document.

Specify a destination for the scanned page. In Figure 34a, the only option available is a new document; if other documents are open in Acrobat, you can append the scanned file to the active document displayed in the program window.

The default option is to create a searchable document, meaning the contents of the document are converted to words and images that you can then use with Search and Find features. Click Settings to open a dialog for changing the conversion options. (See Tip 139 in Chapter 17 for information on choosing different capture settings.)

(Continued)

Checking Your Scan Results

Many of the files you convert to PDF are composed of text and images that you can manipulate using a variety of tools. PDF files created by scans using older versions of Acrobat or from some programs, such as Photoshop, are images only; you can't make any changes to the file's contents. Here's a quick way to tell the difference.

Click the Select tool on the Basic toolbar. Then click an area of text on the document. If you see the flashing vertical bar cursor, you know the page contains text. If you click a text area on the document and the entire page is selected, you have an image PDF.

If you are scanning the document yourself and leave the default selection Make Searchable (OCR) in the Create PDF From Scanner dialog, the document is always converted to images and text.

The Art of Scanning

Acrobat includes filters that you can modify before scanning, or use to make adjustments if your test scan needs tweaking. Here's a rundown:

- Deskew rotates a skewed page so it's vertical. The default setting is automatic.

- Background removal is used with grayscale and color pages to make nearly-white areas white, resulting in clearer scans. The default is Low; you can also choose Medium and High options.

- Edge shadow removal gets rid of the black edges sometimes seen from scanned pages. The default is Cautious; an aggressive option is also available.

- Despeckle removes black marks from the page. Low is the default; you can also choose Medium and High.

- Descreen removes halftone dots, like those from a scanned newspaper. The default is Automatic: Acrobat applies the filter automatically for grayscale and RGB images of 300 ppi or higher.

- Halo removal removes high-contrast edges from color pages. The default setting is On.

If your document contains images, click Image Settings to open the dialog shown in **Figure 34b**. You can change compression and filter options in the Image Settings dialog rather than use the defaults, as shown Figure 34b. Click OK when you have modified settings, and then click Scan to start the conversion process.

Figure 34b Configure settings for images before you start the scan.

Acrobat opens your scanner's dialog. The settings you use depend on your scanner and software; follow the instructions and start the scan. When the scan is finished, your scanner's dialog closes and the scanned document opens in Acrobat. Choose File > Save and save the PDF document.

TIP 35 — Creating a PDF from a Clipboard Image

Your computer's operating system maintains a storage area called a *clipboard*. Content you select and copy or cut from a document is placed on the clipboard, and you can then paste it into another location or another document. You have two ways of using the clipboard contents in Acrobat: creating a new file or adding the clipboard contents to an existing file.

Creating a new document is a very simple process. Select and copy the image or text you want to use for a PDF document in your source program. In Acrobat, click the Create PDF task button and choose From Clipboard Image from the menu.

The image is converted to PDF and opens in Acrobat. A dialog displays explaining that the PDF is an image and that you can use Picture Tasks to perform some functions with the PDF (**Figure 35a**). Click OK to close the dialog and save the file. (See Tip 132 in Chapter 16 for more on using Picture Tasks.

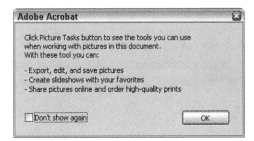

Figure 35a Acrobat notifies you when there are special features about the PDF document you are creating, such as Picture Tasks for image documents.

Note

If you are using a layered Photoshop image, only the selected layer is pasted to the clipboard; you have to flatten the image first before copying it to the clipboard. It is simpler to use the File > Export and select Photoshop PDF commands than to use a layered Photoshop image copied to the clipboard.

(Continued)

You can use the image in an existing PDF document as an image stamp rather than making a separate PDF file for an image. Again, select and copy the image from your source program; it is placed on the system clipboard. Open the PDF document you want to work with in Acrobat. Choose Tools > Commenting > Stamps > Paste Clipboard Image as Stamp Tool. If the Commenting toolbars are open, you can click the as Stamp Tool's pull-down arrow and click Paste Clipboard Image as Stamp Tool button ▣ on the Attach subtoolbar.

Move your mouse over the document. You see the pointer changes to a stamp pointer (**Figure 35b**). Click the page where you would like to insert the image, and the image is pasted to the page. The location on the page where you click determines the center location of the pasted image.

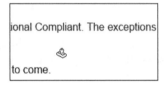

Figure 35b Click the page where you want to paste the image.

The stamp pointer changes to the Hand tool ▨; if you move the pointer over the image the pointer changes to a selection pointer. Click the image on the page to select it (**Figure 35c**). You can drag the image to move it, or drag a resize handle to change the size of the image. Save the file with the added image.

Figure 35c You can select an image pasted to a page to move or resize it.

Note
You can also copy and paste content within a PDF document, such as images. Read more in Tip 83 in Chapter 10.

Attaching Source Files to a PDF

Acrobat 7 contains a feature for attaching source files to a converted document, and also includes a pane for managing attachments.

If you are working in a source program that contains a PDFMaker (such as Word), choose Adobe PDF > Change Conversion Settings to open the Acrobat PDFMaker dialog. Click Attach source file to Adobe PDF in the Application Settings area of the Settings tab (**Figure 36a**). Then click OK to close the dialog.

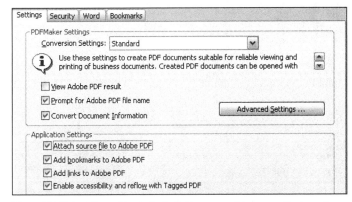

Figure 36a Select the setting to include the source file as an attachment when using a PDFMaker.

You can attach any type of file from within Acrobat, and can place an attachment icon anywhere on your page that your users can click to view the attachment. Click the Attach icon's pull-down arrow on the File toolbar and click the Attach a File as a Comment icon (**Figure 36b**). You can also choose Tools > Commenting > Attach a File as a Comment or click the Attach a File as a Comment 📎 icon on the Commenting toolbar.

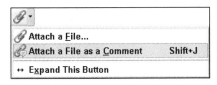

Figure 36b You can choose an attachment option directly from the File toolbar.

(Continued)

Why Bother with Attachments?

Consider your workflow when deciding whether it is necessary to use attachments:

- If you move the PDF document on your hard drive, the attached files or pages automatically move with it, saving you time in moving documents.

- You can attach more information about content in your PDF without having to convert the entire document. For example, create a PDF executive summary and attach detailed documents, spreadsheets, and so on.

- You can search attached files using the Acrobat Search function, which can save you time when you're trying to locate information in a big project.

- You can attach a great deal of accessory material to one PDF document, great for large projects containing multiple information sources.

- You can quickly see information about the attachment in the Attachments pane.

- You can protect attached information when emailing it by using an eEnvelope and security (see Tip 149 in Chapter 18 for information on using secure ePaper).

Move the pointer, which looks like a pushpin, over the document to where you want to display the attachment icon. Browse to the location of the file and select it. Click Select to close the dialog. The File Attachment Properties dialog lets you choose an alternate icon, color, or opacity (**Figure 36c**). Click the General tab to display fields where you can modify the attachment's name, your name, and a description of the attachment. To dismiss the dialog, click Close. You can't attach an open file to a PDF document.

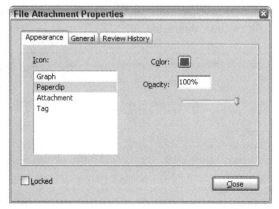

Figure 36c You can specify the appearance and description of an attachment in the File Attachment Properties dialog.

Voilà! The attachment icon is displayed where you clicked earlier, and if you move the pointer over the icon, you can see information about the attachment in the form of a tool tip (**Figure 36d**). Save the document. Files attached using the Attach a File as a Comment tool are also listed in the Comments pane (see Chapter 14 for information about adding comments and Tip 123 in Chapter 15 for working with the Comments pane).

Figure 36d An attached file displays a paperclip icon and a tool tip describing the attachment.

TIP 37 Managing Attached Files

Regardless of whether you attach a document from PDFMaker or embed it within Acrobat using the Attach File as a Comment tool, the attachment is identified by a paperclip icon at the bottom left of the program window.

Click the Attachments tab in the Navigation panel at the left of the program to display the pane horizontally below the Document pane (**Figure 37a**). If the Attachments pane's tab isn't shown, choose View > Navigation Tabs > Attachments.

Name	Description	Modified	Location in document	Size
jimi hendrix painting.pdf		8/14/2004 9:40:51 AM	Page 1	295 KB
089-the-beach2.jpg	Hua Han Beach, Thailand	8/19/2004 3:09:26 PM	Attachments tab	79 KB
man in hammock.psd	Placencia Beach, Belize	8/21/2004 11:06:42 AM	Attachments tab	2,427 KB

Figure 37a Attached files are displayed and managed in the Attachments pane.

The pane shows basic information, including the name, description, size, and date modified. Click the filename and right-click or Control-click to open the shortcut menu, also shown when you click Options on the Attachment pane's toolbar (**Figure 37b**).

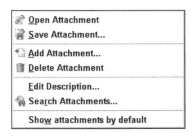

Figure 37b Use the commands or icons to manage the attached files.

Choose a command from the menu for managing the attachment, right-click or Control-click to display a shortcut menu, or use the corresponding icon on the Attachment pane's toolbar. For example, click Open to open the attached file in its native program, or choose Open Attachment from the Options or shortcut menus.

(Continued)

Locating Attachments

For files that you attached before converting them to PDF or those you added through the Attachments pane, the Location in document column lists the location as *Attachments tab*; if you add an attachment in Acrobat using the Attach File as Comment tool, the page number is listed. If you attach a file using the Comment tool (chosen from the File toolbar or the Comments toolbar), the page number is listed.

You can add descriptive labels to any of the listings in the pane. Select the listing, and choose Edit Description to open the Edit Attachment Description dialog shown in **Figure 37c**. Type a description, and click OK to close the dialog and add the information to the Description column of the attachment.

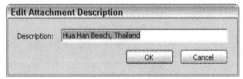

Figure 37c Add a description to the attached document's information to make it simpler for your users to decide which attachments to view.

To open the attached file, double-click a listing in the Attachments pane, click Open on the pane's toolbar, or choose the command from the Options menu. If the attachment is a PDF document it opens automatically. If it is another file format, you see a warning dialog that describes the hazards of opening documents that may contain macros, viruses, and so on. Click Open to proceed, or click Do Not Open to stop the process and close the dialog.

You can save a file independently from the PDF document to which it is attached. Click Save on the Attachment pane's toolbar or select the Save command from the Options menu. In the Save Attachment dialog, choose the storage location for the file and name it if necessary (it uses the name shown in the Attachments pane) and click Save; the dialog closes.

You can add another attachment to the document itself by clicking the Attach File icon on the File toolbar or click Add on the Attachments pane's toolbar or select Add from the menu. The Add Attachment dialog opens; locate the file you want to attach and click Attach. The dialog closes and the file is listed in the Attachments pane. In the Location in document column, the new file's location is listed as *Attachments tab*.

Click Delete to delete an attachment, or click Search to open the Search pane and search the contents of the attached files.

Using Attachments in Earlier Versions of Acrobat

TIP 38

Using attachments is all well and good if you are working in Acrobat 7, but what if your users are working with Acrobat 5 or 6? Fear not, you can still use attachments—you just don't have the fancy pane to work with.

In Acrobat 7, choose File > Document Properties > Initial view and select Attachments Panel and Page from the Show pull-down list. Click OK to close the Document Properties and save the document.

When a user opens the document in Acrobat 5 or Acrobat 6, the information dialog shown in **Figure 38a** appears. Click OK to close the dialog. Choose Document > File Attachments to open the File Attachments dialog (**Figure 38b**). The attachments are listed according to their locations. Those attached as document file attachments are listed first; documents attached using the Attach a File as a Comment tool are listed by page number.

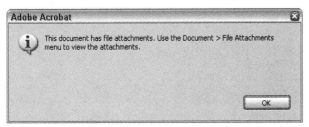

Figure 38a If you specify displaying Attachments in the Document Properties, users can access the attachments in earlier versions of Acrobat.

(Continued)

Please Read Attachments

When you attach files to a PDF, an attachment icon is shown at the bottom left of the Document pane in Acrobat 7. Your intended audience may not have the Acrobat-savvy to understand what the icon means, or even notice it is there! Instead of leaving it to chance, you can change the way the program opens to display attachments.

Click the Options pull-down menu on the Attachments pane and choose Show Attachments by default. Save the file. When it is opened, the document displays in the Document pane and the attachments are automatically displayed at the bottom of the program window in Acrobat 7.

You have to set the option in the Document Properties if you want to notify readers using Acrobat 5 or 6 that there are attachments included with the document.

Whether you choose the page open display from the Attachments pane or the Document Properties, the result is the same. That is, changing the setting in one location automatically changes it in the other location as well.

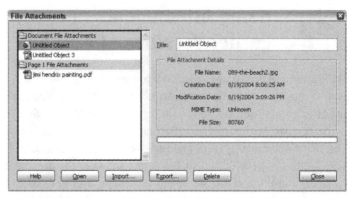

Figure 38b The attachments are listed in the File Attachments dialog in Acrobat versions 5 and 6.

Click the name of a file in the dialog to view details. To manage the attachments, use the buttons at the bottom of the dialog—Open, Import, Export, and Delete.

CHAPTER FIVE

Saving and Exporting

When you have a PDF document open in Acrobat you can perform a wide range of processes based on the document's structure and content. You can define properties for the document, as well as define what your users see when they open your document.

You can generate a wide range of repurposed output using customized export options from a single PDF document. Options include exporting it for use as a Web page or as a Word document, saving its content as an XML document, or exporting it in different image formats.

TIP 39 Finding Information about Your Document

There is a lot more to a document than what you see on the screen or printed page. Use the Document Properties dialog when you want to find or modify information about your documents. Choose File > Document Properties (or press Ctrl+D/Command+D) to open this dialog. It opens to the Description tab by default; if you have modified settings in the dialog, the last tab you worked with displays.

The dialog contains six tabs:

- The Description pane holds information about a document (**Figure 39a**)—how much information depends on the source program that created the original document. Use this screen to facilitate searches (you can search by keyword, for example) and to keep better track of material within an office environment. Click to activate a field and add content to any description element.

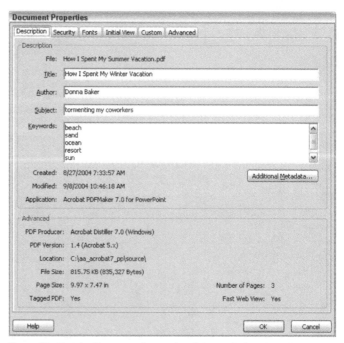

Figure 39a Use the Document Properties dialog to find and modify basic information about your document.

More Info on Info

The lower area of the Description pane (Figure 39a) lists PDF information about the file, such as the tool used to generate the PDF and where the PDF is stored. This area is a good place to check whether the file is tagged (you can read more about tags in Chapter 7). A tagged PDF includes an XML structure that you can use for a range of purposes, such as Web output, reflow, and delivery to accessibility devices.

- The Security pane describes what level of security, if any, has been added to the document, and lists permissions granted to users of the document. If you are the author, and you can use either the document's password or a security certificate, you can change the security settings. In **Figure 39b**, you can see that anyone opening this document has the right to do pretty much anything with the contents. You can read more about Security in Chapter 18.

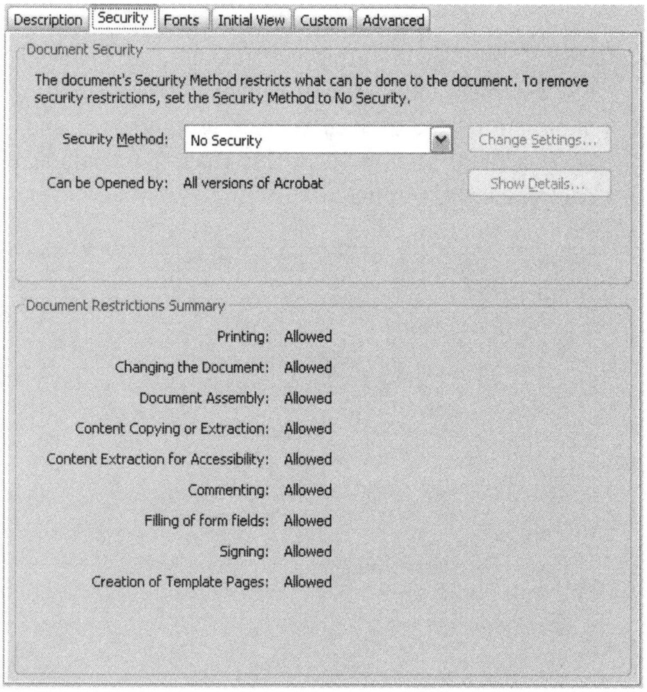

Figure 39b Choose a security method and read properties in the Security tab.

(Continued)

TIP 39: Finding Information about Your Document

Font Information to the Rescue

In situations where you need to expand an original body of work but don't have a template, for example, you can quickly check in the generated PDF and see the fonts in the Fonts pane. Click the (+) icon to the left of the font name to open a list with more information. For each font, you see the name and font type used in the original document; the list displays the font, font type, and encoding used to display the document in Acrobat.

- The Fonts pane (**Figure 39c**) lists the fonts, font types, and encoding information used in the original document. Having this information at hand can be a real timesaver.

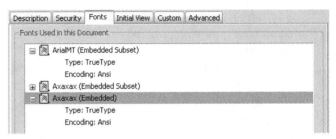

Figure 39c Read information about the fonts embedded in your document.

- Click Initial View to display information that defines how the PDF document looks when it is opened (**Figure 39d**). A range of options related to the document, user interface, and window are available. See Tip 40 in this chapter for information on controlling these options.

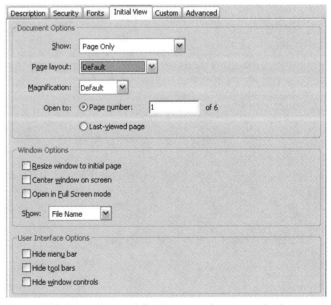

Figure 39d Select options to define how your viewers see the document when it opens.

- The Custom pane lets you add properties and values that identify the content in the document. This information is often used on an enterprise level to organize large quantities of material. Identifying the same document in different versions is a common custom property; in **Figure 39e**, the document uses the custom property *version* and the custom value *1A*. In addition to identifying the content of a document, the custom properties can be used for searching.

More on Custom Properties

Plan ahead when starting a project if you intend to use custom properties. Decide what to name the properties and the range of values, then add the properties as you process each document.

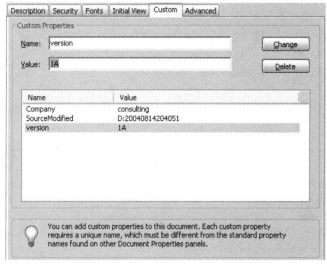

Figure 39e Add additional properties and assign values to be used for indexing and searching.

(Continued)

TIP 39: Finding Information about Your Document

More on Advanced Settings

You can change information about the document as set by the creator—unless the file has security settings that prevent changes.

- The Advanced pane shows PDF settings and reading options. Normally, you won't often change this information, aside from attaching an index to a document (**Figure 39f**). Click Browse to open an Attach Index dialog and locate an index on your hard drive, then click Open to close the dialog and attach the selected index to the document.

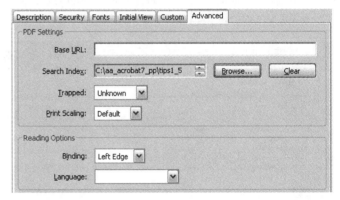

Figure 39f Attach an index, set trapping, and choose a language in the Advanced settings.

When you have finished making changes to the document's properties, click OK to close the dialog. You have to save the file in order to apply the modified properties.

TIP 40 Deciding What Your Reader Sees First

The Initial View pane of the Document Properties dialog lets you modify the Initial View settings. Change the options to control what your readers see when they open your document. Choose File > Document Properties and click the Initial View tab to display the document view settings.

Choose a Show option based on the document's contents and how the reader uses the document (**Figure 40a**). The key to choosing a viewing option is how you want your viewers to navigate the document. What is the most important information for your viewers to note when they open the document? What is the simplest way for them to make their way through the information you are presenting?

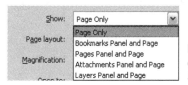

Figure 40a Select different ways of displaying your document from the Show option pull-down list.

- In a long document, you often use a bookmark structure as a way to link content in various locations. For such documents, choose the Bookmarks Panel and Page view.

- In an image-based document, such as a slideshow, you can use the Pages Panel and Page view. That way, your reader can easily browse the document using the thumbnail views of the pages (**Figure 40b**).

Figure 40b Let your viewer navigate through an image-based document using thumbnail views of the pages.

(Continued)

Make Your Content Pop!

Removing access to menus and commands isn't necessarily a bad thing. When screen space is an issue, or if you want your content to jump out at the reader, hiding the menu bar and toolbars helps draw more attention to your document. But be careful when you decide to do this—the next time the document opens, you can only use shortcut keys to control the program. Make sure you provide other types of controls, such as links, from the document.

TIP 40: Deciding What Your Reader Sees First

What's in a Name?

Choose either the document name or the filename to display at the top of the program window. It's a small detail but contributes to a more polished piece of work. After all, what is more descriptive—"Hua Hin Beach" or "hhb040204"? To use a document name, be sure to add the descriptive content on the Description pane of the Document Properties dialog.

- In a short document with multiple attachments, such as an executive summary with attached detailed information in a number of accessory files, choose the Attachments Panel and Page view.

- In a layered document, choose the Layers Panel and Page view; your readers can make their way through the layers in the document (**Figure 40c**).

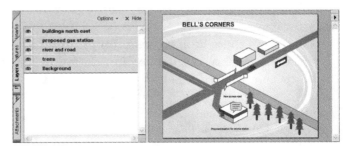

Figure 40c You can show the Layers pane for a multilayered document.

In addition to a default, there are four ways to display the document's pages. Choose an option from the Page Layout pull-down list. The set of page layout options are the same as those found on the status bar below the Document pane. Unless your document's security settings prohibit it, your readers can choose their own page display using the status bar icons (**Figure 40d**).

Figure 40d Choose from several page layout options; the options can be selected from the status bar unless security settings prohibit view changes.

Select an option from the Magnification pull-down list (**Figure 40e**):

Figure 40e You can choose from numerous magnification presets.

- As with the page layouts, the reader can control magnification in the document using the controls on the status bar.

- Choose a zoom option depending on the document's content. Fit Width is common for text documents, for example; the reader sees the entire width of the document and can scroll through vertically to see the rest.

- Use magnifications carefully. A large image is often best presented at full size, and the reader can zoom in for a closer look. In **Figure 40f**, the left side shows a page at 400 percent; the right side shows the Full Page magnification. If you want to use a high magnification for impact (the zoomed version does look rather exotic), be sure to use a high-resolution image.

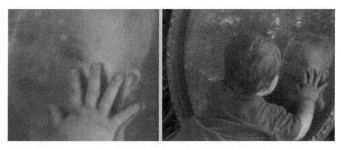

Figure 40f Set magnification according to your content. A full-page screen is usually easier to understand than extreme magnification.

Choose an option that defines how the window will open (**Figure 40g**). Again, the purpose of the document determines which option you'll choose. If you are using a full-page layout, for example, pick the Resize option to show your entire page with the document window fitted around it. This produces the most professional-looking layouts.

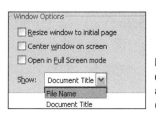

Figure 40g Choose an option that defines how your document will open, and whether or not you show user controls for your documents.

The final options deal with displaying user controls, also shown in Figure 40g. Removing access to menus and commands can make it impossible for your reader to navigate through your document.

Exporting PDF Documents in Other Formats

TIP 41

Editing Export Preferences

Do you find yourself continually exporting the same types of files from Acrobat and making the same settings changes? If so, change the preferences to save yourself precious time. Choose Edit > Preferences (in Mac, Acrobat > Preferences) to open the Preferences dialog.

Click Convert from PDF in the left pane. Select the format you want to modify from the list in the right pane. When you select an option, its settings appear in the dialog. Click Edit Settings to open the same settings dialog you use to export an individual file. Adjust the settings as desired and click OK. Click OK again to close the Preferences dialog. Now your file exports use your modified settings, saving you processing time for each file.

You can use a PDF document for a variety of purposes, and then pass it through various programs. For example, you can create a document in Microsoft Word, convert it to a PDF using PDFMaker, and then export it from Acrobat as an HMTL Web page that includes JPEG images.

To save a PDF document in another file format:

1. Choose File > Save As to open the Save As dialog and click the arrow to open the Save as Type pull-down list (**Figure 41**).

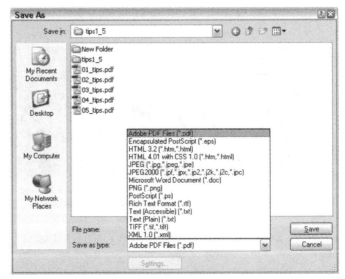

Figure 41 Acrobat offers many file formats you can use for exporting a document.

2. Select a format. The file format extension is appended to the file's name and the Settings button becomes active.

3. Click Settings to open a Settings dialog. The available options are specific to the file format you chose.

4. Adjust the settings in the dialog and click OK to return to the Save As dialog.

5. Click Save. Acrobat exports your file in your chosen format and the Save As dialog closes.

TIP 42 Saving a PDF as a Word or RTF File

Acrobat lets you save a PDF file in two formats that you can then use in Word or other document-processing programs. When the document is open in Acrobat, choose File > Save As to open the Save As dialog, and choose from Rich Text Format (RTF) or Word document (DOC) format based on how you plan to use the content.

Once you choose a format, click Settings to access the options for your desired format (**Figure 42**). A Save As dialog appears; the options vary depending on the format.

Which Format Is Best?

If you want to use the document in Word, export it as a Word document; for use in another document-processing application, use RTF.

Figure 42 Choose export settings for documents, including layout and image options.

Here are some pointers:

- Include Comments is selected by default; deselect it if you don't need comments in the exported document.

- Don't export the images if you don't need them. They add to file size and processing time.

(Continued)

TIP 42: Saving a PDF as a Word or RTF File

- If you want to export images and your PDF file contains both color and grayscale images, choose Determine Automatically from the Use Colorspace pull-down list. If you don't absolutely need the images to be in color, it's a good idea to select the Grayscale option since the files are processed faster and are smaller in size.

- The option for generating tags is selected by default. These tags are not maintained in the exported document; they are used only in the conversion process and then discarded. Leave the option selected.

Note

Image resolution for export defaults to 150 dpi. You can change the resolution depending on the file format chosen; options range from 72 to 300 dpi.

TIP 43
Exporting as HTML, XML, or Text

What if you have a PDF document and need a Web page in a hurry? Or want to use just the text from a document? Easy. You can export the content and images from Acrobat in HTML or XML format. XML describes data and focuses on what the data contains, while HTML displays data and focuses on how data looks. If you want to use a PDF document as a Web page, use one of two HTML formats. But if you want to your document's contents to be used for data exchange in a corporate environment, choose XML format. Choose the accessible or plain text option for output when you don't want any applied styles or formatting.

Choose File > Save As and select a file format option from the Save As pull-down list. Click Settings to open the Settings dialog specific to that format type (**Figure 43a**). If you choose the accessible text option, there aren't any settings you can modify manually.

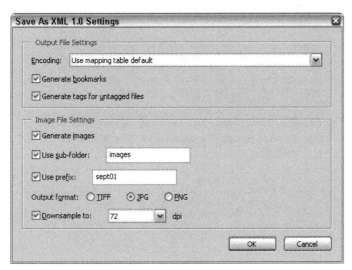

Figure 43a Choose export settings in this dialog for several text-based export options.

- If you're using a specific format, choose it from the pull-down list, or leave the default (Use mapping table default). Bookmarks and tags are generated automatically. Bookmarks, converted to links, are placed at the start of the document.

(Continued)

HTML or XML?

HTML and XML function differently and are used for different purposes:

- If you are saving a PDF document for use on a Web site, use an HTML format. Acrobat does a good job of converting a page and creating styles for the page.

- Computer systems and databases contain data in incompatible formats. Converting your document's data to XML reduces the complexity and creates data that can be read by many types of applications. XML defines the structure of the document and doesn't organize it in the same fashion as HTML will—that is, interpreting the code and displaying images and text in a browser window. Use XML format when you want to export a document for data exchange, such as for use in spreadsheets or databases.

Need More Control?

If you are building a large site, you'll find it more efficient over time to write the code by hand or to use an HTML or WYSIWYG editor. Either approach gives you control over the page's structure as well as style sheet design.

- Choose options in the Image File Settings pane. Acrobat creates a new subfolder named "images"; you can edit this field to suit your purposes.

- Click OK to close the Settings dialog and return to the Save As dialog, and then click OK to convert the file. In the Explorer window, you can see that the file's images are numbered and use the assigned prefix (**Figure 43b**).

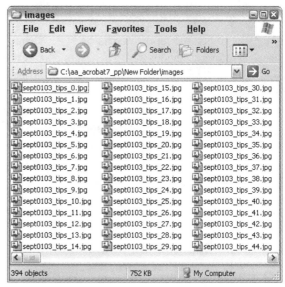

Figure 43b Assign a prefix to exported images to keep track of your efforts.

TIP 44 Saving a PDF as an Image

Often you save a PDF document in a text and image format—as HTML or as a Word document, for example. However, you can also save a PDF document as an image. You might want to do this when:

- You want to use the content as part of another project or process.

- You want to create thumbnail images of pages for use in other documents.

- You need to protect the content in a page. Exporting as an image with security prevents text and other content changes.

To save a PDF as an image, choose File > Save As and select an image export option from the Save As pull-down list. Next click Settings to open the Settings dialog; the Save As JPEG Settings dialog is shown in **Figure 44a**. Modify these options according to your requirements, which vary depending on the file format you selected.

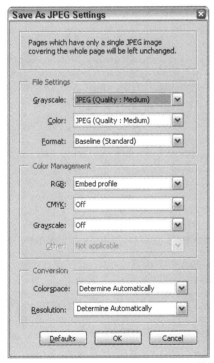

Figure 44a Configure settings for exporting a PDF document as an image.

(Continued)

Check Your Color Space

You can export images to applications, such as Adobe Illustrator, that use EPS (Encapsulated PostScript) files. Take care with the settings, however. If the file is formatted using RGB color space you won't be able to create an EPS file. Instead, you'll see a message telling you that an image uses a color format that won't separate. In this case, you can't export the images as EPS files. The only way to rectify the situation is to use a source image that uses a CMYK color space.

Click OK to close the Settings dialog box and to return to the Save As dialog; click OK to convert the file. Acrobat converts each page of your document to an image. The image will be the same size as the document page.

An image of a document makes a very nice link from another document. When you are building a large project incorporating several types of material, you typically link the documents together. You can use text links, but you can also use an image of the linked document, as in **Figure 44b**. I have a document that is linked to a slideshow. Instead of using text to link, I used a thumbnail-sized image of the first page of the slideshow. Be sure the outcome is worth the effort—don't use an image of an all-text page, for example.

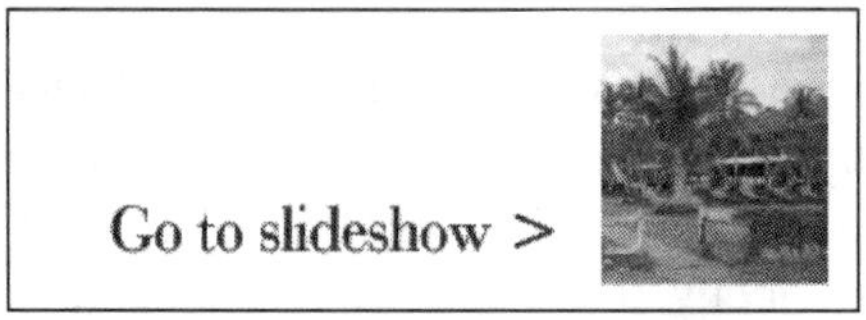

Go to slideshow >

Figure 44b You can use an exported image as a visual link.

TIP 45: Exporting all the Images in a Document

You can export images along with content when you save a document in an HTML version. You can also export the images alone, and specify the extraction size.

Follow these steps:

1. Choose Advanced > Export All Images; the Export All Images As dialog opens. Browse for the folder you want to use to store the images.

2. Choose an image format from the pull-down list at the bottom of the dialog, such as PNG.

3. Click Settings to open the Export All Images As [format] Settings dialog. In this example, as shown in **Figure 45**, the dialog shows Export All Images As PNG Settings. The dialog is similar to that shown in Figure 6a with one addition—you can specify the extraction size by clicking the Extraction pull-down arrow and choosing a size. The default is set at 1.00 inches, which means that all images in the document that are 1 inch in size and smaller are not exported.

(Continued)

Check the Default Size

Extracting all the images from a document is a good idea—but do you really need 100 copies of your company logo? If your logo is placed on each page of a document, for example, setting the extraction size to the logo's size prevents one copy of the image from being exported from each page.

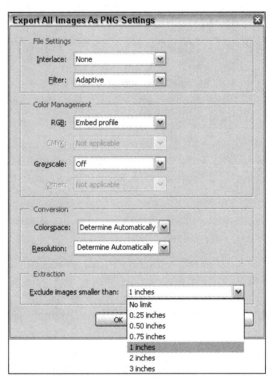

Figure 45 Specify the size of the images extracted from a document.

4. Click Save to export the images to the folder and save them using the file's name and an incremental number.

In the case of JPEG and JPEG2000 formats, images that have a specified compression and resolution aren't affected by the settings you choose in the dialog.

CHAPTER SIX

Printing

You know that you can print any PDF document and it retains the integrity of your original document—that's one of the big attractions of the Portable Document Format, after all.

However, in addition to providing methods for printing and choosing a wide range of options, Acrobat 7 Professional also includes a suite of preflight tools, which are used to evaluate and prepare documents for sending to high-resolution printers.

Some of the preflight tools are useful regardless of the intended output for your document while others are best used for print production jobs.

Picking Pages

You can use Acrobat's Pages pane to select portions of a document to print:

- To select a group of pages, click the first page to select it, hold down the Shift key, and click the last page to select it. Acrobat selects all pages in between as well.

- To select noncontiguous pages, click the first page to select it, hold down Ctrl/Command, and click the other pages you want to print.

Choose File > Print to proceed with your print job.

Print What You See

Suppose you want to print a portion of an image that shows a spectacular palm tree or your dog's face. Resize the program window to show only the content you want to print; use the scroll bars and magnification tools to get the placement correct. Then choose File > Print and click Current View in the Print Range settings of the Print dialog. The area displayed in the program window shows in the Preview area. Choose other print settings, and click OK to print.

TIP 46 Choosing Print Settings

Printing from Acrobat can be much more complex than clicking the Print button: You can control what you print as well as where and how a document is printed. In addition, Acrobat lets you print to a printer or to a file, define a portion of your document for printing, or create a PostScript file.

Choose File > Print to open the Print dialog (**Figure 46**). Here you can choose specific print characteristics, such as the print range and number of copies. Let's take a look.

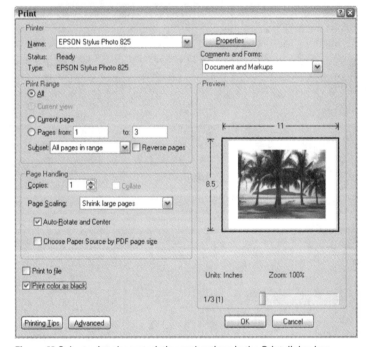

Figure 46 Select print characteristics and options in the Print dialog box.

- Choose a printer from the Name list in the Printer list; on Mac OS, choose an option from the Presets pop-up menu. Your operating system's printer and printer driver installations, as well as your network configuration, determine the Presets and Printer lists. In Windows, click Print to file to create a PostScript file.

Printing

- Specify a print range and options such as page scaling and number of copies.

- Click the Comments and Forms pull-down arrow and choose the document only (the default setting), the document and comments, or form fields. See Tip 125 in Chapter 15 for more on printing comments.

Note

Choose File > Print Setup to set general print options, such as the printer you want to use. The options vary according to your printer and printer drivers. The same settings available from the Print Setup dialog appear at the top of the Print dialog. In Windows, click Properties to set driver options; in Mac OS, driver options are set in the Print Center.

Before printing, preview the page in the Preview area of the dialog. If you like, drag the slider below the Preview area to show the other pages in the document. Click OK to close the dialog and start the print job.

More Printing Options

Look for these other settings in the Print dialog:

- If you are working in Windows, and using a drawing that contains colored lines, such as an engineering drawing, click Print Color As Black to force all non-white color to print as black. This allows the lines to be readily visible on a black-and-white printed page.

- You can quickly change the size of a printed document. Click the Page Scaling pull-down arrow and choose Fit to Paper. Your document is reset at the page size selected in the printer properties.

TIP 46: Choosing Print Settings

Print Troubleshooting 101

These troubleshooting tips won't state the obvious, such as telling you to check whether your printer has paper or that it's turned on. However, I will offer some basic tips and hints that you may find handy in times of stress (usually one minute before a deadline!) If you're having trouble printing a PDF:

- Rewrite the file. Choose File > Save As, and resave the file as itself (don't change the name, and click OK when prompted to overwrite the existing file). I usually save it as itself so I don't get confused by storing multiple copies of the same document. Each time you save a PDF file, it actually saves a version of itself. When you choose Save As and resave it as a PDF, it overwrites all the stored versions, sometimes clearing a stored problem.

- Print the file as an image. Sometimes a document won't print because of errors in interpreting the text or font information. If you print as an image, font and text information isn't required. In the bottom left of the Print dialog, you'll see the Advanced button (**Figure 47a**). Click this button to open the Advanced Print Setup dialog, and then select the Print As Image option (**Figure 47b**). You'll note that the Settings option switches from Acrobat Default to Custom when you click the Print As Image check box. Click OK to close the dialog, and then click OK to try printing again.

Figure 47a Click the Advanced button to open the Advanced Print Setup dialog.

Advanced Print Setup		
Settings: Custom ▼	Delete	Save As
Printer: EPSON Stylus Photo 825	☑ Print As Image	300 ▼
		72
		150
		300
		400
		600

Figure 47b You can print any document as an image; choose from a range of resolutions.

- Re-create the PDF file using a different method; for example, if you originally converted the file using PDFMaker, try again using Acrobat Distiller. Sometimes I have had luck converting a file from within Acrobat that didn't work correctly when originally converted from within Word.

- If you are using a PostScript printer, you can set the printer to display printing errors. Check your printer's documentation. Check that the PostScript Printer Description (PPD) file is up to date, and that you are using the PPD file recommended by the printer manufacturer.

- If you are using a Web file, download the PDF again and try printing once more.

- In a layered document, merge or flatten the layers in the PDF file to determine if a layer is causing the printing issue. To preserve your original, save the document with another name after flattening layers.

- If the document you are trying to print has color separations, print a composite of the document to see if a color plate is causing the problem.

Help!

If you run into printing problems, click Printing Tips at the bottom left of the Print dialog to open Adobe's print troubleshooting document—an excellent and comprehensive reference.

TIP 47: Print Troubleshooting 101

TIP 48 Choosing and Using Fonts

Fonts can be a beautiful thing. It isn't always easy to find the perfect font for a particular project—but you can try! Before converting a document to PDF, make sure your fonts can be used and viewed by others. This tip describes the process for using the PDFMaker in Word. The same methods apply to any program that uses the Adobe PDF printer driver or Acrobat Distiller since the same .joboptions files are used throughout.

Once your masterpiece is created and perfected, check the conversion settings. Choose Adobe PDF > Change Conversion Settings. When the dialog opens, click the Advanced Settings button to open the Adobe PDF Settings dialog; then click the Fonts folder in the left column to display the Fonts settings (**Figure 48a**).

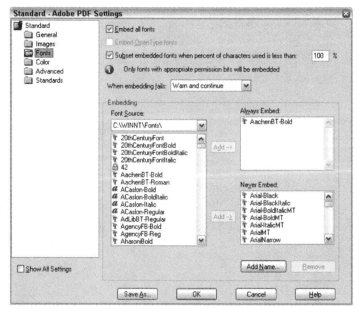

Figure 48a Choose which fonts to embed and add them to the list at the top right. Some font licenses prohibit embedding.

Depending on the conversion settings option you are using, you may find the Embed all fonts, Embed Open Type fonts, or the Subset embedded fonts checkboxes at the top of the pane already selected—the default for the .joboptions file in use.

In the lower portion of the window, select the font you want to embed from the list at the left and click Add. The font is added to the Always Embed list at the right. As you can see in Figure 48a, a font has been added to the list.

Some fonts can't be embedded. A key to the left of the font's name indicates that the font is locked. If you select that font, Acrobat displays a message below the Font Source column stating that the font's license does not permit embedding. In this case, you have two options: Either you must purchase the font for everyone who uses the document, or you should change to a font that can be embedded.

When you have finished, click OK. Before you leave the Adobe PDF Settings dialog, you are prompted to name the .joboptions file. Back in the source program, convert the document to PDF. In Acrobat, the document looks the same, but is it the same? The text shown at the left of **Figure 48b** is the text in the source program; that shown in the right is the text after converting to PDF.

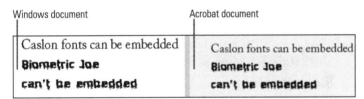

Windows document   Acrobat document

Figure 48b The original Word document is shown at the left; the converted document in Acrobat is shown at the right.

Embedding and Subsetting

Embedding means that information about all the characters in the fonts is automatically attached for use after the document is converted to a PDF. *Subsetting* refers to a percentage of the font's information based on the number of characters used in the document.

When you embed a font, the text in the document using that font displays correctly. You can preserve your content precisely using subsetting. Choose a subsetting value up to 100%, which means that all of the characters used are embedded. It's a good idea to subset at 100%—the difference in file size is hardly noticeable. If you use half of the possible characters in a font and subsetting is set to 100%, all your information is used. If you use half the possible characters in a font and have subsetting set at 25%, other characters may be substituted.

Subsetting is important for documents sent to a print service or press, since it means that your document contains a collection of the font characters actually used in the document. When the document is printed, it uses the information in your document, not that of the printer's version of the font, ensuring precise results.

Documents that comply with PDF/X standards always use subsetting and embedding.

49 Previewing Fonts in Acrobat

Before you finish a document containing text that must be visually correct, experiment with it in Acrobat.

A common error is to preview a document only on your computer using the fonts you have installed. You can't evaluate the embedding/subsetting using your computer's fonts—you need to test how other computers display your document.

By default, Acrobat uses the local fonts (those installed on your computer) for displaying documents. **Figure 49a** shows the text using fonts installed on my computer for my sample document. In the Advanced menu, I deselected the command Use Local Fonts. The results are shown in the lower portion of Figure 49a.

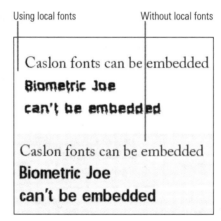

Using local fonts — Without local fonts

Caslon fonts can be embedded
Biometric Joe
can't be embedded

Caslon fonts can be embedded
Biometric Joe
can't be embedded

Figure 49a Where did the fancy font go?

The difference is clear. The first font, Caslon, was embedded. The font used for the second row of text, Biometric Joe, is a locked font and can't be embedded. As a result, if I shipped a document using these fonts, only the first font would display correctly.

You can check the Document Properties for confirmation. Choose File > Document Properties > Fonts. The information for the Caslon font is as you would expect: The dialog states that the font is embedded and also subset.

The substitute font configures itself to simulate the missing font as closely as possible. In the example, although the font looked different structurally, it still used the same color, size, and spacing.

Embedding Fonts

When you are building PDF documents for distribution, try to use a font that can be embedded whenever possible. If a font can't be embedded, such as the one used in this tip's example, Acrobat substitutes with one of two fonts—Adobe Serif MM for a serif font, or Adobe Sans MM for a missing sans serif font (see Figure 4b).

Handling Proofs

Traditionally proofs are printed and then the proof and the original are compared side by side. Instead of printing paper proofs, use the Commenting summary feature to produce a single document that shows the comment in the summary with a connector line to the correction or comment added to the document. Choose either to split the view between two pages (which puts a document page on one page and comments on another), or place the comments and document page on the same page. Read more about comment summaries in Chapter 15.

Look at the font information for Biometric Joe. Although the name and font type are listed, you see the actual font used, Adobe Sans MM, is a substitute for the original (**Figure 49b**).

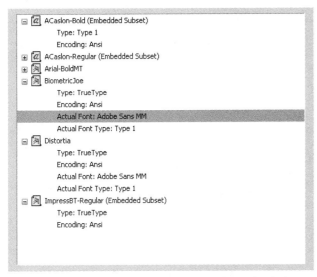

Figure 49b Check the font status in the Document Properties. In the case of Biometric Joe, the original font is replaced by a substitute font.

Previewing Color Separations

Documents going to a printer for a full-color printing use color separation plates. The image is composed of four layers: cyan, magenta, yellow, and black (collectively called CMYK), with each layer containing varying amounts of ink. Overprint colors are two unscreened inks printed on top of each other, such as magenta ink over yellow ink, resulting in a bright orange overprint. If overprinting isn't turned on, only the magenta ink prints.

To preview your images in Acrobat:

- Choose Tools > Print Production > Output Preview, then choose Separations from the Preview menu to estimate the color.

- Click Color Warnings in the Preview menu and then click the Show Overprinting check box to assess the document.

Use this command for a quick check of your document before sending it to the printer to make sure all colors are present. If they aren't, open your source document or Distiller and check the settings, then re-create the document.

TIP 49: Previewing Fonts in Acrobat

TIP 50 Print Production

Acrobat 7 Professional includes a suite of print production tools you can use to evaluate and prepare documents for high-end printing. Choose Tools > Print Production and select an option from the submenu, or select Show Print Production Toolbar to display the set of tools (**Figure 50a**). When the Print Production toolbar is open, the submenu command is Hide Print Production Toolbar. You can also access the toolbar from the shortcut menu. Right-click (Control-click) the toolbar area at the top of the program window and choose Print Production from the toolbar listing.

Figure 50a Choose tools for print production from the toolbar or menu.

Although the tools are intended for high-resolution printing, there are several tools that can be very useful in many business-based production situations as well:

- Click Output Preview 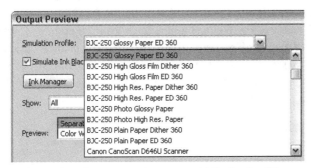 to open the Output Preview dialog. Click the Simulation Profile drop-down arrow and choose options to show you how your document would look using different types of paper, different monitors, different color profiles, and so on (**Figure 50b**).

Figure 50b Simulate how your document would look using different types of paper, monitors, and other types of output.

- To open the Crop Pages dialog, click the Crop tool ; use the settings to crop off unwanted areas of the page. Read more about the Crop tool in Chapter 9.

- Click the PDF Optimizer tool to open the PDF Optimizer dialog. In this dialog, you can choose settings to decrease the size of the file, compress images, unembed fonts, remove unused objects, and other processes. The PDF Optimizer is discussed in Chapter 17.

Soft-Proofing

The Output Preview dialog is used to simulate how your document looks in different conditions. In traditional publishing, you print a hard copy of the document to preview the colors. In Acrobat, you can use color profiles and other settings to show how your document will look in print; this is called *soft-proofing*.

Click the Simulate Ink Black check box to preview how the document would look printed in black ink; click the Simulate Paper White to preview the color of your document printed on white paper. The Simulate Paper White option is used in addition to the Simulate Ink Black option. Not all profiles in Acrobat will support these two soft-proofing options.

In order for soft-proofing to be valuable, your monitor must be calibrated correctly; you should also consider room lighting. For example, bright fluorescent light can cast pink or blue tones on your screen.

Proofreader's Marks

If you are working in print production and need to use traditional proofreading marks, build some custom stamps. Create the proofreading marks in an illustration program, and print as a PDF or export as a PDF. In Acrobat 7, choose Tools > Commenting > Stamp Tools > Create Custom Stamp. In the Select Image for Custom Stamp dialog, click Browse and locate your illustration (now a PDF). Click Select and the stamp is imported. Create a custom folder or add the stamp to your favorites; learn more about stamps in Chapter 14.

TIP 51 Basic Preflighting

Preflighting, the process of reviewing a PDF document to ensure that it meets specific printing requirements, is the traditional realm of the prepress world. But have you ever had to prepare ads for a newspaper or a magazine? Or design brochures? Or create an annual report? I'd bet most people have had these types of experiences.

Preparing a print job, expecially one intended for prepress, can be a laborious and time-consuming process. Acrobat 7 Professional includes a suite of preflight tools you can use to evaluate your files for problems with items such as image compression and transparency.

Choose Advanced > Preflight to open the Preflight dialog (**Figure 51a**) and give the program a minute to load the profiles. The available testing profiles range from standards compliance options, to industry standards for magazines and newspapers, to testing for specific items such as transparency or image resolutions, to compliance with a particular version of Acrobat.

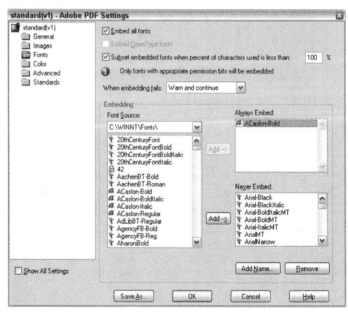

Figure 51a Choose options for testing your document's print output in the Preflight dialog.

Scroll through the list to find the profile you want to use to evaluate the document. When you choose a profile, information displays in the Purpose of the selected Preflight profile section of the dialog below the list.

You don't have to preflight the entire document; click the Preflight only pages check box and type the page range you want to evaluate. Then click the Execute button and the document is tested.

The results of the analysis are shown in the Preflight dialog (**Figure 51b**). Errors are indicated by a big red X; items that comply with the profile you chose are indicated by a green checkmark.

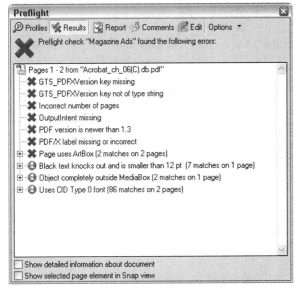

Figure 51b Once your document is analyzed, errors and other information show in the Results display.

More Info

The basic analysis is only the beginning of what you can learn about a document. At the bottom of the Preflight dialog, you can select Show detailed information about document (Figure 51b), which displays an overview of items ranging from fonts and images to layers and color spaces. Use the information to find specific details about errors or content in the document.

Select an object in the document from the Preflight dialog's results list and then click Show selected element in Snap view. A pop-up window identifies the object based on its location on a page. This feature is particularly useful in an image-intensive document to pinpoint an object or item on a page. The Snap view doesn't work with all errors or objects. For example, you won't see a layer error.

Evaluating a Number of Documents

You can evaluate a number of documents for compliance at one time by using a batch process. Read about designing a batch script in Chapter 17.

TIP 52 — Making a Document PDF/X Compliant

PDF-X is the print standard used in PDF and PostScript files to ensure the document meets criteria for high-resolution printing. Unless you're creating an Adobe PDF document for print production, you can ignore the PDF/X options.

Note

You can't create a PDF/X-compliant document using PDFMaker.

Choose Advanced > Preflight or click the Preflight  icon on the Print Production toolbar to open the Preflight dialog. If you choose one of the profiles that require PDF/X-compliance, such as Magazine Ads, the compliance status of the document is defined automatically. All the listings in the Preflight dialog's Profiles list in bold type require PDF/X-compliance.

To convert the active document to a PDF/X-compliant document, click the Convert to PDF/X icon at the lower left of the Preflight dialog. The Preflight: Convert to PDF/X dialog opens (**Figure 52a**). Choose a proposed conversion option, either PDF/X-1a or PDF/X-3, select an output condition from the pull-down list, and specify a trapped key option. Click OK to close the dialog and start the processing.

Figure 52a When converting a document to a PDF/X format, choose the type of conversion and output conditions.

A message dialog displays to tell you whether the conversion was successful (**Figure 52b**). Click OK to close the dialog and display the results in the Preflight dialog (**Figure 52c**). Click the (+) signs to the left of any error message to display more detailed information. You can also see the error in the Preflight: Snap View dialog.

Figure 52b Results of the conversion are displayed in a small dialog.

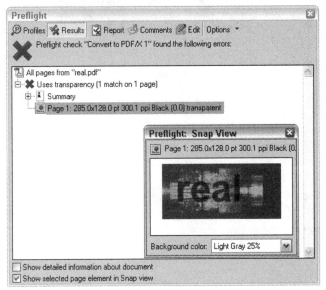

Figure 52c Information about your conversion effort is listed in the Results display in the Preflight dialog. Pinpoint specific problems using the Preflight: Snap View dialog.

Variations on the PDF/X Theme

You can choose from a number of different PDF/X standards. The one you select depends on the final processing of the document:

- A document destined for digital press uses a PDF/X-1a standard; this standard has versions for 2001 and 2003.

- You can also choose PDF/X-3 standards that are 2002- or 2003-compliant; the PDF/X-3 standard includes color usage options—CMYK and spot colors only or calibrated color.

- All compliance options contain an output intent and a printing profile.

- Specific named standards such as Sheetfed Offset (CMYK) are based on best practice guidelines recommended by industry associations.

- Your printer may have custom settings, or recommend you use one of the standards.

Adobe PDF files that complied with both PDF/X-1a and PDF/X-3 standards in Acrobat 6 will default to PDF/X-1a compliance in Acrobat 7.

TIP 52: Making a Document PDF/X Compliant

TIP
53 Managing PDF/X Documents

Preflight Profiles can be edited, and the results of preflighting can be integrated into the document as comments, or made into a separate report.

To share information about a document's status with your workgroup, click Comments 🖼 in the Preflight dialog to transfer the information from the Preflight dialog to the document itself. Acrobat draws a comment box on the appropriate area of the document, adds a comment note to the Comments list (**Figure 53a**). In the example, the image uses transparency so the comment box encloses the entire image.

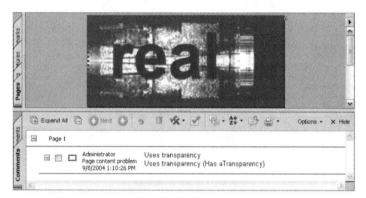

Figure 53a Transfer the results of the Preflight evaluation to the document as comments.

You can also generate a report on the status of the document. Click Report in the Preflight dialog 🖼 to open a Save As dialog. The file uses the document's name and appends _report to the name. Click Save to save the document.

Share and Share Alike

To use a profile provided by your printer, click the Options pull-down menu arrow in the Preflight dialog and choose Import Preflight Profile. When the Open dialog displays, locate the file (which uses the extension .kfp) and click Open. Profiles are added to the Preflight dialog's Profile list in alphabetical order.

You can also share profiles with others. Again, click the Options pull-down menu in the Preflight dialog to open a menu and choose Export Preflight Profile. An Export Preflight Profile dialog opens. Name the file, which uses the listed profile's name by default, and browse to the folder where you want to store the file. Then click Save.

Sometimes the many profiles available in Acrobat don't quite meet your needs. In that case, edit the profile that most closely matches what you need. Click Edit 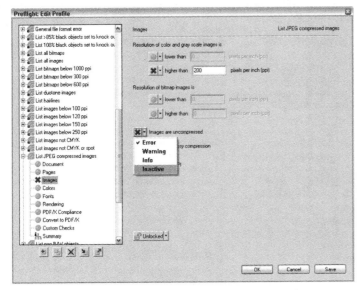 in the Preflight dialog to open the Preflight: Edit Profile dialog (**Figure 53b**). Follow these steps to create a custom profile:

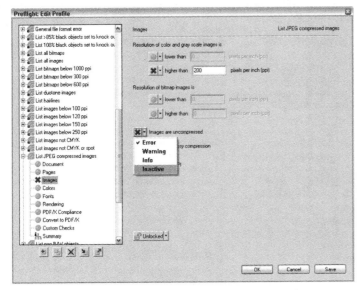

Figure 53b Edit existing Preflight profiles or create new ones.

1. Select the profile that you want to change from the list at the left of the dialog.

2. Open the profile by clicking the (+) to the left of its name. Click the element you want to modify. The sample shows the Images option selected.

3. Click the Locked/Unlocked arrow and select Unlocked to allow you to change the elements of the profile.

Note

When you choose Unlocked, all elements of the profile are unlocked simultaneously.

(Continued)

TIP 53: Managing PDF/X Documents

4. Make the changes in the options at the right of the dialog. For each option, click the pull-down arrow and choose the evaluation setting. You can choose from Error, Warning, Info, and Inactive settings.

5. Click OK to close the dialog; click Save to save the changes and leave the dialog open.

You can also start a new profile from scratch. On the Preflight: Edit Profile dialog, click New ⊞ to open a blank profile. Choose an element from the profile and specify values and evaluation settings (**Figure 53c**). Then name and save the profile. Your custom profile is added to the Preflight dialog's listing in alphabetical order.

Figures 53c When you start a new profile, the categories of options are automatically added to the dialog for your use.

CHAPTER SEVEN

Enhancing PDF Accessibility

Acrobat 7 offers a range of options, tests, tools, and wizards that allow users who are visually or motion-impaired to work with PDF documents. Acrobat provides these features:

- Mouse-free navigation using both keyboard navigation and auto-scroll functions

- Speech capabilities for translating text to spoken words

- Visibility modifications that allow readers to use screen-enhancing software and tools, as well as configure the program to make content easier to view

- Program capabilities that you can use to make a document more accessible

Tags are a key element of making documents accessible and compliant with the Rehabilitation Act, which requires electronic and information technology to be accessible to those with disabilities. Acrobat contains a number of ways in which you can apply tags to a document, evaluate the status of the document, and use the tags for manipulating the document and its contents.

Setting Up Keyboard Access on a Mac

You can set up full keyboard access on a Mac using system-level preferences. Follow these steps to set it up:

1. Choose Apple > System Preferences > Keyboard & Mouse. The Keyboard & Mouse Preferences dialog opens.

2. Select the Turn On Full Keyboard Access option at the bottom of the dialog.

3. Choose View > Universal Access; select either Enable Access For Assistive Devices to use installed screen reader devices or select Enable Text-To-Speech to use the Mac OS speech technology,

4. Choose System Preferences > Quit System Preferences.

When you open Acrobat in a Web browser, keyboard commands are mapped first to the Web browser. Some keyboard shortcuts may not be available for Acrobat, or may not be available until you shift the focus to the PDF document.

TIP 54 Navigating a Document Using Keys

For the user, the important issue is getting around a document, so the most basic accessibility feature is keyboard navigation. Common shortcuts for moving around the program appear in **Table 7.1.** Some shortcuts have more than one option; I have listed the most common or the one I prefer. Check the Acrobat Help menu for the complete list of optional key combinations.

Table 7.1 Common Shortcuts for Moving Through a Document

To do this...	In Windows, press...	In Mac OS, press...
Go to the previous screen	Page Up	Page Up
Go to the next screen	Page Down	Page Down
Go to the first page	Shift+Control+ Page Up	Shift+Command+ Page Up
Go to the last page	Shift+Control+ Page Down	Shift+Command+ Page Down
Scroll up	Up arrow	Up arrow

Scrolling a Document

You can automatically scroll through a document. Scrolling is useful if you're scanning for a particular piece of information, such as an image or table. Choose View > Automatic Scroll, or press Control/Command+Shift+H. The document starts scrolling from the position currently in the Document pane; use the keyboard shortcut to pause the scroll or click the page with your mouse; as long as you're pressing down the mouse button, the page stops. Release the mouse button to start scrolling again. The scrolling stops when you reach the end of the document.

- The Automatic Scroll feature uses the Continuous page layout option, which is applied automatically when you select the command or press the keyboard shortcut.

- Be sure to click the Hand tool before starting. If you are using the mouse to pause the scrolling, each time you click the page Acrobat not only pauses but also applies the tool selected.

- Press the up arrow key to increase the speed or the down arrow key to decrease it. Use the number keys to change speed; 0 is the slowest and 9 is the fastest.

- Reverse the direction of the scroll. Press the minus key (-) on the keyboard or number pad.

- Press Esc to stop the scrolling.

TIP 54: Navigating a Document Using Keys

Choosing Document Colors

Making Form Fields More Visible

A form designer's goals are typically ease of input and a pleasing appearance. However, it can be difficult to visualize form fields if they aren't colored or identified in some way. In that case, the only way to know an active field exists is to move the pointer over the areas until you see the pointer change to an I-beam cursor.

Change preferences to set form field visibility:

1. Choose Edit > Preferences > Forms. On a Mac, choose Acrobat > Preferences > Forms.

2. Click the option Show background and hover color for form fields.

3. Click the color swatch to choose a custom color.

Click OK to close the Preferences dialog. The form fields on the document are now identified by the selected background color; as you move the pointer over a field, Acrobat places a black outline around the field.

If you use a custom color on a document that contains colored form fields, the colors are combined.

Before distributing a document that will be used by vision-impaired users, you should test the settings using the methods described in this tip to see how your document looks. You may be surprised.

You can check your document using custom color and text visibility options. Choose Edit > Preferences > Accessibility to display the Accessibility preferences dialog (on a Mac, choose Acrobat > Preferences > Forms). In the Document Colors Options section check the Replace Document Colors check box to activate the accompanying options (**Figure 55a**).

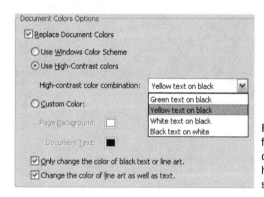

Figure 55a Choose from a number of options to create high-contrast color schemes.

There are several types of color options you can select:

- Use Windows Color Scheme (Windows)—Applies the custom scheme a user may set in the operating system.

- Use High-Contrast colors—Bright green or yellow text on a black background is easier to see than black text on a white background. To select from common high-contrast color schemes, check this option and then select color options from the pull-down menu.

- Custom Color—Check this option to select colors for your document. To choose a page color, click the color swatch and select an option from the standard palette, or click Other Color to open the Color Picker and choose a custom color; click OK to close the dialog.

- Line art and black text changes—The final two options are used for modifying the color of black text and line art. If you don't want to change the color of text that is already colored, click Only change the color of black text or line art; to change the color of line art, click Change the color of line art as well as text.

Click OK to close the Preferences dialog and apply the color scheme. **Figure 55b** shows portions of the same page; the left image shows a page before color changes, the right after applying a Yellow text on black High-Contrast scheme.

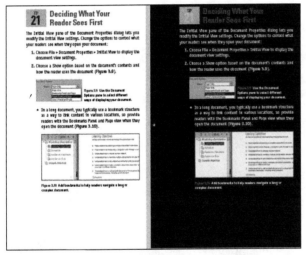

Figure 55b Changing the appearance of a standard document (left image) to a high-contrast color scheme (right image) can be a valuable tool for vision-impaired users.

Colors to Avoid

If you know that vision-impaired users will be viewing your documents, be careful with the colors you choose. One of the biggest problems is light-colored backgrounds. While a pale background behind a title looks attractive on a white background, if you use a high-contrast color scheme, for example, the text becomes virtually illegible. The light background and the light text used for high-contrast schemes are similar in color, thus making the text hard to read.

Set It Here, Set It There

The Accessibility Setup Assistant brings together settings from a number of panes in the Preferences dialog.

For example:

- The Reading Order options are also available in the program preferences. Choose Edit > Preferences > Reading Order and select a preference in the Reading Order options. On a Mac, choose Acrobat > Preferences > Leading Order.

- The Confirm before tagging documents option is also on the Reading preferences in the Screen Reader Options.

Acrobat 7 Professional offers a wizard you can use to set up Acrobat for use with screen readers. The wizard contains five consecutive dialogs. Choose Advanced > Accessibility > Setup Assistant to open the Accessibility Setup Assistant (**Figure 56a**).

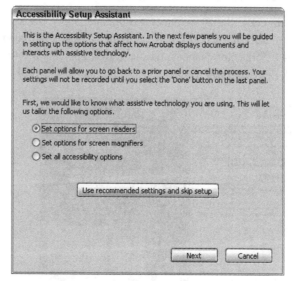

Figure 56a Use the Accessibility Setup Assistant to choose screen reader options rather than selecting preferences in multiple panes of the Preference dialog.

Progress through the wizard by clicking options on each pane and then click Next to move to the next numbered pane; click Done when you have made selections from the fifth pane. Look for these features on each pane:

- Pane 1. Choose the device you are working with: a screen reader, screen magnifier, or all options. You can also click the Use recommended settings and skip setup button to close the wizard and apply the preprogrammed settings.

- Pane 2. On this pane choose a high contrast color scheme, text smoothing, and a default zoom for document viewing. Since some assistive devices can have problems with Acrobat's use of different cursors for different tools, you can check Always use the keyboard selection cursor to specify your preference.

- Pane 3. Choose tagging options. You can choose to let Acrobat infer the reading order or specify an option. Also on this pane, choose to override reading order in a tagged document, or confirm tagging in an untagged document.

- Pane 4. Select an option for viewing large documents. You can choose to deliver the visible pages or the entire document, or you can let Acrobat decide. If you prefer, you can have all the pages delivered for a small document. Click the Maximum number of pages in a small document field and type a number. The default is 50 pages.

- Pane 5. The fifth and final pane gives you an option to disable document auto-save (**Figure 56b**), which can cause the document to reload and begin reading from the start of the document. You can choose to reopen the document from the last viewed page—which is terrific when you're working with long documents. Finally, you can also choose to open a PDF document in Acrobat or a browser; opening a document in Acrobat is less confusing for some assistive devices.

Click Done to close the wizard and apply the settings.

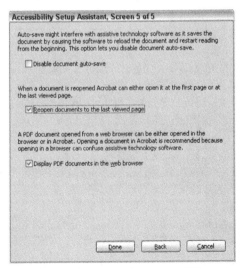

Figure 56b The final pane of the Accessibility Setup Assistant lets you disable auto-save.

TIP 56: Using the Accessibility Wizard

You can have Acrobat read a document aloud. This is a terrific feature when your goal is to make your documents more accessible, because Acrobat simulates some features of a full-blown screen-reader program. But be warned: A document that appears to be a simple, well-planned page isn't always simple for a reader. For example, a screen reader may read a document from left to right, even if there are multiple columns on the page. The solution in that case is to use articles, described in the tip following this one.

To set reading preferences, choose Edit > Preferences > Reading, or Acrobat > Preferences > Reading on a Mac (**Figure 57**). In the Read Out Loud Options section, choose a voice, pitch, and volume. In Windows I prefer to listen to "LH Michelle," but you can also choose from "LH Michael," "Microsoft Sam," and "Sam." On a Mac, you have a choice of numerous voices, some of which aren't even human!

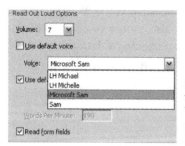

Figure 57 Make your selections in the Read Out Loud Options section. Windows users can choose from one of four voices: LH Michael, LH Michelle, Microsoft Sam, and Sam.

Check Read form fields to have text fields, check boxes, and radio buttons in fillable forms read aloud.

Click OK to close the Preferences dialog and apply the voice settings. You have to return to the preferences to make adjustments. Unfortunately, you can't modify the settings and listen to the outcome of your adjustments at the same time.

Once you have selected a voice and its settings, choose View > Read Out Loud. Choose Read This Page Only or Read To End of Document. The reading starts.

Pause and resume the reading using the menu commands or use shortcut keys:

- Ctrl/Control+Shift+C to pause/resume
- Ctrl/Control+Shift+E to stop

TIP 58 Articles

Articles are areas on a page that you define to give you control over how the viewer reads your page. The key to working with articles is understanding how we read a page and then simulating that as closely as possible for all our viewers. Articles allow you to design a document both for visual appearance and for ease of reading using magnified views.

If you are zoomed into a document at a high magnification, how can you tell where you are on a page? Or know that you are reading the middle column of a complex page, such as a magazine article?

It is much simpler to add articles to a document than to reformat an optional version of the document. Follow these steps to control a reading path through a document using articles:

1. Choose Tools > Advanced Editing > Article Tool or click the Article tool 🔲 to select it if you have opened the Advanced Editing Toolbar. The pointer changes to crosshairs.

2. Click and drag a rectangular marquee in your document to draw the first article box. When you release the mouse, Acrobat draws the first article box, numbered 1-1 (**Figure 58a**). The Article tool draws a shape on the page irrespective of the contents. Anything within the margins of the box becomes part of the article.

Article number

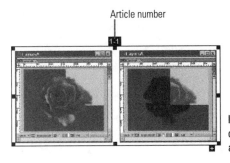

Figure 58a Articles are defined by boxes and automatically numbered.

(Continued)

Using the Articles Pane

You can also use the Articles pane to read articles in a document. Choose View > Navigation Tabs > Articles to open the Articles pane, which lists the articles in the document. Click the article you want to read. Double-click the article's title or icon to start reading at the beginning of the article. Acrobat displays that article in the Document pane.

You can't use the Articles pane in a Web browser; you must use it from within Acrobat on either a computer or a handheld device.

The Shape of Articles

When you select an article box, handles will appear at the sides. Drag the handles to resize the box. You can also drag the entire article box to another location on the page. The content on the page and the article box aren't one and the same—article boxes "float" over the page and display whatever page content is enclosed within the box. If you add an article thread and want to change its order, shift the location of the boxes on the page.

3. Continue adding article boxes; as you draw boxes around pieces of text or images, Acrobat numbers the articles consecutively. The sequence of boxes using the same article number is called an article thread (**Figure 58b**).

Figure 58b Draw a series of boxes with the Article tool to identify consecutive areas on the document.

4. Press Esc (or Return) or select another tool to stop the article drawing. The Article Properties dialog opens (**Figure 58c**).

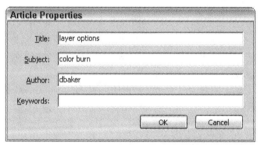

Figure 58c Name the article thread and add other information if desired.

5. Enter information about the article in the dialog. You must name the article, named "Untitled" by default, but the other information is optional.

6. Click OK to close the dialog.

Add additional article threads, and save the document when you have finished. As long as you add articles to your document in the logical order in which the content should be read, you can be sure that readers will move through your document as you intended, even when the view is magnified.

Reading Articles

When you have finished adding a set of articles to a document, use the Hand tool or keystrokes to read the articles. Click anywhere on the page to start reading an article—you see the pointer change to the follow article pointer (the Hand tool is overlaid with a down arrow.) You can scroll through the page using the mouse wheel or dragging the Hand tool down the page.

To navigate through the article:

- Press Enter/Return to go to the next page in the article.

- Shift-click or Shift+Return in the article to return to the previous page.

- Ctrl/Option-click in the article to go to the beginning.

At the end of the article the pointer changes to the end article pointer (the Hand tool is overlaid with an up arrow.) Press Enter/Return or click to return to the view displayed before you started reading.

TIP 59 Basic Document Tagging

Some program features used to enhance accessible use, such as articles and reflow, don't work properly or predictably unless a document is tagged, which means it has a logically defined structure. Tags are invisible and are a part of the document's information. They define relationships among elements in the document, including tables, lists, images, and text.

Tagging can be done in the source document (if you're using a PDFMaker) or in Acrobat. To tag a document using a PDFMaker, like the one used in Microsoft Word, choose Adobe PDF > Change Conversion Settings. The Change Conversion Settings dialog opens to the Settings tab. In the Applications Settings section of the Settings tab, select the option Enable accessibility and reflow with Tagged PDF, and then click OK. Click Convert to Adobe PDF or choose Adobe PDF > Convert to Adobe PDF. Word creates your PDF file.

Open the document in Acrobat and choose View > Navigation Tabs > Tags to display the Tags panel. Click the Tags icon ⊞▣ Tags to display the document's tags in a hierarchy (**Figure 59**). The figure shows a section of the Tags panel for a table. You see the parent tag Table contains tags for the <Tbody> (table body,) which contains tags for the table rows <TR>, which contains tags for table cells <TD>, which contains tags for column heads, and finally the cell's text.

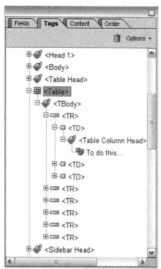

Figure 59 A tagged document displays its tag content in a hierarchy.

Planning Documents for PDF Accessibility

The key to successful tagging of a document as well as making it comfortable for a user working with a screen reader is to use your source programs' features efficiently. Plan ahead. Here are a few examples:

- Configure the document pages correctly. Don't add blank lines to make a space.

- Check the styles attached to inserted material such as images and charts.

- Group tables and charts or convert them to an image before conversion to prevent creating individual tags for each line and word segment.

Many document-creation programs don't offer tagging options. You can easily add tags from within Acrobat:

1. Check for preexisting tags by choosing Advanced > Accessibility > Quick Check. The Accessibility Quick Check looks for a document structure (tags). An untagged document displays a message stating the document isn't structured and may cause a problem with reading order. Click OK to close the Quick Check results message.

2. Choose Advanced > Accessibility > Add Tags. Acrobat processes the document and adds tags. An Accessibility Report displays in the How To pane area at the right of the document pane in the program window. Refer to the following tip for information on working with tags and reports.

3. Check the document again by selecting Advanced > Accessibility > Quick Check. The new message will state there are no accessibility problems with the document, meaning it is tagged.

4. Choose File > Save to save the document with its tagged structure.

A Structure and Tags Aren't Equal

Some programs create a structured document that often is fine for reading in Acrobat. For example, creating a Word document using styles in a heading hierarchy is an example of a structure. A structure doesn't provide some of the qualities in an accessible document such as word spacing; you must tag a document in order to make it compliant with accessibility standards.

TIP 59: Basic Document Tagging

TIP 60 — Reporting on and Repairing a Document

In addition to tagging your document, you can have Acrobat perform a complete assessment of a document and generate a report with repair hints. Use these advanced evaluation methods if you are preparing documents that must comply with government or other regulatory accessibility standards.

Choose Advanced > Accessibility > Full Check to evaluate a document. If the document isn't tagged, a message displays telling you to add the tags first and then proceed with the reporting. Tip 59 in this chapter describes how to add tags. When the document has been tagged, the Accessibility Full Check dialog opens (**Figure 60a**).

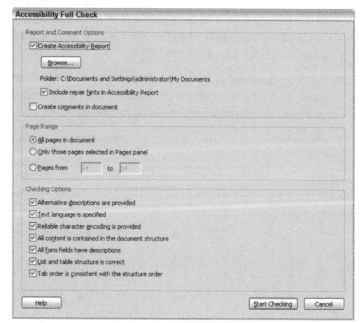

Figure 60a Select the document elements you want to evaluate for accessibility compliance.

Select from the options according to your requirements:

- Report and Comment Options—Check to create a report, and click Browse to define a storage location for the report (which is automatically named using the PDF document's name). The option Include repair hints in Accessibility Report is selected by default. I recommend you leave this setting selected since it can save a great deal of time repairing your document.

- If you are the type of person who likes to see what's what close up, click Create comments in document. When the report is finished, all errors and irregularities are shown on the document in comments.

- Page Range—Choose either the visible page, a specified range, or the entire document.

- Checking Options—The default option is to check all options for compliance. You can check for options such as alternative descriptions, text language, encoding, form field descriptions, list and table structures, content inclusion, and whether the tab order is consistent with the order of the document's structure.

Click the Start Checking button to start the evaluation. When the check is complete, the results appear in summary in a dialog (**Figure 60b**). Click OK to close the dialog.

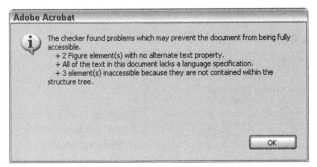

Figure 60b A summary of the accessibility check is shown in a dialog after the test is completed.

(Continued)

Make a Pretest

Processing a very long document can take a considerable length of time. If you are working with a long document and aren't sure of the accessibility status, choose a few representative pages to test instead of processing the whole file. If the returned list of repairs isn't too extensive, you can proceed with testing the entire document. If it reads like Santa's gift list, you have a good indication of where to start looking for errors and making repairs.

TIP 60: Reporting on and Repairing a Document

Customize Your Accessibility Test

Accessibility reports can take a long time to process. Before running the report, customize the Checking Options on the Accessibility Full Check dialog. For example, if your document doesn't contain tables or lists, then deselect the List and table structure is correct option. If you don't need a specified text language, deselect the option, and so on.

The Accessibility Report opens in the How To pane to the right of the document pane in the program (**Figure 60c**). The report is an HTML document, and contains links within it to help you identify and correct errors. If you left the option Include repair hints in Accessibility Report selected in the dialog before running the evaluation, the report includes information on how to repair your document. Click Hide to close the Accessibility Report when you have finished. You can retrieve the report any time you wish. Choose Advanced > Accessibility > Open Accessibility Report. In the Open Accessibility Report dialog that displays, browse to the location you specified for the report's storage and select the file. Click Open to close the dialog and display it in Acrobat in the How To pane's area to the right of the document pane.

Figure 60c Use the Accessibility Report to evaluate and correct errors in your document.

TIP 61 — Using Document Tags

Once a document is correctly tagged and in order, you can examine the contents of the document using the Tags panel. Choose View > Navigation Tabs > Tags to open the panel. Drag the panel to the left of the screen to dock it with the other Navigation tabs.

You can find a specific location in a document using the Tags panel. Open the main document tag and scroll through the list to find the parent tag containing the item you wish to see. Click the tag in the Tags panel to select it, and then right-click or Control-click to open the shortcut menu. You can also click Options on the Tags panel to display the menu (**Figure 61a**).

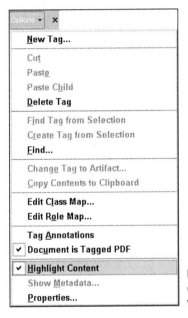

Figure 61a Choose from a variety of options to modify the contents of your document's tags.

(Continued)

What Does It Mean?

If you look at the tags in the Tags panel, such as those shown in this tip, you see a variety of icons to the left of the tag names. These icons indicate the type of tag, which can range from Paragraphs to Forms to References to Table Headings. The content contained within a specific tag is not identified by a tag icon, but instead shows information about the content of the tag, such as an image or text.

Touching Up Properties

When correcting the accessibility status of a document, you can modify the properties of individual tags. Select the tag in the Tags panel, and from either the Options menu or the shortcut menu choose Properties. The TouchUp Properties dialog opens; make changes to the properties, such as the type or the alternate text, and then click Close.

Click Highlight Content. The tag or its content you select in the Tags panel is surrounded by a colored box in the document. In **Figure 61b**, the <L> tag representing the list in the document is selected. I opened the first level of the tag, and you can see three <LI> or list item tags, representing each of three items in the list. In the Document pane at the right of the figure, you see four list items selected by a gray box. It isn't necessary to select all four list items: Selecting the parent list tag automatically selects the child tags.

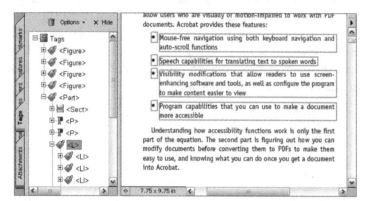

Figure 61b Use the tags in your document to locate content quickly and precisely.

TIP 62 Reflow

Readers using assistive devices or very small screens like those on personal digital assistants (PDAs) often experience a problem called *reflow*. When you zoom in closely to a page, what happens? You see a few words and maybe an image (**Figure 62a**). Not only do you have to scroll back and forth to see the entire line, but also it's difficult or impossible to understand where you are in the document at any given time.

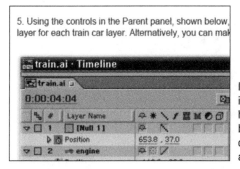

Figure 62a You can zoom into a document at very high magnification, but then it is difficult to determine where you are on a page.

If the document is tagged, you have more viewing options available. You can control how the page reflows to make viewing the content simpler, whether in Acrobat or on your PDA, by choosing View > Reflow. Use the Zoom tools or shortcut keys to zoom in to the size you want to view. As you zoom in and out of the Document pane, the size of the document changes. The text automatically wraps itself to the next lines, and you don't need to use the horizontal scroll bar to read the text (**Figure 62b**).

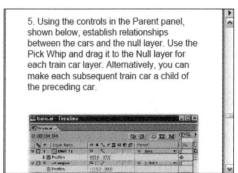

Figure 62b Choosing Reflow Page wraps the content of pages automatically, regardless of the magnification used.

(Continued)

Using Alternate Reading Orders

The Accessibility Quick Check suggests that you try other reading orders by modifying choices in the Reading Order options in the Reading preferences dialog. The default setting is to allow the program to infer the reading order. Sometimes this works; sometimes it doesn't. Often reading errors occur. You can also choose to read from left to right and from top to bottom, or to use the reading order from the raw text stream. These options can make a difference in some circumstances.

The process is fairly reliable. However, with a complex document such as one using numerous columns, images, and text boxes, the page isn't necessarily presented in the optimal reading order. For example, a person reading the entire page may read a sentence, refer to the image, and then return to the next sentence. In a reflow view, the document is read as presented—that is, in the order the content appears on the page. The content can be controlled using articles, which is discussed in Tip 58.

CHAPTER EIGHT

Working with Acrobat Forms

One of the coolest features in Acrobat 7 Professional is the ability to design a form that grants form fill-in rights to users working with Adobe Reader 7. A form can now be used with even greater versatility by the literally millions of people that use Adobe Reader 7.

Acrobat 7 Professional offers two methods of forms creation depending on your operating system. For both Windows and Mac, you can construct forms using the Forms tools. If you are working with Windows, you have access to the entire Adobe Designer 7 program, integrated as part of Acrobat 7 Professional.

What makes up a form? What's the point? What's the best way to design a form? And how do you automate the processes you can program into a form field?

These are big questions. You have the same flexibility in designing forms in Acrobat as you do in creating and designing PDF documents of other types. You can design a form from scratch, based on a document you create in another program, or based on a PDF document. If you are working with Adobe Designer, you can choose any of these three options, or use a template, as we describe in Tips 72 and 73. The option you choose is based on your expertise and your existing source materials.

Don't approach form design casually. Plan ahead, storyboard the form, and decide what you want it to do. See how to construct and troubleshoot a simple form, and how to add features to let your users work with your forms easier.

As with other tasks you perform in Acrobat, you can customize how you fill in forms, and set a wide range of forms preferences as well.

TIP 63 Getting Started with Forms

Like many things in life, planning ahead is the key to designing a good form in Acrobat. Forms are made up of a number of components, which can include:

- Graphic and image content, such as backgrounds or logos
- Form fields such as text entry fields, radio buttons, pull-down lists, and more
- Document structure information such as tags and alternate text
- Programming used for calculations, form data transmittal, and so on

If you are starting a new form:

- Define what sorts of data you need to collect, and decide what type of fields can be used. For example, do you want your users to type "Yes" or "No"? If so, adding Yes/No radio buttons may be a simpler choice.
- Decide if you are creating a single form, or if it is to be part of a suite of forms. If you are building a number of forms for your company, such as personnel records, vacation records, sick forms, and so on, plan ahead. If you use the same naming structure for all the forms, your users can import and export data into and out of forms quickly, saving everyone time.
- Decide how large or small the form should be. If your form is designed for onscreen use, a form that fits well and reads clearly at 800 x 600 ppi resolution works for the majority of users. If the intent is to print the form as well, decide how many pages and what size margins are required for a logical print size.
- Decide if you want to create the form field's appearance in the source program or in Acrobat—this choice defines whether you add tables and cells in your source program, or leave sufficient space to add the fields in Acrobat (**Figure 63a**).

See What You've Got

Sometimes forms are so beautifully designed that it is difficult to see the actual fields you need to fill in. You can set preferences or, on a form-by-form basis, use the options in the Document Message Bar, the yellow bar that displays automatically above the Document pane when a form PDF is opened:

- Click Highlight Fields to make all fields light yellow. If the designer has set a color for the fields you can't highlight them, but a highlight isn't necessary as you can clearly see a colored field.
- To show required fields, which must be filled in for you to submit the form, click Highlight Required Fields. Any required fields on the form are framed with a red outline.

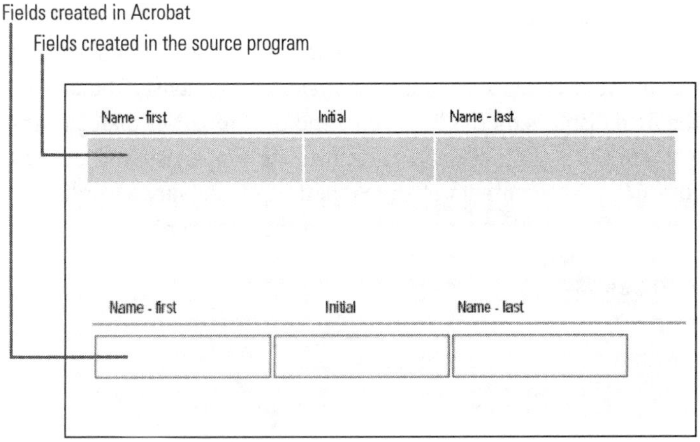

Fields created in Acrobat
Fields created in the source program

Figure 63a Do you want to create the field appearance in your source program or in Acrobat?

- Create the basic structural components in a source program and then convert it to PDF. It's simpler to lay out labels, graphics, and other visual elements beforehand. Be sure to consider the font size you intend to use once your form is converted to a PDF form (**Figure 63b**).

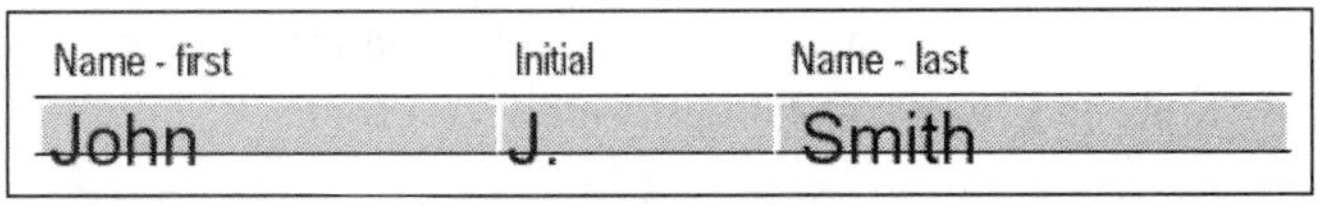

Figure 63b Be sure to consider details such as the font size you want to use for text fields when designing the layout of the form.

Convert the source file to a PDF document; you can then add and configure the form fields in Acrobat Professional 7.

If you are working in Windows, and using Adobe Designer 7, you have several options for forms design (check out Tip 72). Of course, you still have to plan the required data and the form appearance in advance.

Building a Form in Acrobat

Setting a Standard

Adding individual form fields and then configuring each one is very time-consuming—not to mention unnecessary. Add a field to your document, and configure it as you like. Right-click/Control-click to open the shortcut menu and choose Use Current Properties as Default. Whatever settings you've used for the field, such as border color or font, are set as the default for subsequent fields. Then add the remaining fields, either using the shortcuts or adding each field individually.

Do you want a different look for a radio button than for a check box? No problem. Each set of default properties you define applies only to a specific type of form field.

Acrobat includes a toolbar of form field creation tools. Click the Form Field tool to select it on the toolbar, drag a marquee on the document where you want to place the field, and release the mouse. The outline for the field displays on the document, and the Properties dialog opens for you to name the field and customize its properties and options (**Figure 64a**). The contents of the Properties dialog vary according to the type of form field you are applying to the document.

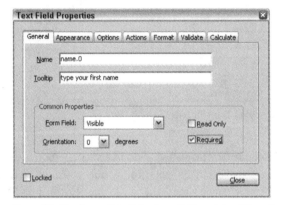

Figure 64a The Properties dialog for a field contains different options depending on the type of field you are creating.

Choose Tools > Advanced Editing > Show Forms Toolbar. The available tools and their common uses are:

- Button tool ▦—Use a button to initiate actions that can be used for everything from printing a document to submitting a form or playing a sound. Buttons are discussed in Chapter 12.

- Check Box tool ☑—Where your user can choose one or more options, use a check box. For instance, if your form includes a list of favorite holiday destinations, your user might like to specify all three choices of Hawaii, Jamaica, and Tahiti.

- Combo Box tool ▦—You can offer a list of items in a pull-down menu or let your user enter a custom value. For example, your order form can include several choices of countries where you commonly ship your products, as well as an option for customers to type their country name.

- List Box tool 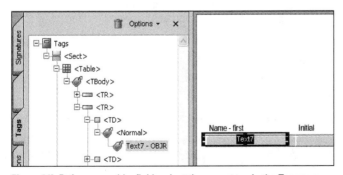—Create a list of items from which your user can select; usually list boxes are designed to allow for multiple selections. For example, when building your dream car at an online site you can choose any or all items from a list of accessories—of course, that doesn't mean you can afford them, but it is nice to dream.

- Radio Button tool —Add radio buttons when you want the user to make a single choice among two or more items. An example is a customer service form that lets the user choose among a range of responses, from "terrific" to "terrible."

- Text Box tool —Use this tool to create a field in which your users can type text, such as their names, addresses, or favorite colors.

- Digital Signature tool —Use this tool to add a special type of field used to apply a digital signature to the document. Learn more about digital signatures in Chapter 18.

When adding form fields to a document where the tag structure is very important (like one that connects to a database, for example), make sure that:

- You open the Tags pane, click the Options menu, and select Tag Annotations.

- You select the tag in the Tags pane that you want to be the parent of the form field you intend to add to the document (**Figure 64b**).

Figure 64b Before you add a field, select the parent tag in the Tags pane.

TIP 64: Building a Form in Acrobat

See What You are Building

Choose Edit > Preferences > Forms (or Acrobat > Preferences > Forms) and click the preference Show field preview when creating or editing form fields. Then close the Preferences dialog. Now when you work on your form fields, you see the structure and content.

TIP 65 Configuring Form Fields

Regardless of the type of form tool you use, form fields share many features in common; some configuration options are used for only certain types of fields. For example, you don't find a Calculate tab in a Check Box Properties dialog, nor will you find a Validation tab in a Button Properties dialog.

Here's a brief rundown of the configuration tabs you can use with form fields in Acrobat 7 Professional:

- General tab—This tab is common to all types. You add a name and tool tip in this tab of the dialog, as well as define whether the field is visible or invisible. In addition, you specify if a field is *required* (an entry is mandatory) or if the field is read only. You may want to make the user's name field required, for example, or specify calculated text fields as read only (**Figure 65a**).

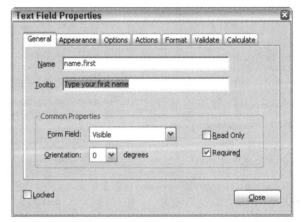

Figure 65a All types of form fields offer the General tab, where you name the field and choose other basic characteristics.

- Appearance tab—This tab is common to all types of form fields. You configure the color of the border and fill, as well as other characteristics, such as text.

- Options—All form fields have an Options tab; the contents vary according to the type of field. Buttons, for instance, contain options for choosing labels and images for their display;

a Check Box field allows you to choose the appearance of the object, such as a checkmark or a star; Combo Box and List Box fields include areas where you can insert lists of items; a Radio Button field allows you to choose the style of the button and whether or not it is automatically selected (**Figure 65b**).

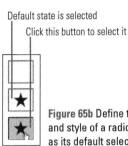

Default state is selected

Click this button to select it

Figure 65b Define the appearance and style of a radio button, as well as its default selection state.

- Actions—All form fields have this tab, and it looks and works the same in all types. Actions are activities Acrobat performs in response to some sort of interaction. For instance, clicking a button that opens another document is an action, as is typing a number in a form field that then shows a calculation in another form field. Actions are described in several tips in this chapter, as well as in Chapters 12 and 13.

- Format—Some types of form fields, such as Text Box and Combo Box fields, include this tab in their properties dialogs. Click the pull-down menu and choose a type of formatting to apply to the text your user enters in the field (**Figure 65c**).

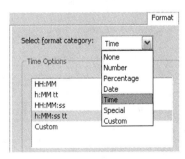

Figure 65c Define how the text entered in a Text Box or Combo Box is formatted.

(Continued)

TIP 65: Configuring Form Fields

- Validate—You can restrict what your user enters in a field, such as a number or characters added in Text Box and Combo Box fields. Choose options in the dialog or use custom JavaScript validation scripts.

- Calculate—Perform a number of arithmetic functions using this tab of the dialog. (See Tip 66 for information adding calculations to a form).

- Selection Change—This tab is seen only in List Box Properties. You set the behavior that occurs when the list box's selection changes.

You don't have to draw, name, and position form fields individually if you are adding a group of fields to your PDF form document. Draw and configure the first field; then right-click/Control-click to open the shortcut menu and choose Create Multiple Copies to open the dialog. Choose how many fields you want to add horizontally and vertically. Click OK to close the dialog and Acrobat adds the extra fields. See Tip 101 in Chapter 12 for more information on adding multiple fields and using alignment tools for manually aligning objects.

For example, if you were building an order form, how many similar fields would you have to add and configure if you added them manually? A whole lot, right?

The value of using an automated method when building a form is how the fields are named (**Figure 65d**). The original field at the upper left was named pen_blue. Adding the other fields automatically appends .0.0 and .0.1 to the fields in the top row, and 1.0 and 1.1 to the fields in the second row.

Figure 65d Add multiple, prenumbered fields with Acrobat's handy, convenient automatic feature.

When you use the automatic feature to add fields, the fields are also automatically spaced on the document. If necessary, you can manually align them as well. Refer to Tip 91 in Chapter 11 to see how grids and guides can assist in placement of objects on the page.

TIP 66 · Creating Forms That Make Sense

Building forms can be fun (and creative!), but the process has its share of headaches. Calculations can be a particular hurdle in building forms—particularly order forms. In this tip, I'll show you how to plan and add calculations using a sample order form.

Rather than explaining how to build the form step by step, I'll describe the workflow in general terms that may be useful to your work; check out the sidebar for some hints to make the job simpler.

Let's say we're setting up a PDF form that allows customers to order citrus fruit online. The oranges are priced at 77 cents apiece, lemons go for 47 cents each, and you can buy a lime for a mere 40 cents. We need a way for the customer to order multiples of each fruit, and then have the totals calculated.

Here goes:

1. Import the form structure. The example we're using consists of a table, labels, and a background we created in Microsoft Publisher and then converted to a PDF document.

2. Add the first text field, Quantity. In the Text Field Properties dialog, click the Format tab and choose Number from the pull-down list. Set the decimal places to 0—you can't buy .25 of an orange, after all (**Figure 66a**).

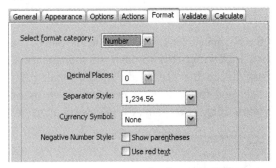

Figure 66a Be sure to use a number format for fields that require calculation.

(Continued)

Just Juicy Fruits

If you have planned your adventures in form-building (as described in Tip 63), you know in advance what you need to calculate and which fields are involved. In my example, I have three products—oranges, limes, and lemons. My customer types an amount in the Quantity column, and the total for each product automatically displays in the Price column. Not only that, but a Subtotal, Tax, and Grand Total are automatically calculated as well. This very simple form shows you many of the ways you can plan and work with calculations.

3. Add the remaining text fields. Plan how to add multiple fields so the new fields' names make sense (**Figure 66b**).

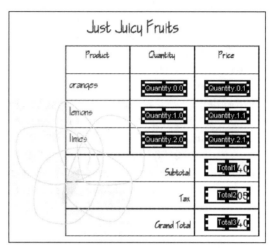

Figure 66b Add groups of fields to the form depending on their use to make sure the automatic names are meaningful and useful to you.

4. Customize the appearance of the additional fields as necessary. The values in the Price column all need decimal places since they calculate a dollar value, and the SubTotal and Grand Total fields need a $ sign as well. In the Format tab, shown in Figure 66a, change the Decimal Places value to 2 and select the $ sign from the Currency Symbol pull-down list.

5. Change the alignment for the currency fields. Select the fields and right-click/Control-click to open the shortcut menu. Click Properties to open the Text Field Properties dialog. Click the Options tab, and from the Alignment pull-down list, choose Right (**Figure 66c**). Now the fields' values will align.

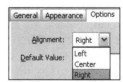

Figure 66c Users are accustomed to seeing dollar values aligned to the right; you can easily set this option.

6. Add the first field calculation. The three products' values are the Quantity * Price. Double-click the first price field, named Quantity.0.1, to open its Properties dialog. Click the Calculate tab, then click the Custom calculation script button and click Edit to open the JavaScript Editor. Enter the calculation script for the first product:

```
var a=this.getField("Quantity.0.0");
event.value=a.value*.77;
```

The script names a variable for the first field, var a, which is a programming "container" that holds whatever value your user types in the field, be that 1 orange or 100 oranges, for example. The rest of the first line makes a reference to the field, and then names the field in parentheses and quotations. The second line then defines an action that will take place in your form, which is to multiply whatever number your customer types in the field times the price per orange, which is $.77. Click OK to close the JavaScript Editor and return to the Properties dialog. The script is displayed in the dialog (**Figure 66d**). You can now close the Properties dialog.

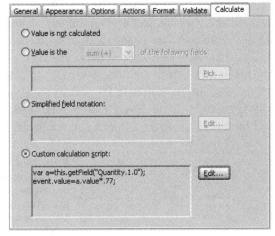

Figure 66d After you write a custom JavaScript, it is shown in the field's Properties dialog.

(Continued)

JavaScript Pointers
JavaScript lets you assign actions to links, bookmarks, and in the case of the sample project in this tip, form fields. Here are some tips for using Acrobat JavaScript:

- Drag the dialogs away from your form on the program window so you can see your fields' names to type them correctly in the script. Alternatively, you can select them from a dialog.

- Before you close the JavaScript Editor, select and copy the script so you can paste it into the other products' Price field scripts.

- If you are using custom scripts, add and customize the scripts for all fields to keep focused. It's like using a batch file for your brain.

TIP 66: Creating Forms That Make Sense

7. Repeat with the other product fields that need a custom script. In the sample, the Price fields for the second and third product use a custom script. For each, paste the JavaScript into the JavaScript Editor and customize it. You need to change:

- The name of the variable; I used var b and var c
- The name of the field
- The variable's value
- The price for each product

8. Add other custom scripts. You also need a similar custom script for calculating the tax. Again, you can paste the script into the JavaScript Editor and customize it. Give the variable its own name, use the SubTotal field, and use the tax rate in the calculation. Here's an example:

```
var d=this.getField("Total1");
event.value=d.value*.12;
```

9. Add calculations for the Subtotal and Grand Total fields. The totals fields are simpler! Double-click the Subtotal field to open its Properties dialog and click the Calculate tab. You want a total of the three calculated fields. Click the "Value is the" radio button; click the pull-down menu and choose Sum (**Figure 66e**). Then click Pick to open a small dialog listing all the fields in your document. Choose those you want to add, which in this case are the three Price fields for the products, and click OK. Back on the Calculate tab, you can see that the chosen fields are added to the dialog (**Figure 66f**). Repeat with the Grand Total field, using the SubTotal and Tax fields.

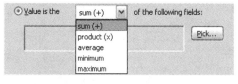

Figure 66e Some calculations can be done by picking fields from the form, such as a sum.

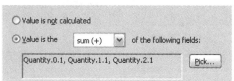

Figure 66f When you choose fields, they are listed on the Calculate tab.

10. Save the form. It's time to test your work—that's coming up in the next tip.

Simplify Your Form Building, Simplify Your Life

Consider these ideas as you build a form:

- Make sure the design of the document can accommodate the size of the fields you intend to use.

- Set options that are common to all fields, such as the font and appearance, when you build the first field.

- Develop a system for adding extra fields. The sample project has three products, so I added a text field for the first product's quantity, and then added two multiple fields for the quantities of the other two products. The result is a sequence of numbered fields that make sense. Then I created a multiple for each of the products to use for calculating the total cost of each item. These fields' names are also logical.

- Rename fields if it makes sense to you. The set of three Total fields (Subtotal, Tax, and Grand Total) were renamed manually.

- When you want to change one property of several fields, such as the alignment, don't change each field individually. Shift-click to select the fields (in the sample, all the fields in the Price column) and then open the Properties dialog using the shortcut menu. When you change the alignment, the change is applied to all the selected fields.

- JavaScript is written for each field separately; calculations aren't allowed for a number of selected fields.

TIP
67

Testing and Tweaking Your Forms

Before you send your forms out into the world to gather information for you, give them a test run. Here's a checklist you can use to make sure your forms are ready for public use:

- Click the Hand tool and add values to all your text input fields. Then press Enter/Return or click another field to check the calculations.

- Make sure to cipher the calculations manually to verify that the scripts are written correctly. For example, if you need a value of 3 * 50, the result must be 150 or there is an error.

- Check to see when and where values change. If you are using my method of copying and pasting JavaScript from one field to another, it is a simple error to forget to change the variables and target field names; in that case, when you type a value in one product's field, the result should change in the appropriate field. Ordering a bunch of lemons shouldn't change the value of the oranges.

- Lock down fields that your users can't type into. In our sample project, all the fields in the Price column are calculated; you can click the Read Only check box on the General tab to prevent users from trying to add content to those fields themselves.

- Test the calculation order. The fields are added to the calculation order according to how you add them to the form, which may not be correct. First, click the Text Box tool on the Forms toolbar to activate the fields so you can see the names. Then choose Advanced > Forms > Set Field Calculation Order to open the dialog shown in **Figure 67a**. Your calculated fields are listed in the dialog in the order of calculation. Click a field and then click Up or Down to rearrange the order. In the figure, you can see that the field for calculating the first product's price is at the end of the list, rather than at the start where it belongs.

Who Took My Fields?

Sometimes it seems your fields disappear from the document. They aren't lost. Only those fields created with a selected form field tool are active on the document at any time. If you have a collection of text fields, for example, and click the Button tool, only buttons are active; other fields are hidden.

Figure 67a Make sure the calculations are performed in the right sequence.

- Test the tabbing order for your form. You would like your users to tab in a logical way, usually from left to right, top to bottom. Click the Pages tab in the Navigation pane to open the Pages pane. Click the page thumbnail, and choose Page Properties from the Options menu to open the Page Properties dialog (**Figure 67b**). Click Tab Order and choose an option. Our sample project uses a standard format of left to right, top to bottom.

Figure 67b Specify how your users can tab through the fields on your form.

Once you have evaluated your form, take a few minutes and consider your users. Here's some more ideas you should take into account:

- Are any of your users going to be working with assistive devices like screen readers? If so, be sure to add a descriptive tool tip that screen readers will read (see the sidebar).

- What can you do to make it simpler for your users to work with your form? Think about adding Reset and Submit buttons (see Tips 68 and 69).

TIP 67: Testing and Tweaking Your Forms

Sending Form Data Automatically

Let's say I am creating a form for my company, which sells reproductions of old movie posters. To make the form easier for my users to work with, there are several actions I can attach to buttons. One common action is a button that submits the data to a specified address. Instead of having to open an email program, starting a new message, and then attaching the file, my users simply click the button and have the information sent to me automatically.

Here's a quick way to add a Submit button:

1. Create or select the form field you want to attach the action to—in this example, a button field named submit (**Figure 68a**).

Figure 68a Include a button that allows your users to easily send the form's information to you.

2. Right-click/Control-click the button and choose Properties from the shortcut menu. The Button Properties dialog opens. Click the Actions tab.

3. Select the Submit a form action from the Select Action pull-down list (**Figure 68b**). Click Add, and the Submit Form Selections dialog opens.

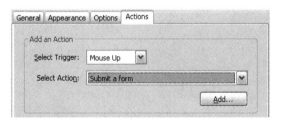

Figure 68b Choose the Submit a form action from the pull-down menu.

4. Enter an address for submission. The address can be a URL, an FTP address, or an email address. When you type the address, be sure to type the entire URL, including the protocol—that is, "http" or "ftp." If you specify a server, and the server returns

data using form data format (FDF) or XML form data format (XFDF) formats, the URL must end with the suffix #FDF.

5. Choose submission options. You can send the form data, the PDF document itself, or the content as HTML, and also specify what content is sent.

6. Select the Convert dates to standard format option to export all form dates in a uniform format regardless of how they are entered in the form.

7. If you want to define only a specific number of fields, click Only these in the Field Selection section of the dialog and click the Select fields button. The Field Selection dialog opens (**Figure 68c**).

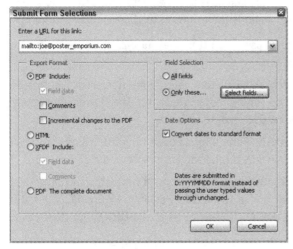

Figure 68c Select the fields you want to include or exclude from the list in this dialog.

8. Choose the fields for export and click OK to return to the Submit Form Selections dialog. Click OK to close the Submit Form Selections dialog and return to the Button Properties dialog.

9. The Submit a form action now appears in the field's Actions list. Click Close to close the Button Properties dialog and apply the action.

10. Click the form field to test the action.

So Many Formats— Which Is Best?

When you are configuring the export format for the data in the Submit Form Selection dialog (Figure 68c), consider where your users are working with the form and what your data requirements are:

- Use the Incremental changes to the PDF option when exporting digital signatures and want to choose specific fields to return data.

- Use the PDF export option to receive the entire form; this option preserves digital signatures, but you can't select specific fields to return.

- If your users are working with Adobe Reader, you must choose either FDF or XFDF export formats.

TIP 69 Handling Field Contents

When you design a form, be sure to consider how your users interact with the form. Ask yourself what you can do to make their work simpler and more efficient. In addition to adding a Submit button, you can add two other common actions attached to buttons that can make working with your form easier:

- Reset a Form—This action deletes content added to a form. Your users can click the button and have the content of the fields removed so they can start over, without having to choose any menu items.

- Import Form Data—This action brings data from another form and adds it to the form open in Acrobat. Your users can click the button and open a dialog to find an FDF file they use repeatedly and have the form data added to the form automatically, again without having to choose any menu items.

Offer your users a button that automatically resets the contents of the form:

1. Select a button on your form, right-click/Control-click the button, and choose Properties. The Button Properties dialog opens. Click the Actions tab.

2. Select the Reset a form action from the Select Action pull-down list. Click Add, and the Reset a Form dialog opens.

3. All the fields in the document are listed in the Reset a Form dialog and are selected by default (**Figure 69a**). Deselect fields that you don't want to reset and click OK to close the dialog.

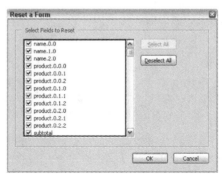

Figure 69a You can specify the fields you want to reset in this dialog.

4. Click Close to dismiss the Button Properties dialog. Acrobat removes the content in the fields according to the selections you made in step 3.

You can use menu actions attached to buttons to import or export form data. Here's how:

1. Choose the button you want to use for the action.

2. Right-click/Control-click the button, choose Properties, and then click the Actions tab in the Button Properties dialog.

3. Select the Execute a menu item action from the pull-down menu and click Add.

4. In the Menu Item Selection dialog, choose File > Form Data > Import Data to Form (**Figure 69b**). Click OK, and then click Close to dismiss the Button Properties dialog.

Figure 69b Consider adding a button action that automatically allows your users to locate data to import or export from the form.

5. Save and test the form.

Follow the same steps to create a button for exporting form data—but this time choose File > Form Data > Export Data to Form in the Menu Item Selection dialog.

Even if the form's designer didn't include automatic actions that you click to insert content into a form, you can do it easily from within Acrobat 7 or Adobe Reader 7. See the sidebar "Exporting and Importing Form Data" to learn how.

TIP 69: Handling Field Contents

Completing a Form and Using Auto-Complete

Filling Out Forms

To fill out an Acrobat PDF form, you move the pointer inside a field on the form and click. You'll see the I-beam, which tells you that the form is active and that you can start to type. Other types of fields using buttons, checkmarks, and so on show variations of the Hand tool, such as a pointing hand. Click an option to select it, and then press Tab (or Shift+Tab) to go to the next (or previous) field. When you have finished, click the Submit button, if it exists. Alternatively, you can print the form, or export the data to a separate file, depending on your rights.

In Acrobat 7, users can fill in a form and submit the actual form (or just the data it contains) to a database, Web site, or email address. Acrobat lets users save the completed form, save the content to reuse another time, or print the contents. You can even set preferences to have Acrobat assist your users by suggesting information used in similar form fields. If you fill out the same type of form numerous times, such as health or dental insurance, reusing the information saves a lot of time.

When you start filling out a new form, you'll see a dialog that suggests using Acrobat's Auto-Complete feature to help fill in the form fields more quickly. When you use this feature, as soon as you type the first few characters of a word in a form field, if the characters match what you have entered in another form, Acrobat automatically enters the rest of the text (**Figure 70a**). The automatic text is selected; you can easily delete or change it if you need to.

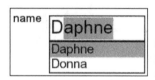

Figure 70a You can choose from a list of matching field entries when you use the Auto-Complete feature.

To enable this feature, choose Edit > Preferences (Windows) or Acrobat > Preferences (Mac OS), and choose Forms from the Preferences list. At the lower part of the window, you see the Auto-Complete options. Click the pull-down arrow and choose an option. Your choices are Off, Basic, and Advanced. Make your selection, and also specify whether you want Acrobat to retain numerical data like phone numbers. Then click OK to close the dialog.

The Basic Auto-Complete process suggests choices when you start typing an entry. A pull-down list offers probable choices; the option listed first appears in the field automatically. In the example shown in Figure 70, the names starting with D are displayed as soon as I type the letter D. If you want to choose another name, click that name to select it from the list.

The Advanced Auto-Complete feature takes the process one step further. Once you start typing and see the auto-entry list, simply move your pointer over the choice you want to use and press Tab. Acrobat fills the field with the selection you specified and moves the pointer to the next field.

To remove entries from the auto-entry listing, click Edit Entry List below the Auto-Complete options in the Forms preferences dialog to open the Edit Entry List dialog. Select the entries you don't want on the list, and click Remove to delete them. To delete the entire list, click Remove All.

(Continued)

Other Preferences for Forms

Acrobat provides several other preferences for forms. Try some of the options—you may find that they increase your form's processing speed and make working with forms simpler.

Choose Edit > Preferences > Forms (on Mac, Acrobat > Preferences > Forms). The top portion of the resulting dialog contains a set of forms preferences:

- Automatically calculate field values—Calculates the content of numerical fields when you enter the data. Often this feature is programmed into the form.

- Show focus rectangle—Shows which form field is currently active (or has focus). This is a very useful preference especially in forms that have narrow fields or a great deal of information on one page (**Figure 70b**).

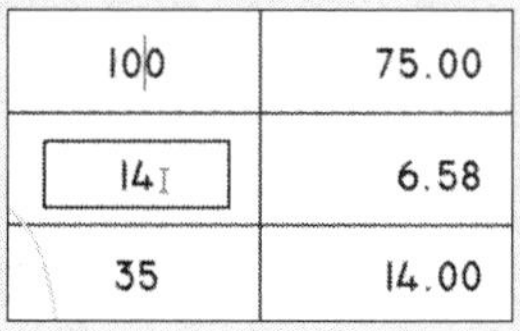

Figure 70b When you move your pointer over a field you automatically see which field is active when the focus rectangle option is used. In the figure, the field showing "14" is below my pointer and outlined.

- Keep forms data temporarily available on disk—Retains the information you add to a form online. This is a useful preference if you fill in forms over the Internet; you can't store the data permanently, but you can reuse it during a session.

- Show text field overflow indicator—Displays a plus sign when you try to type too much text into a text field. The number of characters allowed in a field is defined by the form's designer (**Figure 70c**).

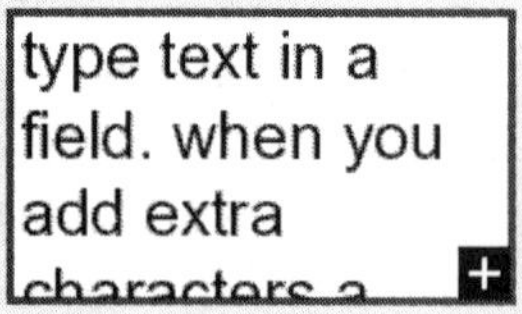

type text in a
field. when you
add extra
characters a

Figure 70c You can instantly see if a user has typed more text into a field than you allowed in the form field's design when you specify using the text overflow indicator.

- Always hide forms document message bar—Hides the message bar that displays by default when you open a PDF form. Use this setting when you work with forms regularly; closing the message bar gives you a bit more room on the screen (**Figure 70d**).

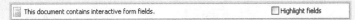

Figure 70d Save precious screen real estate by hiding the form's document message bar.

- Highlight Color—Displays color for form field backgrounds and borders when your user clicks the Show Highlight check box on the Document Message Bar. Click the color swatches in the Highlight Color section of the preference pane to choose colors that highlight both field backgrounds, as well as required fields. The color appears in required form fields only when a user submits the form. The fields in a form are highlighted in whatever color you specify in the preferences (**Figure 70e**).

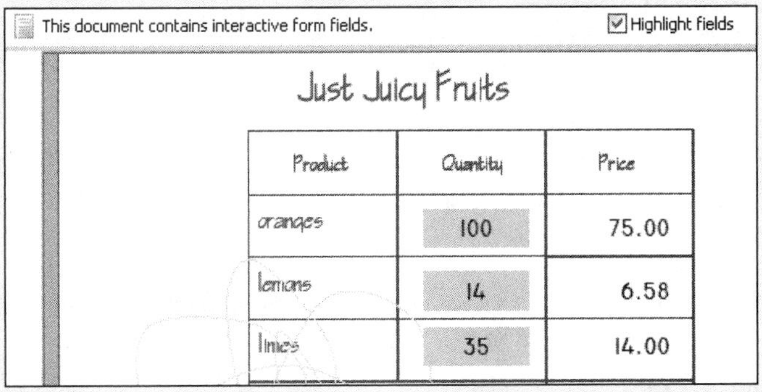

This document contains interactive form fields. ☑ Highlight fields

Just Juicy Fruits

Product	Quantity	Price
oranges	100	75.00
lemons	14	6.58
limes	35	14.00

Figure 70e Set a preference to automatically color all the fields you can use in a form—now you can clearly see how much work you have to do!

These are useful preferences when you work with a lot of forms and find screen glare hard on your eyes, or when you work with large forms and want to see how much work you have left. You can use colored backgrounds for the form fields regardless of how the form is designed; the form's designer doesn't have to assign a color.

71 Collecting Form Data

You've created your form, and now you want to circulate it to your users, giving them an email Submit button to return information to you. Then what do you do? Two things—first create a workflow to manage the form's distribution, and then create a way to store and display the information. In this example, I'll show you how to use a spreadsheet.

Acrobat provides a data collection workflow so you can control the process:

1. Click the Forms task button and choose Initiate Form Data Collection Workflow from the pull-down menu, or choose Advanced > Forms > Initiate Form Data Collection Workflow, or File > Form Data > Initiate Form Data Collection Workflow.

2. The Workflow wizard opens. Proceed through the three screens in the dialog:

   • The first pane explains the process. Click Next.

   • In the second pane, invite recipients by typing their email addresses or click Address Book Address Book to open your email program's address book and select recipients. Click Next.

   • In the third, and final pane, preview the email message (**Figure 71a**). You can click the fields to modify the message or subject. Click Send Invitation.

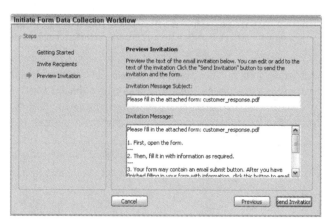

Figure 71a Use the wizard to set up a workflow for form distribution and data gathering.

Working with Acrobat Forms

3. The wizard dialog closes, and the invitations and forms are emailed.

When your recipients receive the form, they complete it and click the Submit button to email the results back to you. Depending on the format you chose when you created the form, the data returns in XML, FDF, PDF, or XFDF formats. As you receive responses, save them in a folder.

Now it's time to build a spreadsheet to display the results:

1. Click the Forms task button and choose Create Spreadsheet From Data Files, or select the command from the File > Form Data menu to open the Export Data From Multiple Forms dialog.

2. Click Add Files; the Select File Containing Form Data dialog opens. Locate the folder you created to store the form data, and select the files you want to incorporate into the spreadsheet. Click Select to close the dialog, and the list now appears in the Export Data From Multiple Forms dialog (**Figure 71b**).

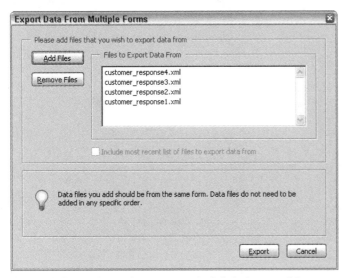

Figure 71b Choose the results you want to include in the spreadsheet.

(Continued)

TIP 71: Collecting Form Data

3. Click Create Spreadsheet. In the dialog that opens, locate the folder on your hard drive where you want to store the spreadsheet and then click Save.

4. When the process is complete, the Complete dialog displays; click View Spreadsheet Now to open Excel, or click Close and View Later.

The spreadsheet generated by the sample project used in this tip is shown in **Figure 71c**. Several of the columns are collapsed to show you more of the content. You can see values from radio buttons displayed, as well as content from text fields.

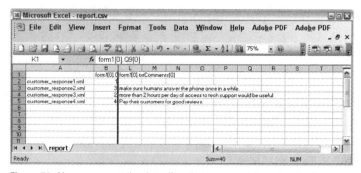

Figure 71c You can export the data directly to a spreadsheet for viewing.

TIP 72 Starting an Adobe Designer Project

Adobe Designer is a forms-designing program that is integrated and accessible either as a separate program or from within Acrobat Professional 7. It is available only in Windows. To access the program from within Acrobat Professional 7, use one of these actions, and follow the prompts:

Who's Got the Copy?

If you build a PDF form in Acrobat Professional 7 and then open the form in Adobe Designer, a copy of the file is opened and your original document is preserved.

- For a blank form, click the Forms task button to display its pull-down menu and choose Create New Form.

- To make an interactive form from a static form, first open the form in Acrobat. Click the Forms task button to display its pull-down menu and choose Make Form Fillable in Adobe Designer (**Figure 72a**).

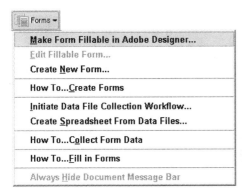

Figure 72a Choose from several methods for opening Adobe Designer when you are working in Acrobat Professional 7 in Windows.

- If you have an interactive form open in Acrobat, click the Forms task button to display its pull-down menu and choose Edit Fillable Form.

- If you want to edit an existing form, open the form in Acrobat and then choose Advanced > Forms > Open Form In Adobe Designer.

(Continued)

Instead of working through Acrobat, you can work directly in Designer 7. Open the program from the Start menu like other programs, and the Welcome Screen displays. You can choose a new blank form, open an existing form, or work from a template. Let's look at using the templates:

1. Click New From Template 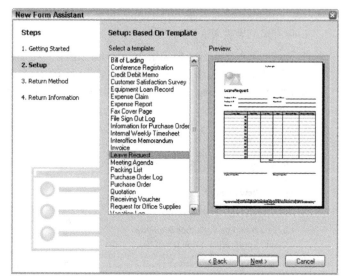 on the Welcome Screen and click Close. The Welcome Screen is replaced by the New Form Assistant (**Figure 72b**).

Figure 72b Choose a template to customize in Adobe Designer. In this tip we are using a Leave Request Form template.

2. Choose a template, in this example, a Leave Request Form, and click Next.

3. Select how you want the information returned to you on the Return Method pane of the dialog (**Figure 72c**). The form data can be sent electronically, which is the default. You can give your users the option of returning the data electronically or printing and mailing the form (the option used in this example). They can be allowed to fill in the form and print it only, or they can print the blank form and fill it out manually. Click Next.

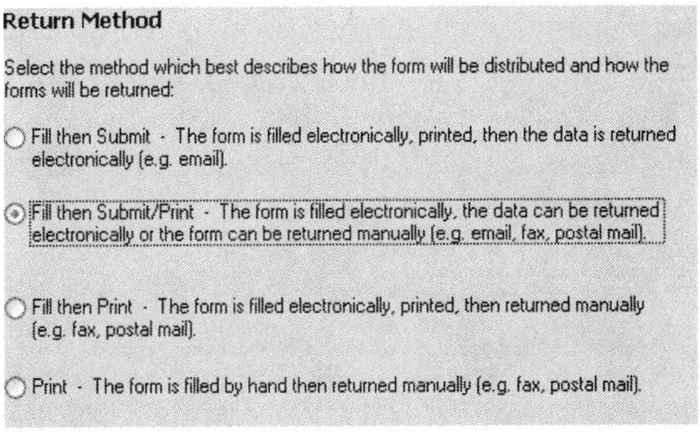

Return Method

Select the method which best describes how the form will be distributed and how the forms will be returned:

○ Fill then Submit · The form is filled electronically, printed, then the data is returned electronically (e.g. email).

◉ Fill then Submit/Print · The form is filled electronically, the data can be returned electronically or the form can be returned manually (e.g. email, fax, postal mail).

○ Fill then Print · The form is filled electronically, printed, then returned manually (e.g. fax, postal mail).

○ Print · The form is filled by hand then returned manually (e.g. fax, postal mail).

Figure 72c Select a Return Method. You can automatically create fields that include actions for printing or returning data.

4. The options on the Return Information pane reflect the choice you made in the Return Method pane. This example uses the option that allows users to both transmit information and also print the form. Type an email address on this pane (**Figure 72d**) and click Finish.

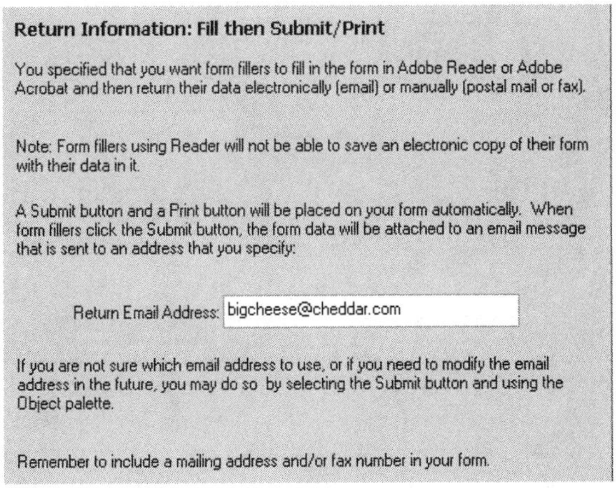

Return Information: Fill then Submit/Print

You specified that you want form fillers to fill in the form in Adobe Reader or Adobe Acrobat and then return their data electronically (email) or manually (postal mail or fax).

Note: Form fillers using Reader will not be able to save an electronic copy of their form with their data in it.

A Submit button and a Print button will be placed on your form automatically. When form fillers click the Submit button, the form data will be attached to an email message that is sent to an address that you specify:

Return Email Address: bigcheese@cheddar.com

If you are not sure which email address to use, or if you need to modify the email address in the future, you may do so by selecting the Submit button and using the Object palette.

Remember to include a mailing address and/or fax number in your form.

Figure 72d If you choose an option that automatically returns the form data to you by email, type an email address in this pane of the wizard.

(Continued)

A Form for Every Purpose

You can create basic forms either in Acrobat or in Adobe Designer. In addition to the basic type, you can build static, dynamic, and interactive forms. Each type has different characteristics:

- An interactive form can be filled out online using either Acrobat or Adobe Reader 7. Interactive forms can contain buttons for common activities like printing or saving data to a file.

- A static form, as the name suggest, displays the same layout regardless of how much data you enter into it—fields don't change size to accommodate their contents. Static forms are used with Form Server, an Adobe server product, to merge the form with data.

- A dynamic form can change its configuration and layout according to how much data is added to it, and is also used in conjunction with Form Server to merge the form and data. In addition, a dynamic form can be interactive.

TIP 72: Starting an Adobe Designer Project

5. The New Form Assistant closes and the form displays in the program window in the Body Pages view (**Figure 72e**). Choose File > Save and save the form. Alternatively, you can save the form in different formats. Choose File > Save As and choose a form type from the Save as type pull-down list.

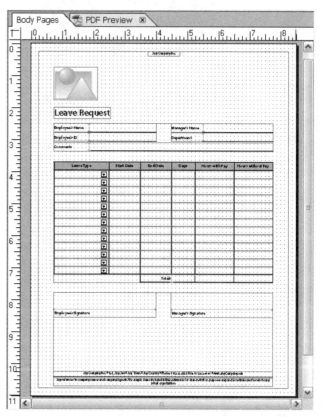

Figure 72e Your new form opens in Adobe Designer 7 in the default working view, called the Body Pages view.

TIP 73 Customizing a Form in Adobe Designer 7

Adobe Designer 7 is a wonderfully complex program with all the features you could possibly want for building and configuring forms. In this tip, I'll mention some of those features as we make a very brief and introductory tour around the form created using a template, described in the previous tip.

- The default working view is the Body Pages view, and includes grid lines. You can toggle them on and off by clicking the Show Grid button ▦.

- Use the controls in the Standard toolbar to change page view and zoom options ▭▭▭⊕ 150% ⊡⊕. These tools look and work the same as those found in Acrobat 7.

- Click an existing form field on the Body Pages view to make it active (**Figure 73a**). The field is surrounded by a hatched line. When you activate a field, information about the field is displayed in the status bar at the bottom of the program window.

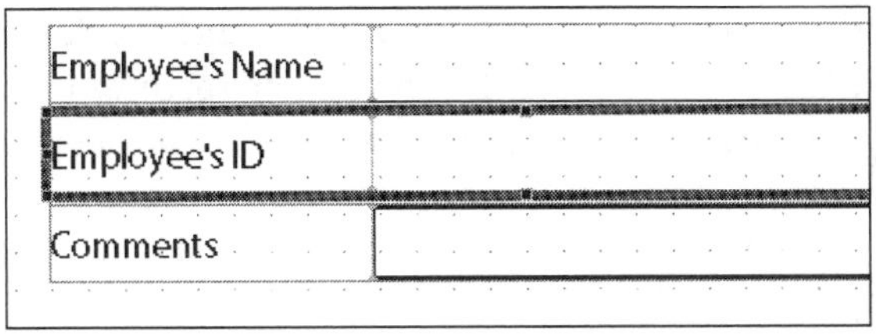

Employee's Name	
Employee's ID	
Comments	

Figure 73a Click a field to select it and display its information in the program.

- Information about the selected field is also displayed in the Field tab of the Object palette, docked at the right side of the program window by default. You can click the pull-down arrow and choose a different type of field from the list (**Figure 73b**).

(Continued)

Ever-Expanding Text Fields

A dynamic form can contain dynamic text fields that grow according to the amount of text you type into them. When the text exceeds the default size of the field; scroll bars display. The field may extend across two pages of a form. If you want to add more information to the field, click the field on either page—all the text is activated.

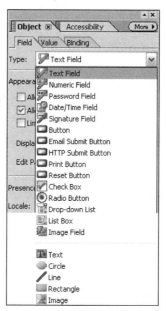

Figure 73b Choose a type of form field from this pull-down list.

- All the palettes include a More button More ▸—click to choose options to hide the palette or open the Help menu.

- To see how your document looks as a PDF, click the PDF Preview tab Body Pages PDF Preview at the top of the workspace to toggle the view. In this view the contents are added to the fields as well. For example, click a pull-down arrow on a list form field to see the contents added by the template (**Figure 73c**). Click the Body Pages tab to return to the default working view.

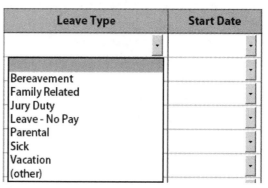

Figure 73c You can see the details of the form field in the PDF view; in this example the template added types of leaves to the pull-down list form field.

- Click the Hierarchy tab docked at the left of the program window to display the contents of the form according to its structure. Open and close Header and Body labels to see the contents; click a field in the listing to display it on the Body Pages view (**Figure 73d**).

Figure 73d Track the content of your form using the entries in the Hierarchy tab. In the figure, the text field txtEmpName is active both in the Hierarchy tab and on the Body Pages view.

- Delete fields on the form by selecting them and pressing the Delete key. To move a field, drag it into its new position (**Figure 73e**). You can resize a field as well by dragging from a corner. When you move an object, use the Snap to Grid tool on the Standard toolbar for easy alignment.

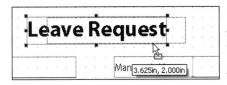

Figure 73e Reposition a field by dragging it. As you move, the object's position displays in a tool tip.

(Continued)

If you design a form that contains barcodes, your users can't add information to the fields. Instead, use an interactive barcode field so the components of the barcode change to encrypt the data entered in other fields. A paper form barcode is created using its own special field, and saves time ordinarily spent on manual data entry. To use paper form barcodes, you must use the Adobe Paper Forms Solution, an enterprise-level server product.

- Replace content in a field, such as the default image added by the template. Click the object on the Body Pages to select it; the Draw tab in the Object palette is activated (**Figure 73f**). Click the Folder icon  to open a dialog, locate and select the image you want to use, and click Open. The image is replaced at the size defined by the template. You can choose several sizing options, as shown in the figure.

Figure 73f Locate and set options for images in this tab of the Object palette.

- As you are learning to work with Adobe Designer 7, be sure to keep the How To palette active; this tab is docked at the lower right of the program window (**Figure 73g**). Click a More Info link in the default display in the tab, or click the Choose a topic pull-down arrow and select an option from the list.

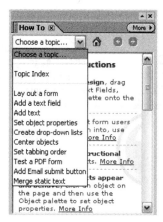

Figure 73g Keep the How To palette active as you are learning how to use the program.

CHAPTER NINE

Transforming a PDF Document

Acrobat 7 Professional isn't a document-editing program. Although you can convert content from spreadsheets, word processing, image editing, and other types of programs, Acrobat isn't meant to do extensive editing of the document's content.

Instead, Acrobat offers a number of tools you can use to manipulate the content of a document, such as combining elements from various documents, as discussed in the tips in Chapter 4. Using Acrobat as a controlling mechanism, you combine documents and add pages from other documents and other sources.

You can combine and manipulate the contents of a single document or a binder created from several PDF documents by substituting pages from one document for those in another in a number of ways, or changing the orientation and size of the pages.

Adding Document Pages

If you choose a PDF document, the pages are added immediately. If you choose another type of file, the document is converted to PDF before the page is inserted into your document. This is a great time-saver, since you don't have to reopen the document's source program and the file, convert to PDF, and then return to Acrobat.

Sometimes when you combine content from several documents, you have pages of information you don't need. You can easily delete a single page or a group of pages. Although you can combine several documents into a single PDF file called a *binder*, you don't have to combine complete documents.

To remove a page from a document:

1. Open your document and click the Pages tab at the left of the screen to display the Pages pane. The pages are shown in small images, called *thumbnails*. The first page is displayed in the Document pane. In the Pages pane, you can see that the third thumbnail is highlighted and that a red box surrounds some of the page contents (**Figure 74a**). This means that page 3 is showing in the Document pane, and the visible portion of the page is outlined with the red box.

page-view box

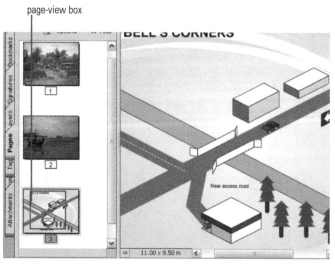

Figure 74a The document's pages are shown in the Pages pane; a page-view box in the thumbnail indicates what content is displayed in the Document pane.

2. Select the page you want to remove by clicking its thumbnail in the Pages pane. The thumbnail is highlighted, and the page displays in the Document pane.

3. Delete the selected page: click the Options menu in the Pages pane and select Delete Pages or choose Document > Delete Pages. The Delete Pages dialog opens (**Figure 74b**).

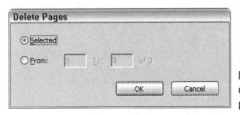

Figure 74b Select an option for deleting a page or pages.

4. The default option is to delete the selected page. If you prefer, you can click the From option and enter the range of page numbers you want to delete, and then click OK.

5. A confirmation dialog opens; click OK to confirm the page deletion. The dialog closes, and Acrobat deletes the page or pages from your document.

Inserting pages is almost as simple as deleting them. You can quickly add particular pages to a document using the Pages pane:

1. In the Pages pane, click the page *before* the location where you want to insert additional pages.

(Continued)

Power Deleting

Instead of using commands to delete multiple pages, use the thumbnails and keyboard keys. Click the thumbnail of the page you want to delete; hold the Shift key and click multiple pages to select them, and then press Delete on the keyboard. The confirmation dialog opens asking if you really want to delete the pages. Click OK and the pages are gone.

Insert Pages in Front

Sometimes you need to insert a new page before an existing page in your document. For example, you may need to add a cover page to a catalog or marketing brochure. In the Insert Pages dialog box, simply click the Location pull-down list and choose Before, then click OK to close the dialog. Acrobat adds the page to your document precisely where you want it.

2. In the Pages pane, choose Options > Insert Pages, or choose Document > Insert Pages from the main menu. The Select File To Insert dialog opens. Locate the file you want to use and click Select. The dialog closes, and the Insert Pages dialog opens (**Figure 74c**).

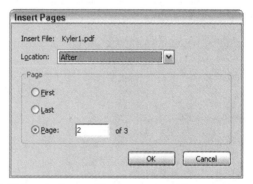

Figure 74c If you select the page thumbnail, the Page option is already enabled when you open the dialog. The new document page will be added at the location you specify, in this case, after page 2.

3. Specify the location where you want to add the document. The default is After; because I selected a page before opening the dialog, the Page radio button is automatically selected and 2 appears in the text box. The page will be inserted after page 2.

4. Click OK to close the Insert Pages dialog. Acrobat adds the page to your document.

TIP 75 Extracting Content

Suppose you have a multipage document and you want to remove a part of it for another purpose, such as combining it with other information for another document. In this tip, I'll explain how to separate, or extract, a portion of a document.

To extract a single page or a group of consecutive pages, first select the thumbnail(s) in the Pages pane. Then choose Extract Pages from the Pages pane's Options menu, or choose Document > Extract Pages. The Extract Pages dialog opens (**Figure 75a**). Because I selected the pages in the Pages pane in the sample, the page numbers (4–6) already appear in the dialog.

Figure 75a Preselected page thumbnails are listed in the Extract Pages dialog when it opens.

Use the options to manage your documents:

- Click Delete Pages After Extracting if you want to separate the content from the original document permanently.

- Click Extract Pages As Separate Files if you want to create individual PDF documents from each page you select in the dialog.

Click OK to close the dialog. If you chose the option Extract Pages As Separate Files, a Browse for Folder dialog opens for you to select the location to store the new document(s). Acrobat extracts the page(s) and creates a new document for each selected page, automatically saving the document in your specified folder. The document is saved with the page number appended to it. For example, if you extracted pages 4-6, the new documents are named as shown in **Figure 75b**.

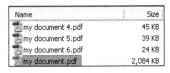

Figure 75b If you extract each page to a separate document, the page number from the original document is appended to the name.

(Continued)

Let's Have Some Order

You can readily extract several nonconsecutive pages from the same document. First, group them together. In the Pages pane's thumbnails view, click and drag the pages you want to extract until they are in sequence. Click the thumbnail of the first page you want to move to select it, and then drag it up or down to the appropriate location. A solid line appears above a thumbnail as you drag up or down. As the page is moved, a solid line shows where it will relocate if you release the mouse.

Once the content is extracted, return the original document to its initial order. Choose File > Revert to open the dialog. Click Revert to return to where you started before the extraction, with the pages in their original order.

For a document with only a few pages, reordering them is a quick and convenient way to assemble the pages for extraction. For a very large document, it would be simpler to extract groups of pages and then recombine them into one new document.

What's in a Name?

Sometimes when working on large projects I leave the default "Pages from" names. It helps to organize content, the location of some documents, and where they originated.

Dialog or Drag and Drop?

Here's a real timesaving process that's terrific for visual people. Rather than combining document content through dialogs, you can do it visually using the Pages pane.

Here's how:

- Start with two documents, one to which you want to add pages (the recipient) and the other from which you're taking pages (the donor).

- Choose Window > Tile > Horizontally to display both documents.

- Click the Pages tab on each document to show the thumbnails.

- Select the page thumbnails from the donor document's Pages pane and drag them to the recipient document's Pages pane.

- Release the mouse when you are in the right spot and the job is done.

- Organize and arrange the pages.

You can readily display the Pages panel from two, three, or even more documents on the screen and drag pages between the documents. Visually combining documents works best when the content is visual. For example, a long report that contains very little except text is difficult to work with if you're relying on thumbnails. On the other hand, if you are working with large images or slideshow pages, the process works very well.

If you don't choose an extraction option, or choose the Delete Pages After Extracting option, when you click OK to close the dialog box the content is processed and opened in Acrobat. As **Figure 75c** shows, the document filename includes the "Pages from" prefix. Save the extracted document; save the original if you extracted the pages from it permanently.

Figure 75c The new document is named according to its source.

TIP 76 Replacing Pages

Say you have a PDF document and realize you need to do some edits that are simpler to make in the source program, such as rewriting a block of text on a page or some other non-Acrobat work. After you make your changes and convert the document to PDF, you can use the Replace Pages dialog to substitute the new page in your original PDF document.

In Acrobat, open the document in which you want to replace the page. You work from the Pages pane; click to select the thumbnails for the page or pages you want to replace, or you can set the pages in the dialog. Choose Options > Replace Pages from the Pages pane's menu. In the resulting browser dialog, locate the new PDF file and click Select. The dialog closes, and the Replace Pages dialog opens (**Figure 76**).

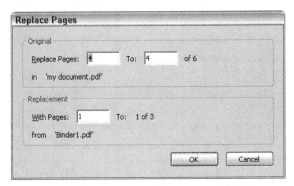

Figure 76 Specify the pages to replace in the original document as well as those to use from the replacement document in the dialog.

Specify the page numbers in both the Original and Replacement sections of the dialog. If you preselected thumbnails in the Pages pane they are shown when you open the dialog. Click OK. When the confirmation dialog opens, click Yes. The dialog closes and Acrobat replaces the original page with the new one.

Delete and Insert or Replace?

What's the difference? It depends on what else is on the page.

For example, you may have a page with a large number of comments, links, or form fields on it. If you merely inserted an edited version of the page and deleted the one you want to remove, you'd lose all your comments and links. When you use the Replace command, Acrobat replaces the underlying page, keeping the overlying content (such as comments, links, or form fields) untouched.

TIP 77 · Cropping and Rotating Pages

Acrobat lets you import a document in one layout and then customize its appearance. However, if you combine several documents from different sources, you may find discrepancies in the page sizes or orientations. A neat feature in Acrobat is the ability to crop and rotate pages to get them looking just so.

If you are cropping a single page, display it in the Document pane; if you are working with more than one image, select their thumbnails in the Pages pane.

Choose Options > Crop Pages from the Pages pane. If you're working from the Document pane, choose Document > Pages > Crop. If you happen to have the Advanced Editing toolbar open, click the Crop tool to select it. Then click and drag to draw a marquee the size of the area you want to crop on the document page. Double-click within the cropped area. The Crop Pages dialog opens. If you opened the dialog by using the Crop tool, the area you drew on the document page is already shown in the Crop Pages dialog.

The page appears as a thumbnail at the top right of the Crop Pages dialog, and the Crop radio button is selected by default in the Crop Margins area of the dialog. Click the Units pull-down list to change the measurement used in the cropping from the default inches.

Adjust the crop settings using the four margin fields (**Figure 77a**). As you change the values, the cropping outline in the preview image changes to reflect the new values. You can type values in the fields, or use the arrows to adjust the settings. Check Constrain Proportions to crop the page equally on all four sides.

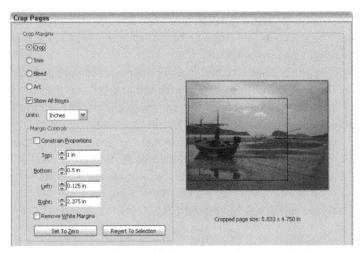

Figure 77a You can see crop margins in the sample as you specify the amount to crop in the Crop Pages dialog.

Cropping Multiple Pages

You can crop several pages at once. Select the pages in the Pages pane—the files can be contiguous or spread throughout the document.

Once in the Crop Pages dialog, you can see the selected pages listed at the bottom in the Page Range section. If you do this, make sure the content of the pages is laid out the same.

Note

If you are having a hard time defining a precise margin, drag the Crop Pages dialog out of the way and you can see faint dotted lines overlaying the page where the crop margins are set.

Acrobat 7 also lets you change the page size to display the contents instead of cropping the page (**Figure 77b**). Click the Page Sizes pull-down arrow and choose from a wide variety of page sizes; or select the Custom option and type a specific size for the page. If you use a specified page size, the crop settings are grayed out.

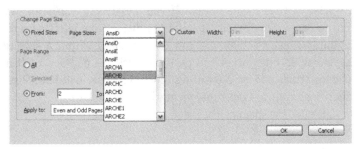

Figure 77b Instead of cropping a page, you can resize the page using one of numerous page size presets or use a custom page size.

(Continued)

TIP 77: Cropping and Rotating Pages

Finally, specify the page range you wish to crop. If you preselected pages from the Pages pane, they are identified in the fields. You can also specify whether to crop all pages, only even pages, or only odd pages by choosing an option from the Apply to pull-down list.

Click OK to close the dialog, and Acrobat resizes the page. You can see the effects of the cropping in the Document pane, as well as in the Pages pane's thumbnails.

Save the document to preserve the cropping. You can't undo a crop by choosing Edit > Undo or using the shortcut Ctrl+Z or Command+Z. If you change your mind after cropping, choose File > Revert to return to the uncropped version of the document.

Change the orientation of a document so you don't have to turn your neck sideways to read a rotated page. Select the page in the Pages pane. Choose Options > Rotate or Document > Rotate > Pages to open the Rotate Pages dialog. Then choose a direction from the Direction pull-down list (**Figure 77c**).

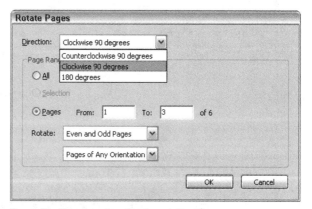

Figure 77c Choose a direction for rotating the page.

Select a Page Range option. If you preselected a page or pages in the Pages pane before opening the dialog, the Selection option is automatically active. You can choose pages within a selection according to orientation and position. Click the pull-down list and choose either odd or even pages; click the lower pull-down list to specify portrait or landscape orientation.

Click OK, the dialog closes, and Acrobat rotates the page.

TIP 78 Configuring the Pages Pane

The default layout of the Pages pane displays a single column of small thumbnail pictures of the pages. The default is fine for most kinds of work when you have a document consisting of several pages. However, when working with a very large document, you might want to make the thumbnails smaller and increase the number of thumbnail columns to see more at once. If you have to be able to see the content of the thumbnails, you'll want to increase their size.

To increase or decrease the size of thumbnails, choose Options > Enlarge (or Reduce) Page Thumbnails. Use a thumbnail size that is meaningful. In **Figure 78**, the thumbnails are set to the smallest size available—so small that they are of limited reference value. Conversely, you can enlarge thumbnails to the size of the Document pane, but that pretty much defeats the purpose.

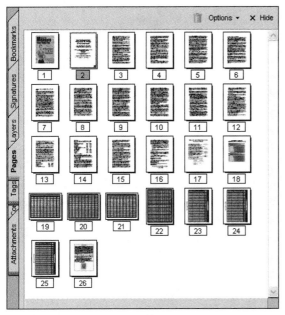

Figure 78 You can change the size of page thumbnails in the Pages pane. These thumbnails are too small for you to see their content, but you can look at various page sizes and orientations.

(Continued)

Managing Thumbnails

You can choose to embed or unembed thumbnails. Which is best? Embedded thumbnails add to a file's size. On the other hand, if you embed the thumbnails when you're working with large documents, opening, closing, resizing, and scrolling through the Pages pane is much speedier. Embed thumbnails from the Pages pane by choosing Options > Embed All Page Thumbnails; unembed by choosing Options > Remove Embedded Page Thumbnails.

Be careful when using embedded thumbnails. Although they give you an instant view of the pages, changes you make to your pages are not updated in embedded thumbnails. To display the thumbnails with your changes, you have to unembed the old ones first and then re-embed the edited ones.

Bigger or Smaller?

Decrease the size of the thumb-nails when working with large documents. This gives you a better overview of the content and can reveal such problems as irregular page sizes.

Increase the size of the thumb-nails when working with images or slideshows. You can quickly sort through, reorder, and change pages working from the Pages pane when you see the content clearly.

Resize the Pages pane to see your thumbnails if necessary. Move the pointer over the right margin of the panel. When it changes to a double-ended arrow and vertical bars, click and drag to the left or right to adjust the size of the pane.

You can change the display of the page in the Document pane from the Pages pane. Click and drag the lower-right corner of the page-view box displayed on the page's thumbnail to increase or decrease its size; increasing the size shows more of the page in the Document pane while decreasing the magnification. Decreasing the size shows less of the page in the Document pane while increasing the magnification.

You can also drag the page-view box around the thumbnail. The content outlined by the page-view box on the thumbnail is shown in the Document pane.

CHAPTER TEN

Touching Up and Modifying a Document

One of the greatest advantages of working with documents in Acrobat is the ability to combine material from a wide range of sources into one document. Bringing content together from a range of programs can produce a cohesive collection of information; using Acrobat's touch-up and modification features results in a document that is also visually integrated.

For example, you can bring together material from a range of programs and then add page numbers, headers and footers, or backgrounds to unify the content.

Love that illustration, or want to quote a block of text from an Acrobat document? If the security settings for a document allow changes, you can reuse most of its components (such as text or images) in a PDF file.

In addition to creating a cohesive-appearing document, Acrobat offers a number of touch-up tools you can use for making simple corrections. You can adjust text, images, reading order, and objects right in Acrobat.

79 Adding Page Numbers

When you combine pages for a project, you end up with one document. Page numbers are shown on the status bar below the document in the Document pane and are numbered in logical order—that is, the first page is page 1, the second is page 2, and so on. Depending on the size and purpose of the document, you often have to renumber pages, or even number pages in sequences.

In a sample 18-page document, I have several sections that I want to number separately; each section will start with text and a letter (such as Sample A-), followed by page numbers. Sounds complicated, doesn't it? Acrobat can handle it.

Here's what you do:

1. In the Pages pane, select the pages for the first section (I am using pages 3–5 in my example.) Choose Options > Number Pages to open the Page Numbering dialog. The Selected option is already active because I selected the pages in the Pages pane (**Figure 79a**).

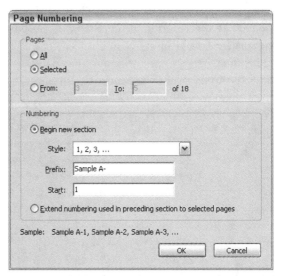

Figure 79a Save time in the dialog by preselecting the pages in the Pages pane. The numbers are automatically defined in the Page Numbering dialog.

Numbering Nuggets

Keep these things in mind when numbering your masterwork:

- Whenever possible, remove visible page numbers from source material before converting it to a PDF. Using Acrobat-based page numbering is easier when the pages contain no numbers to conflict with the numbers displayed on the status bar or in the Pages pane.

- Consider the document's use. Many documents need simple page numbering. However, if you are assembling a technical manual, you will likely use prefixes identifying content based on chapters, systems, and so on.

- If you are building a book structure, consider how the book will look when printed. Books use front matter like a table of contents and other introductory material that is numbered differently from chapter content.

2. Leave the Begin new section option selected in the Numbering section of the dialog. Then click the Style pull-down list to choose a page format. As shown in Figure 79a, our example uses numbers for the page renumbering.

3. Enter a value in the Prefix field, as well as punctuation if desired. The numbering starts at "1" by default, as shown in the Start field. Click OK to close the dialog.

Acrobat modifies the page numbers; as **Figure 79b** shows, we now have pages Sample A-1 through Sample A-3. The remaining pages in the document are renumbered as well.

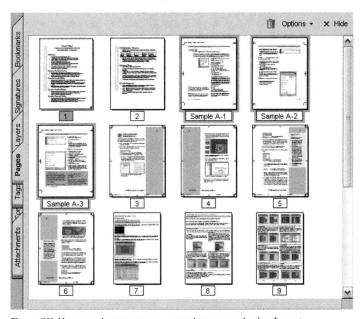

Figure 79b You can choose among several page-numbering formats.

In the status bar, the page numbers reflect both the page count as well as the numbering you added (**Figure 79c**).

Figure 79c The status bar displays both the logical numbering as well as the custom numbers.

TIP 79: Adding Page Numbers

TIP
80

Applying Headers and Footers

Modifying Headers & Footers

To modify headers or footers after you've applied them to the document, choose Document > Add Headers & Footers, then make the changes. Be sure the option Replace existing headers and footers on these pages is checked. When you click OK to close the dialog, a pop-up dialog asks you to confirm the changes; click OK again and your headers and footers are modified. If you want to delete a header or footer, open the dialog, select the text in the text entry boxes, and delete it; then click OK to close the dialog. The header or footer will disappear. You can also edit the content using the TouchUp Text tool (covered in Tips 84 and 85).

Along with assigning page numbers to documents, you can add precise headers and footers to the pages. When adding them in Acrobat, you should avoid using source documents with visible headers and footers to prevent confusion. Let's add some footer information, including custom text, to a sample document:

1. From the main program menu, choose Document > Add Headers & Footers. The Add Headers & Footers dialog opens (**Figure 80a**). Headers and footers use individual tabs in the dialog; each contains the same options. First, click the Footer tab. At the top of the dialog are three text entry boxes, which will hold the content that you want to be left-justified, centered, or right-justified on the document page.

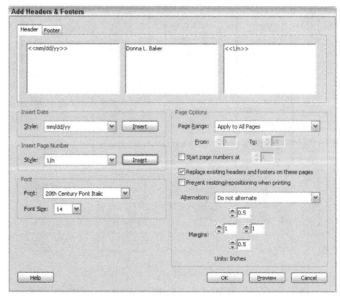

Figure 80a Add custom headers and footers to a document to provide a unified appearance.

2. Choose the font and font size from the pull-down lists below the header/footer content boxes. You have to preview the page to see font effects—they aren't displayed in the dialog.

3. Make entries in the Insert fields as desired. The example uses a date, page numbering, and custom text, shown in Figure 80a. Before adding either an automatic entry or custom text, click the text entry box where you want to add the content on the dialog:

- To insert the date or page numbers, click the Style pull-down list under the Insert Date or Insert Page Number option, respectively, choose a format, and click Insert.

- To add custom text, click the text entry box where you want to add the text (left, center, or right) and type.

The final layout shows the blocks of text in the correct areas. To remove text, select it in the text box and press the Delete key.

4. In the Page Options section, make selections as required for your document. You can specify page ranges, page numbering and the starting number to use for page numbering, margins, and whether to use even or odd pages only. To use a nonstandard value for the margin settings, type the number in the field. The value you set for the top margin applies to headers; the bottom margin value applies to footers.

(Continued)

Fun with Headers & Footers

Experimenting with headers and footers can be an interesting and useful way to guide readers through your document. This book, for example, displays either the chapter or tip title in the footer, depending on the page number. You can duplicate the same look in Acrobat.

In the Add Headers & Footers dialog, enter the footer information for the right-hand, odd-numbered pages into the right-aligned field. Choose Odd Pages Only from the Alternation listing in the Page Options area of the dialog and click OK to apply.

For the left-hand pages, reopen the dialog and repeat with the even-numbered page information, choosing Even Pages Only from the Alternation listing, and entering text in the left-aligned field.

TIP 80: Applying Headers and Footers

5. Click the Preview button at the bottom of the dialog to see the layout of the footer elements in a pop-up Preview window. You can see the selected font and font as well if the font size is large enough (**Figure 80b**). Click OK to close the Preview window.

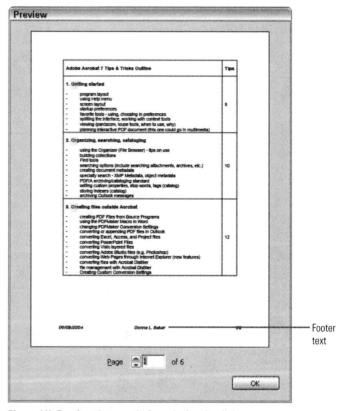

Figure 80b Preview the page before closing the dialog.

6. Click OK to close the dialog and apply the footer. The content and numbering are applied to the page in the area specified.

TIP 81 Adding Watermarks and Backgrounds

A good way to create a cohesive-appearing document you have constructed from multiple source documents is to use a watermark or background. Watermarks overlay the page content; backgrounds are—to state the painfully obvious—applied to the background of the page behind the content.

In this tip, we show you how to apply and configure a graphic background, as well as a text watermark. It is important to plan ahead. Before you start, create the background content and save it as a PDF file if you intend to use an image; if you are using text for a watermark or background, you can create it right in the dialog—a terrific new feature in Acrobat 7.

Open the document to which you want to apply the background or watermark. Our sample document has seven pages, each containing one large image.

1. Choose Document > Add Watermark & Background to open the dialog shown in **Figure 81a**.

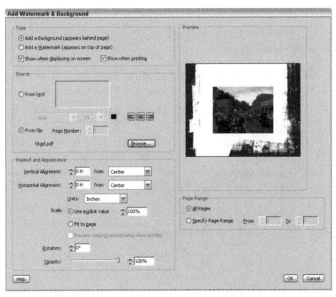

Figure 81a Add text or graphic watermarks and backgrounds from the same dialog.

(Continued)

Removing Backgrounds

Acrobat is designed to protect the integrity of your document, and once the file is saved with the background, you can't remove it. If you aren't sure about the background, or want to use the document both with and without a background or watermark, save the file with another name.

There is a tricky workaround for the permanent background. Follow these steps:

- Open a blank document in Word or some other program and save it as a PDF.
- Open the PDF file in Acrobat with the undesired background.
- Choose Document > Watermark & Background to open the dialog.
- Click Browse, locate the blank PDF document, and select it.
- Click OK to close the dialog. The blank page replaces the background.

Image Protection

Do you have a need for distributing large numbers of images? And do you spend a great deal of time adding a watermark to the images? Save yourself a whopping load of time by combining the content into a PDF document and adding a watermark through Acrobat. Add text or use your watermarking image and adjust the transparency.

2. Choose Add a Background or Add a Watermark in the Type area, and then specify where you want the background or watermark to display (it can be shown on screen and in print).

3. Click Browse to select a source document to use for a graphic background or watermark. If the document has more than one page, select the page you want to use (**Figure 81b**).

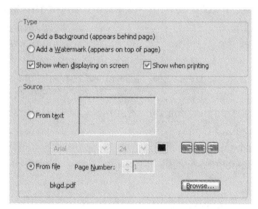

Figure 81b Choose the type of content you want to add, and then locate the PDF file you want to use.

4. Select the range of pages you want to receive the background or watermark.

5. Modify the position, appearance, and size of the background or watermark content as desired. Then set the horizontal and vertical alignments and rotation. Adjust the opacity by using the slider (**Figure 81c**).

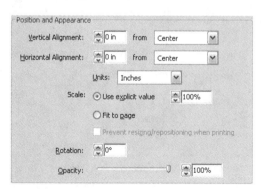

Figure 81c Adjust the location and appearance of the text on the page.

6. Check your adjustments in the Preview area. When you are satisfied with the results, click OK to close the dialog and apply the background or watermark.

You can add both a background and a watermark to the same document. In the same example, I have added both a graphic background and a text watermark.

1. In the Add Watermark & Background dialog, select the Add a Watermark radio button.

2. Then click the From text radio button in the Source area of the dialog (**Figure 81d**).

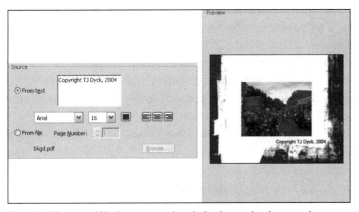

Figure 81d You can add both a watermark and a background to the same document.

3. Type the text to use for the watermark in the text field.

4. Choose font and color characteristics, and adjust the text location as required.

5. When the text is just right, as shown in the preview area of Figure 81d, click OK to close the dialog and apply the watermark.

Pages Here and Pages There

If you want to apply the background to pages that are scattered throughout a document, arrange them in the Pages pane in a continuous sequence before opening the Add Watermark & Background dialog. Or you can reapply the command several times to apply the background throughout the document.

If you have one page in particular that you aren't sure about, move that page to the start of the document. In the Add Watermark & Background dialog, the first page is shown in the preview area.

82 Selecting Text in a PDF

If you need to reuse content on a PDF document, but you didn't create it and you can't get a copy of the source document, you can use Acrobat's tools to select and repurpose the content. Sometimes you'll want to combine pieces from several PDFs into a single document, in which case it's much more efficient to work with the PDF files rather than the source material.

Acrobat provides a single Select tool that behaves differently depending on what you are selecting on a document. Acrobat provides a single Select tool that behaves differently depending on what you're selecting on a document. You don't even have to change tools to select different types of content! The Select tool ⌖ Select is located on the Basic toolbar.

You use this tool to select text, images, and tables. In addition to the tool being dynamic and changing depending on the object over which it is placed, it also provides a small pop-up menu of options you can select, again reflecting the type of object. In this tip we'll learn how to select text. Read about selecting images in the following tip; selecting tables is described later in Tip 86.

> **Note**
> *Don't confuse the Select tool on the Basic toolbar with the Select Object tool located on the Advanced Editing toolbar. The Select Object tool selects items like links and form fields.*

Follow these steps to select text:

1. Click the Select tool on the Basic toolbar to make it active and then click and drag over some of the text you want to select. The text is highlighted in gray, and small arrows display at the upper left and lower right of the selection (**Figure 82a**).

Arrow handle

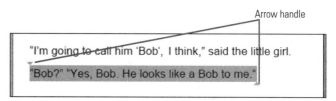

Figure 82a Grow or shrink a text selection using the arrow handles.

Note
If you prefer precise selections, click the text where you want the selection to start, and then Shift-click where you want the selection to end; the text between the two points is selected.

I Want It All...

If you want to select all the text in a document, select a word or paragraph with the Select tool, then right-click (Control-click on a Mac) and choose Select All Text from the shortcut menu.

2. Click and drag either arrow to add text to the selection. Hold the pointer over the selected text for a couple of seconds until the Select Text icon displays (**Figure 82b**).

Select Text icon

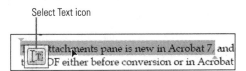

Figure 82b Hold the pointer over the selected text for a couple of seconds and the Select Text icon displays over the text.

3. Now move the pointer over the icon to display the menu listing options you can choose depending on the content selected (**Figure 82c**). For general use, click Copy to Clipboard.

 **Figure 82c** Choose from the two default text selection options.

4. Open the document you want to add the text to and paste it in place.

The Select tool is also great for selecting precise words and phrases to use for links (discussed in Chapter 12) and bookmarks (discussed in Chapter 13).

Copy That

The better you understand some of the intricacies of text selection, the faster you can get your work done. Here are some tips:

- Choose Edit > Preferences > General (on a Mac, Acrobat > Preferences > General) and click Enable text selection for the Hand tool. This way when you hold the pointer over text in a document it automatically works as the Select tool. There is a difference in how the selection process works depending on whether you enable the Hand tool for text selection: If you have the preference set, when you pause the pointer over some text, it changes to the Select tool and you can drag to select text.

- If you are copying and pasting text and intend to send it on to others, be aware that unless the recipient's computer has the same font it can't be preserved. Acrobat substitutes the closest match.

- When a document is tagged, you can use the Copy With Formatting option. This option is especially useful if your document contains columns.

- Selecting text on two pages? And irritated because the footer text is included? Check the document's tags. In a correctly tagged document, footer text uses a different tag.

- If the text isn't behaving as text, maybe it isn't. Scanned text that hasn't been captured behaves like an image. To learn more about scanning, see Tip 34 in Chapter 4; capturing text is covered in Chapter 17, Tip 139

- If you can't copy text, check to see if the document has security settings. The author may have specified that copying is restricted.

TIP 83 Reusing Images

You can reuse individual images from a document if permission is given by the document author. Begin by clicking the Select tool on the Basic toolbar. The Select tool automatically changes to an arrow when the pointer is held over an image. Then, click to select the image, which is highlighted. If you want only a portion of the image copied, drag a marquee with the Select tool.

When you release the mouse, the area you surrounded by the marquee is highlighted. Wait a second or two, and the Select Image icon displays on top of the selected image (**Figure 83a**).

Select Image icon

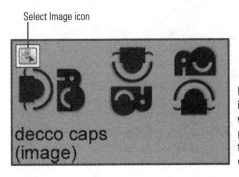

Figure 83a Select an image on the document; when you hold the pointer over the selection the Select Image icon displays over the image.

Move your pointer over the icon and the menu opens. The only option available for a selected image is to copy it to the clipboard (**Figure 83b**).

Figure 83b Click the menu option to copy the image to the Clipboard.

Click outside the selected image or click another tool to deselect an image. Once you have the image or image segment copied, you can reuse it. You can also save the image as a file. Select the image in the document, and then right-click to open the shortcut menu. Choose Save Image As, name the image, and specify the save location.

(Continued)

Snapshot? Maybe Not

If you need to modify or index the text you're copying, don't use the Snapshot tool; use the Select tool instead. Content copied with the Snapshot tool creates a graphic, uneditable image of whatever it captures, whether it's images or text.

Drag and Drop Shot

You don't have to mess around with copying and pasting when you're moving images. Open the recipient document next to the document with the image and arrange the documents on the screen. Then, select the image in the PDF document and drag it to the other document.

What if you want to reuse some of the content on a page that contains both text and graphics? You can copy and paste each element separately, or you can use the snazzy Snapshot tool. Here's how:

1. Select the Snapshot tool 📷 on the Basic toolbar.

2. Select the content from the page:
   - Click anywhere on the document to capture the visible content on the Document pane.
   - Drag a marquee around a portion of the page.
   - Drag a marquee around a portion of an image on the page (**Figure 83c**).

Figure 83c Using the Snapshot tool, you can drag a marquee to select a portion of the image.

You see a flash as the image's colors are inverted within the marquee and the content is captured. The selected area is surrounded by a dashed line until you deselect the tool or select another tool.

3. An information dialog appears telling you that the content has been copied to the clipboard. Click OK.

   Note
   The information dialog isn't something you really need to see more than once. Fortunately, the dialog includes a check box that you can click to hide the message. Go ahead. Click it.

4. Paste the clipboard content wherever you need it, or use it to create a new PDF document.

TIP 84 Editing Text in a PDF

Here's a common scenario: You send deluxe information packages in PDF format to a select few clients. To customize the packages with the recipients' names, you could generate multiple source documents. But do you have to make separate PDF files for each client? Or suppose you publish a catalog and want to maintain a current date on the catalog whenever you send it to your prospective clients. Do you have to re-create the PDF each time you need to modify the date?

No and no. You can easily tweak the text in Acrobat using the TouchUp Text tool, hidden in the Advanced Editing toolbar. Choose Tools > Advanced Editing > Show Advanced Editing Toolbar. You can click the pull-down arrow to the right of the displayed TouchUp tool to open the TouchUp toolbar if you like. Both toolbars and the pull-down menu are shown in **Figure 84a**.

Figure 84a Open the Advanced Editing toolbar to find the TouchUp Text tool and the TouchUp toolbar.

Select the TouchUp Text tool from the Advanced Editing toolbar or the TouchUp toolbar and click the tool within the text you want to edit. The paragraph is surrounded by a bounding box. Drag the I-beam pointer to select all or part of the paragraph, or position the I-beam within the text you want to edit (**Figure 84b**).

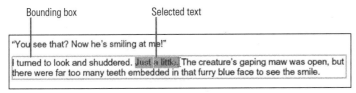

Figure 84b The block of text is identified by a bounding box. Select all or part of the text within the bounding box.

(Continued)

Gimme a Break!

Adding new text to an existing paragraph is all well and good, and adding extra lines of text is fine too, but what happens if the line of text grows too wide for the page's layout? In previous versions of Acrobat you had to add one line of text at a time.

Well, Acrobat 7's TouchUp Text tool handles this tricky layout problem with panache. In addition to adding text, you can also add line breaks. Click the location on the text block where you want it to break, and then right-click or Control-click to open the shortcut menu. Click Insert > Line Break. Then press Enter or Return to wrap the text to the next line. Check out Tip 87 on using the TouchUp Object tool to see how to make the reformatted paragraph fit.

You can use the same method to insert other items, including soft hyphens, nonbreaking spaces, and em dashes.

If you need to select an entire paragraph, instead of dragging the cursor choose Edit > Select All to select all the text in the bounding box, or use the shortcut keys Ctrl+A or Command+A. Type the replacement text or add new text at the position of the I-beam pointer. Click outside the highlighted area to deselect the text.

In addition to touching up existing text in a document, you can add new text using the TouchUp Text tool. With the TouchUp Text tool active, Ctrl-click/Option-click within the document where you want to add the text. The New Text Font dialog opens with the default options: Arial text and horizontal writing mode. Select the font and writing mode (horizontal or vertical), and click OK (**Figure 84c**).

Figure 84c Select the desired font and writing mode for your inserted text.

Note

If you select a vertical writing mode (shown in the dialog in Figure 84c) and the font doesn't write vertically, you'll get an error message that the requested font with the requested writing mode doesn't exist in your system. Click OK to dismiss the dialog. You have two choices: Either use the font horizontally or find another font that can be used vertically.

The default text "New Text" displays on the page. Select it, and then type the new text (**Figure 84d**). Click outside the new line of text to finish the process. The text is de-selected and the new line of text is complete.

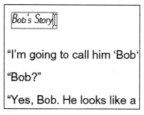

Figure 84d Your text appears just as you specified.

TIP 85 Modifying Text Attributes

You can modify properties of new text as well as text already in the document, including:

- Font and font size

- Fill and stroke options

- Font embedding and subsetting

- Spacing between words and characters

- Baseline adjustments

With the TouchUp Text tool, first click the row of text or select the words or characters you want to edit. Then right-click/Control-click the text to open the shortcut menu and choose Properties. The TouchUp Properties dialog opens (**Figure 85a**).

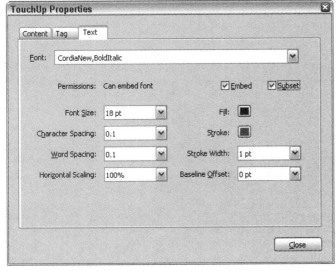

Figure 85a Change the properties of the text in the TouchUp Properties dialog.

(Continued)

Editing Text

Sometimes it's simpler to modify a source document than it is to edit text on the PDF document. But for small or simple text changes, you can work in Acrobat. Acrobat offers three different tools to work with text.

Use the Select Text tool to select text for copying and pasting into another document. On the Advanced Editing toolbar, use the TouchUp Text tool to modify and edit text, or to add new text to a page. You can also use the Text Box tool on the Advanced Commenting toolbar, discussed in Chapter 14.

The Look of Letters

It can be great fun to experiment with the text attributes and change the way your text looks, but be aware of how you are changing the effect of your document. As professional page designers know, the appearance of the text influences readers almost as much as the content itself. Fonts communicate messages, and even something as subtle as character spacing can give a different feel than you intended. Wild changes like adding strokes and fill colors to your text can tilt a document on its ear—which may be just what you are looking for.

Click the Font pull-down list and choose a font if necessary. The fonts used in the document appear first; other fonts on your system are listed below a blank space (**Figure 85b**).

Figure 85b Choose a font from the TouchUp Properties dialog.

Adjust other text attributes as desired and as the font's attributes allow, shown in Figure 85a. As you make adjustments, the changes are automatically previewed in the selected text. Click Close to dismiss the dialog and apply the settings.

TIP 86 Reusing Table Information

Tables are not generally considered exciting, although they are an important and necessary part of business documents. Until Acrobat 6 it was difficult to deal with tables in PDFs; Acrobat 6 included a Select Table tool, and Acrobat 7 takes your table manipulation capabilities to new heights.

Suppose you have a PDF document containing tables, and you need to use the table information but don't have the original source file. Or suppose you want to cut a table out of a PDF document to use as a separate PDF file. In earlier versions of Acrobat, the only way to reuse table data was to export the content as a rich text format (RTF) file, and then reassemble and restructure the table in Microsoft Word or Excel.

How you select table information differs depending on whether or not the document is tagged. In this tip, you see how to work with an untagged document. Read about tagged documents in this tip's sidebar.

Using the methods you learned in Tip 82, select your text and expand your selection area to include some or all of the content from the table. If you see a Select Table icon when you move the tool over the table, you can automatically select all the content.

Wait a couple of seconds for the Select text icon to display over the selected table content. Move the pointer over the icon to open the menu, and choose an option (**Figure 86a**). You can also right-click or Control-click the selected text to open the shortcut menu and choose the same options, and the shortcut menu includes other text manipulation options as well.

Figure 86a Select all or a portion of the table for exporting.

(Continued)

Why a Table Is a Table

Spreadsheet programs are designed using a structure called comma-separated values (CSV). Exporting the content from the table using the CSV process pastes the content from a cell location in the Acrobat table to the equivalent location in the spreadsheet.

Tag It

If your document is tagged and you merely want to copy and paste a table, don't spend time selecting tools, selecting text, and selecting commands. Instead, open the Tags pane and click the table's tag. Choose Options > Copy Contents to Clipboard from the Tags pane's menu. Then open the document in which you want to use the table and paste it in. The table is pasted and includes its data as well as any formatting such as borders, fonts, and so on. How cool.

Using Tables in a Tagged Document

Tagging a document can be really beneficial—if, as with most things in life, you know how to use those tags to best advantage.

When a document is tagged, Acrobat 7 automatically recognizes the structure and gives you yet another Select tool to use for your document manipulation enjoyment. Click the Select tool on the Basic toolbar and move it over a table on your document. The icon changes to crosshairs and a grid. Click once and the entire table is selected.

As with other select tools, if you hover the pointer over the table, the Select Text icon displays; move the pointer over the icon to open the menu. In addition to the options available for a table selected in an untagged document, you can select a Copy with Formatting command.

Regardless of the menu you use, Acrobat automatically recognizes the text as belonging to a table format, which gives you three table-specific options in addition to the customary Copy to Clipboard command. You can:

- Choose Save As Table; the Save As dialog box opens. Name the table, and choose a format from the pull-down list (**Figure 86b**). Then click Save.

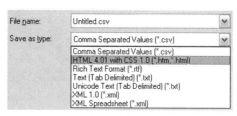

Figure 86b Choose an exporting format for saving the table.

- Choose Open Table in Spreadsheet. Your spreadsheet application, such as Excel, opens and displays the imported table in a new worksheet (**Figure 86c**).

	A	B	C
1	To do this...	In Windows, press...	In Mac OS, press...
2	Go to the previous screen	Page Up	Page Up
3	Go to the next screen	Page Down	Page Down
4	Go to the first page	Shift+Ctrl+Page Up	Shift+Command+PageUp
5	Go to the last page	Shift+Ctrl+Page Down	Shift+Command+PageDown
6	Scroll up	Up arrow	Up arrow
7			

Figure 86c An exported table is converted to an active Excel worksheet.

- Choose Copy As Table to copy it to the clipboard. Open the document you want to paste the table into, and choose Edit > Paste.

In both Word and Excel, the tables taken from the PDF document are editable and ready to use.

TIP 87 Object TouchUps

An object you create in Acrobat, such as a link or a form field, can be selected with the appropriate tool, or with the Select Object tool, as described in Chapter 12. And by using the TouchUp Object tool, you can select content imported as part of the document, such as text, images, and multimedia objects.

The TouchUp Object tool 🖻, located on the TouchUp subtoolbar of the Advanced Editing toolbar, can be useful when you're organizing content on a page. For example, if you have added extra text to a page and need to shuffle the location of the following paragraph, use the TouchUp Object tool to select the text and drag it to a new location (**Figure 87a**).

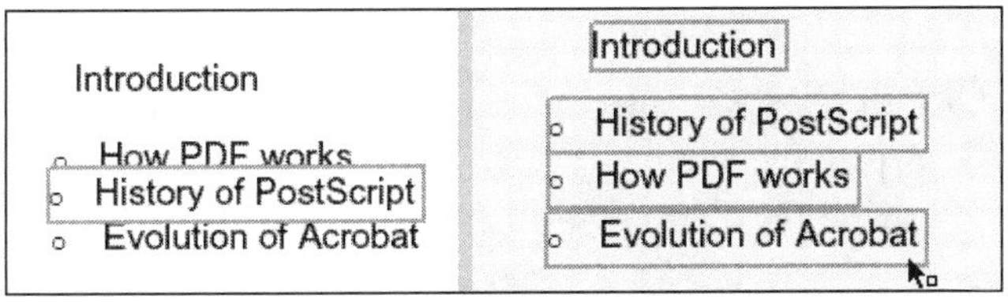

Figure 87a You can add a new line of text on your document using the TouchUp Text tool and then shift adjoining objects to correctly space the content.

Here are some tips:

- You can cut, copy, and paste objects.

- Although you can't select an object on one page and drag it to another page, you can cut an object from one page and paste it to another page.

- You can select more than one type of object at the same time.

(Continued)

What Else Does It Do?

Glad I asked. In addition to cut, copy, paste, and move options, you can use the TouchUp Object tool to do other types of editing in your document. Select an object or objects, and then from the shortcut menu, click:

- Delete Clip to remove any objects that are clipping the selected object.

- Create Artifact to remove the object from the reading order so it isn't identified by the Read Out Loud feature or a screen reader program.

- Edit Image to edit a bitmap in Photoshop, or Edit Object to edit a vector object in Illustrator. The commands change based on the object type.

- TouchUp Properties to open the Properties dialog, where you can edit the object's content, tag, and text information.

- Hidden objects are revealed when the TouchUp Object tool is selected in the toolbar (**Figure 87b**).

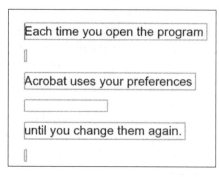

Figure 87b Not all objects are visible on a document. In this example, extra spaces and tabs added in the source document are actually separate objects in the PDF document.

- Click and drag the tool over objects on the page to select all the objects within the marquee. Ctrl-click or Option-click an object to add it to the selection.

- Click to select an object, and then right-click or Control-click to display the shortcut menu. Choose Select All, and Acrobat selects all the objects on the page.

Note
For those who prefer to work with mouse and shortcut keys, click the first object with the TouchUp Object tool, and then press Ctrl+A or Command+A to select the page's or document's objects.

TIP 88 Touching Up Reading Order

Yet another reason for using a tagged PDF document is to organize its reading order. You can use the TouchUp Reading Order tool to define individual content elements on a page and then order them as desired.

Select the TouchUp Reading Order tool 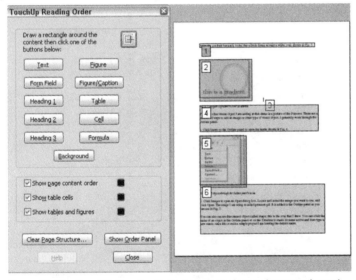 in the TouchUp subtoolbar of the Advanced Editing toolbar, or choose Advanced > Accessibility > TouchUp Reading Order.

Click the page with the tool. The TouchUp Reading Order dialog opens, and the content of the page is shown in separate gray numbered blocks. The numbers identify the document's reading sequence (**Figure 88a**).

Keep It Organized

It's often easier to work with the reading order if you are zoomed out of the page. However, that's hard on your eyes. To easily select content, see what you are doing, and control the reading order assignment, arrange the dialog, page, and Order pane across the program window. Select objects by clicking them on the Order pane.

Figure 88a The TouchUp Reading Order tool shows how a document is read by identifying components of the page and numbering them in sequence. Use the dialog to change the identification of components in a document.

(Continued)

Order, Please

By default the reading order of a page is assigned from left to right, top to bottom. You can assign a different order. Choose Edit > Preferences > TouchUp. Click the TouchUp Reading Order pull-down menu and choose an alternate order.

Here are some tips for using the tool and touchup process:

- Decide how you want to handle images with captions. Screen readers define a caption within a figure tag as a part of the image and it isn't read. On the other hand, using the figure/caption tag separates the caption from the body text.

- Need some bookmarks? Tag selections as headings and then convert the heading tags to bookmarks. See tips in Chapter 3 for using bookmarks in various Office programs; see Chapter 14 to learn how to work with bookmarks in Acrobat.

- Use the Cell tag to identify a table cell if it is split incorrectly.

- Extra spaces, lines, tabs, and so on added in the source document are identified in the reading order. Either tag the offending object as a background element, also known as an artifact, or remove it altogether (**Figure 88b**).

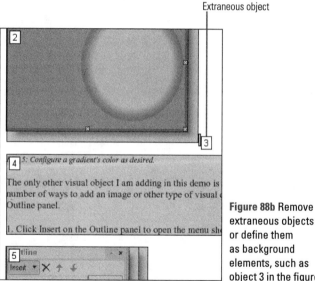

Extraneous object

Figure 88b Remove extraneous objects or define them as background elements, such as object 3 in the figure.

- If your page is a mess of extraneous and incorrect tags, click Clear Structure and then rebuild the page's structure.

- Change the reading order quickly in the Order pane. Click the icon to the left of the number of the object you want to move and drag it up or down. A horizontal bar displays on the pane showing the position where the object will be placed when you release the mouse (**Figure 88c**).

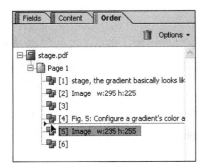

Figure 88c Reorder the reading order in a document by dragging objects up and down in the Order pane's list.

Choosing an Editing Program

Before you can edit from Acrobat, you need to specify the programs you wish to use for editing images and text. You make your choices in the Preferences dialog. Choose Edit > Preferences > TouchUp (on a Mac, Acrobat > Preferences > TouchUp) to open the dialog.

For both the image and text editor selections, click the appropriate button, either Choose Image Editor or Choose Page/Object Editor, to open a browse dialog. Locate the program you want to use and select it. Click Open to close the dialog and assign the program to the function. Then, click OK to close the dialog and set the preferences.

TIP
89 Round-trip Editing an Image

What if you have a terrific document and it is ready to send to a client when you realize you should have tweaked an image or added a text layer? Can you still make your deadline in time? You can if you are working in Acrobat, which supports round-trip editing! Round-trip editing lets you work from Acrobat, make changes to content in another program, and then integrate those changes automatically in the PDF document. You can use the TouchUp Object tool and use a designated source program, such as Photoshop, to make changes that are then returned to the PDF document—round-trip editing at its finest. You can even select several images and change them all at the same time. Follow these steps to change image content:

1. Select the TouchUp Object tool and then select the image or images you want to edit.

2. Right-click or Control-click and choose Edit Image. Photoshop opens, and displays the image or images.

3. Make your changes. If you have added any layers, choose Layer > Flatten Image to flatten the layers.

4. Choose File > Save. The image is saved, closed, and replaced in Acrobat (**Figure 89**).

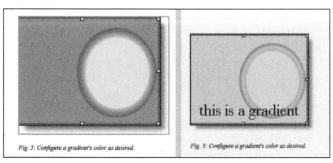

Fig. 5: Configure a gradient's color as desired.   Fig. 5: Configure a gradient's color as desired.

Figure 89 The original image shown at the left has been edited from Acrobat. As seen in the right of the figure, the image has been scaled and recolored, and a text layer has been added.

Watch out for some things that can make your editing experience less than miraculous:

- A resized image's location will often need tweaking in Acrobat. Use the TouchUp Object tool to reorganize the content if required.

- Transparency is preserved only for masks specified as index values in an image using indexed color.

- When you change image modes, such as from RGB to grayscale, your image may not be saved automatically; instead Photoshop opens a save dialog to save the image as a Photoshop PDF separate from your original PDF document.

- Not every image can be read. If you see a checkerboard instead of your image, you can't edit using the round-trip method. Check your Photoshop configuration.

- If the image looks a little odd when it opens in Photoshop, check the pixel aspect ratio. Acrobat instructs Photoshop to use pixel aspect ratio correction for previewing.

Keep the Connection

The image connection exists only as long as the object is selected in Acrobat. If you are working with an image in Photoshop and then deselect the object in Acrobat, you have to start over.

TIP 89: Round-trip Editing an Image

CHAPTER ELEVEN

Drawings and Layers

One of the super features of Acrobat 7 Professional (Windows) is its ability to handle professional drawings produced by programs such as AutoDesk AutoCAD, and other complex material such as Microsoft Visio drawings and high-end print files. To handle the job, you can choose from a variety of tools and processes that help you in your quest for document management nirvana.

New in Acrobat 7 Professional is a PDFMaker for AutoCAD with which you can convert all layers, filtered subsets, or selected layers into a layered PDF document.

When you have a PDF open in Acrobat, you can examine imported drawings using a set of measuring tools. You can also create your own drawings in Acrobat, and use grids and guides to assist you. A number of Acrobat's commenting tools are used for drawing. In this chapter I'll describe the tools available on the Drawing Markups toolbar; see Chapter 14 for general information on working with comments.

Layered documents generated by AutoCAD or Visio can be used in Acrobat, and you can attach actions to the layers as well as define how your users see the document.

Hundreds of Layers

Often engineering and other technical drawings have dozens, if not literally hundreds, of layers. How do you keep them all straight? In AutoCAD you can work with layer filters, and the PDFMaker gives you that convenience as well.

Organize the layers sets for your users' convenience. For example, in a construction drawing you might want to build separate layer sets for plumbing, electrical, telephone and network, and so on.

Acrobat 7 Professional includes a Windows-only PDFMaker for Auto-CAD. As with other PDFMakers, an Adobe PDF menu and a three-button toolbar are added to the program. You can convert all layers or some of the layers from an AutoCAD drawing to a PDF document.

Here are some tips for working with the AutoCAD PDFMaker:

- Page size and plotting information is transferred from AutoCAD to the PDFMaker automatically to ensure the PDF document uses the right page size.

- You can flatten the drawing into a single layer, retain some layers, or retain all layers—choose the option in the first pane of the Acrobat PDFMaker dialog.

- You select the layers to add from the Layers in Drawing list; to add the layer to the Layers in PDF list, simply click Add. Until a layer is added to the Layers in PDF list from the Layers in Drawing list, the Add PDF Setting button is grayed out (**Figure 90a**).

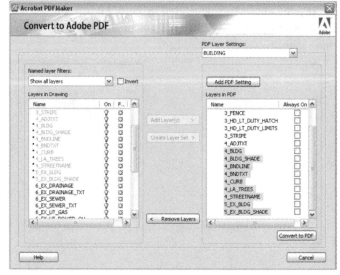

Figure 90a Select the layers you want to convert to PDF. In a large drawing, use the Named layer filters menu to make the job easier.

- If you make a mistake in adding layers to the Layers in PDF list, you can reorder the layers using the up and down arrows. To remove a layer, first select it and then click Remove Layers, or press Delete.

- Settings you created in the past are listed (such as layer selections or layer filters) in the PDF Layer Settings menu; these settings can be reused, edited, renamed, or deleted. First click the setting you wish to use; then click Rename to rename it, or click Remove to delete it. Click OK to close the dialog and return to the Acrobat PDFMaker dialog. The selected PDF Layer Settings are displayed in the dialog.

- PDF settings are stored in the AutoCAD file itself. After you convert an AutoCAD drawing to PDF (be sure to choose to save the PDF settings), you have to resave the AutoCAD drawing again to actually store the PDF settings.

- Use the Named layer filters options in the Acrobat PDFMaker dialog (located above the Layers in Drawing list) to select a filter fitting specific criteria. If you want to use all layers except those filtered on your named criteria, click the Invert option.

- Click Create Layer Set to add a folder to the Layers in PDF list, and then add layers to the folder (**Figure 90b**).

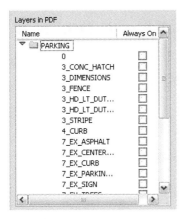

Figure 90b Create folders to store layer sets in the finished PDF.

(Continued)

TIP 90: Using the AutoCAD PDFMaker

After you convert the document to PDF, when you open it in Acrobat, you see the layers in the original AutoCAD drawing arranged in layer sets, which makes it much simpler for users to view specific parts of a drawing (**Figure 90c**).

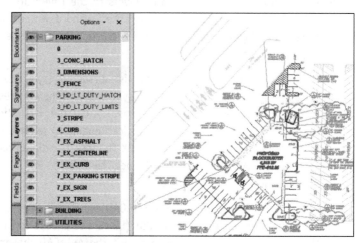

Figure 90c When the converted drawing is opened in Acrobat, you see the layer sets defined in the PDFMaker.

TIP 91 Using Grids and Guides for Assistance

If you have worked with image, illustration, or layout programs, you know about grids and guides. Acrobat 7 includes both these handy features, along with rulers to help you position content precisely, and to assist in measuring and examining drawings.

Grids are sets of vertical and horizontal lines that overlay a document. The lines of the grid, which use spacing that you specify, aren't printed.

Choose View > Grid to display the grid. If you want to be able to move an object and have it "snap" to the grid (align itself automatically with the grid lines), choose View > Snap to Grid (**Figure 91a**). As you drag an object you see it jump to align with the grid lines horizontally and vertically.

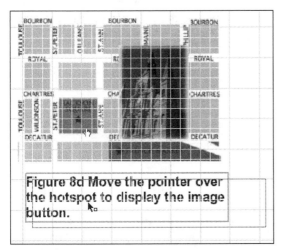

Figure 91a Using the grid to snap content to precise locations on the document, you see a dotted line where the object will snap to when you release the mouse.

Guides are custom lines that you can add either vertically or horizontally to help with positioning. To use guides, turn on the rulers first by choosing View > Rulers. Click the horizontal ruler at the top of the Document pane with any tool and drag downward to place a horizontal guide; drag right from the vertical ruler at the left of the Document pane with any tool to place a vertical guide.

(Continued)

When Objects Misbehave

Whether the grid is displayed or not, the Snap to Grid feature can still be active. If you are moving content on your page—images, text, form fields, drawings—and you can't seem to nudge it into position smoothly, click the View menu and see if the Snap to Grid option is checked. Uncheck the setting and you can nudge to your heart's content.

Making the Grid Work for You

The grid is only as valuable as its settings. In many documents, setting the Offset preferences may be the most important setting. For example, if you have one-inch margins on a page and set the grid to .4 inches vertically, there is no grid line that lines up with your left margin, as the grid lines show at .4, .8, and 1.2 inches. If you instead set the Offset at 1 inch, the grid lines are offset by the amount you specify in the preferences, and a grid line is sure to line up with your margins.

To reposition your guide, click the Select Object tool on the Advanced Editing toolbar and drag the guide line. When you drag, the Select Object tool switches to a cursor (shown in **Figure 91b**). Toggle the guides on and off using the View > Guides command. Use the Select Object tool and drag horizontal guides up to the ruler or drag vertical guides left to the ruler to remove them.

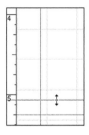

Figure 91b Use any tool to drag a guide from the rulers; use the Select Object tool to reposition the guides.

Both grids and guides can be customized in the Preferences dialog. Choose Edit > Preferences or Acrobat > Preferences and choose the Units and Guides option in the list at the left of the dialog to display the customization settings (**Figure 91c**).

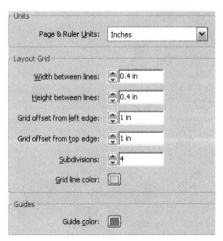

Figure 91c Customize grid and guide lines according to the document you are working with.

Click the Units pull-down menu and choose an option other than the default inches if required. Select options for grid spacing, color, and position of the grid. Use the arrows for each setting to increase or decrease the values, or you can type a value in the text boxes.

Not sure where the grid should start? You can use the Info pane to tell you exactly where to set the Offset values for the grid preference. Choose View > Navigation Tabs > Info to open the pane (**Figure 91d**). As you move the mouse over the page, you see the values change in the pane; note the horizontal or vertical value at your desired location and then use the value to set the Offset preference. Of course, you can use the Info pane for other purposes as well, such as checking the size and location of a button, form field, or drawn object.

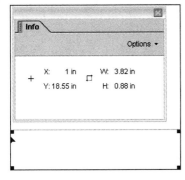

Figure 91d Use the Info pane to define a location on a page, as well as the dimensions of drawn objects on your document.

TIP 91: Using Grids and Guides for Assistance

Where Did It Go?

A measurement is an elusive thing. Unless you specify the measurement as a comment, the object you draw will disappear when you start another measurement or select another tool. You can define the measurement as a comment by clicking the Measurement Markup option in the dialog. When you type text in the Annotation field, it is shown as a comment when the measurement is complete, as shown in Figure 92b. Read about working with and configuring comments in Chapter 14.

Measuring Objects

Acrobat 7 Professional includes several tools you can use to measure the distance and area of objects in a PDF drawing. You most often use these tools with CAD drawings or with documents being sent to a printer.

Open the Measuring toolbar by choosing Tools > Measuring > Show Measuring Toolbar (**Figure 92a**). Of course you can select an individual tool from the menu, but my strong preference is to open any toolbar I am working with to save time. You can also right-click or Control-click the toolbar well at the top of the program window and click Measuring.

Figure 92a Open the Measuring toolbar for convenience. The toolbar contains three tools, used to measure distance, perimeter, and area.

Each tool measures in a different way:

- Click the Distance tool ⊢ to measure the distance between two points by clicking the location for the first point and then dragging to the second point and clicking the mouse again.

- Click the Perimeter tool ⊣ to measure the distance between several points. Click each point you want to measure and then double-click the last point to finish the measurement.

- Click the Area tool ◺ to measure the area within line segments. With the tool, click each point you want to measure and then click the first point again to complete the measurement area.

Note

To stop the drawing process before completing a shape, press the Esc key on your keyboard or select another tool from the toolbars. To constrain the segments to straight lines as you draw, hold the Shift key as you drag and click the mouse.

When you click a measuring tool, the Distance/Perimeter/Area Tool dialog opens. The name of the dialog depends on the chosen tool (**Figure 92b**). After you have completed measuring with one of the three tools, the values appear in the dialog.

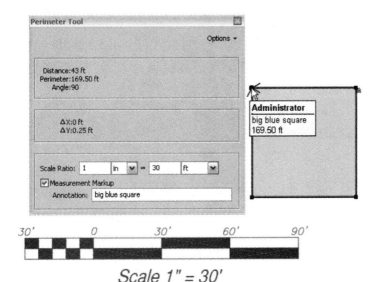

Figure 92b The values of the measured area are shown in this dialog; change the scale to match your drawing. You can also assign a note to the measurement, as shown here.

Many times drawings are constructed to scale, which you can set in the dialog by typing the ratio values in the fields and choosing a unit of measurement from the pull-down lists.

Viewing Metadata

Visio and AutoCAD drawings may have metadata embedded in them. These elements are custom information added in the source program which is then included with the converted PDF document. To view custom metadata from a CAD application, choose Tools > Object Data > Object Data Tool. Your pointer changes to crosshairs when you mouse over an object containing metadata; click to select the object and the Object Data dialog opens. The contents of the embedded data are shown in the dialog. Click the Options button in the dialog to view a list of actions you can take, such as zooming to the selected object, counting similar objects, or copying the content to the clipboard.

TIP 92: Measuring Objects

TIP 93 — Drawing and Marking Up Shapes in Acrobat

Another Dimension

You can use the Dimensioning tool ⊟, found on the Drawing Markups toolbar, to measure distances between two points or areas on a page. For example, use the tool to add a line between two points when you want to point out the width of a parking spot on a drawing or the distance between two graphic elements on a brochure layout. Click the tool in the Drawing Markups toolbar and drag from the line's starting point. When you release the mouse, the line finishes, and a text box displays for you to type a note. Each end of the line includes an anchor point and arrow.

Some people have a need to doodle on paper. What happens if you take their paper away? Well, just put a mouse in their hand and open a PDF document because you can draw all sorts of objects, including the aforementioned doodle, using the Drawing tools.

Choose Tools > Drawing Markups > Show Drawing Markups Toolbar or right-click/Control-click the toolbar well and choose the toolbar from the list. The Drawing Markups toolbar contains a Drawing sub-toolbar. You can see the two menus as well as the pull-down list in **Figure 93a**.

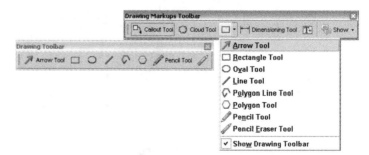

Figure 93a Use the Drawing Markups, including Drawing tools, to add visual comments to your documents.

Drawing markups are forms of comments. To use a tool, click to select it on the toolbar, and then draw points, click and drag, or scribble (in the case of the Pencil and Pencil Eraser tools). For shapes such as a polygon or clouds, click the starting point to close the shape. When you complete the drawing, you can double-click it to open a note, where you can type information about your doodle (**Figure 93b**). If you want to show some text on the document in a text box, use the Text Box tool . Click to select the tool in the toolbox and then drag a marquee on the page. A yellow text box the size of the marquee is added to the document; click the box and type your message.

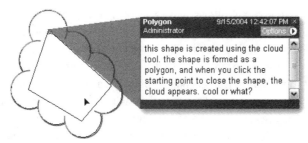

Figure 93b Drawing Markups and drawn shapes are types of comments; type remarks in a note box.

A callout is a specific form of drawing markup that you can use to pinpoint a specific location on a drawing (**Figure 93c**). Click the document with the Callout tool ⌨ and a yellow note box appears; type your note, and then click anywhere on the page away from the note box to resize the box and display the arrows. You can drag the box around the page and reposition the arrow's point by dragging as well.

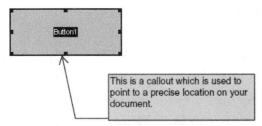

Figure 93c Use a callout to display a remark about a specific location on a page or drawing.

Note
See Chapter 14 for information on how to change and customize the appearance of any drawing or drawing markup object.

TIP 93: Drawing and Marking Up Shapes in Acrobat

TIP 94
Working with a Layered Document

Acrobat 7 Professional allows you to work with layered documents created in Visio and AutoCAD. Unfortunately, layered documents created in programs such as Adobe Photoshop are not supported.

This tip uses a document with three named layers created in Microsoft Visio 2003. Our document displays a graphic of kitchen cabinets with three alternate color schemes for the tile. The default view (**Figure 94a**) shows some of the content of all layers simultaneously (looks a bit messy, doesn't it?). If you come across a document like this, have a look at the bottom left of the Acrobat window. If you see a "layer cake" icon 📚, you know the document is layered. Click the Layers tab in the Navigation pane to open the Layers pane. If the Layers tab isn't visible in the Navigation pane, choose View > Navigation Tabs > Layers to open the tab.

Figure 94a The default view of the document shows the contents on all visible layers at once.

In **Figure 94b**, you can see that our document has three named layers; each corresponds to the individual layer's color scheme.

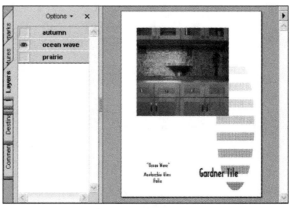

Figure 94b Toggle a layer's visibility on and off by clicking the eye icon in the Layers pane. Here just one layer is visible.

You can toggle a layer's visibility on and off by clicking the eye icon—when the eye is visible, the layer is visible. In the figure, only the *ocean waves* layer is set to visible, and the content on the layer appears on the Document pane.

As with other documents, you may be able to make changes to the content (depending on the rights granted by the document's author). Our sample doesn't have security attached, so you can add comments to it or export it in another file format from Acrobat.

To see what a layer contains, right-click it on the Layers pane and choose Layer Properties to open the dialog (**Figure 94c**). The Layer Properties dialog lists information about the layer, including its original name, visibility, print status, and export status. Keep in mind that settings applied to the original layered document cannot be changed. For example, our sample document uses the Prints When Visible setting; only a blank page prints unless the layer's eye icon is toggled to Visible.

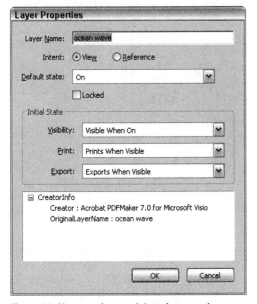

Figure 94c You can view each layer's properties. The properties are set in the source program, not in Acrobat.

Show Them What You've Got

Your users may not be aware that your carefully constructed document contains layers, although the Layer Cake icon displays at the bottom of the program window. To make sure they know the layers exist, set the initial view. Choose File > Document Properties and click the Initial View tab. Click the Show pull-down arrow and choose Layers Panel and Page. Save the document to preserve the initial view choice.

TIP 94: Working with a Layered Document

Different Types of Layers

What you see in the Layers pane depends on how the original document was constructed and converted. In some cases, a document is converted with *preserved* layers, as in our example. In other cases, the document layers may be *flattened* or locked. In a flattened document you see a single layer like a regular PDF document. A locked document, on the other hand, displays the layers individually, but they can't be edited in any way.

Bookmarking a Layered Document

Acrobat lets you attach bookmarks to layers, which you can use in different ways. For example, you can distribute the same information using different languages without having to provide documents in different languages, or you can show customers samples in different colors in the same document. Use bookmarks in conjunction with layers to give readers control over what they see and print. Use actions to extend the function of a bookmark beyond just pointing to a location in your document.

Our sample document has three layers, each having a different color scheme and details.

Follow these steps to bookmark a layered document:

1. Open the Bookmarks pane and add three bookmarks. At this point, if you click any bookmark it displays the same location on the same page.

2. Select each bookmark and name it (**Figure 95a**). To minimize confusion, name the bookmarks and arrange them in the same order as the layers listed on the Layers pane.

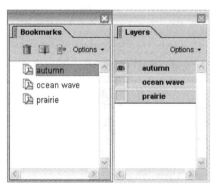

Figure 95a Use a set of bookmarks linked to layers in a document.

3. On the Layers pane, toggle all layers but *autumn* to off by clicking the eye icons. Set the destination view for the *autumn* title bookmark to display only the *autumn* layer, as shown in Figure 95a.

4. On the Bookmarks pane, right-click/Control-click the *autumn* bookmark to select it and open the shortcut menu. Choose Properties to open the Bookmark Properties dialog and then click the Actions tab.

5. From the Select Action pull-down menu, select Set Layer Visibility and then click Add. The action automatically appears in the Actions section at the bottom of the dialog (**Figure 95b**).

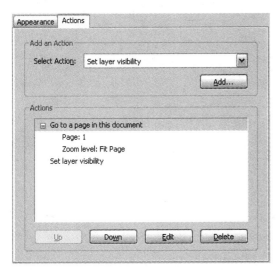

Figure 95b Choose the Set layer visibility action in the Actions tab.

Note
A bookmark's action is to display a page as shown in the bottom of the window in Figure 95b. You can delete the action or leave it as is. In this case, it doesn't make any difference.

6. A notification dialog appears to tell you that the target layer state of the selected actions will be set to the current state. In other words, set the destination layer you want to see as a result of clicking a bookmark and leave the rest hidden. Click OK. The action is added to the Actions list.

7. Click Close to close the Bookmark Properties dialog.

8. Repeat with the other layers. Be sure to hide all layers except for the one you are attaching to the bookmark.

TIP 95: Bookmarking a Layered Document

CHAPTER TWELVE

Controlling Documents with Links and Buttons

Acrobat 7 Professional provides several tools for linking labels to content, including bookmarks, links, and buttons. Learn about bookmarks in Chapter 13.

A PDF, with all its features, more closely resembles a Web site than an ordinary printed document. Would you go to a Web site and scroll through innumerable pages of content to find information? Would you be comfortable using a Web site that didn't have some sort of navigational structure? Of course not! You expect a Web site to come complete with a system of links that allows you to click through the site to find information.

Although people tend to use Acrobat just to convert documents to the PDF format so they can be shared, once you have converted your masterpiece, you can easily add links of different types or buttons to guide readers through your document.

In this collection of tips, you'll see how links and buttons work. You'll learn how you can use them to perform a variety of actions, from jumping to another page in a document, to opening a document, to playing a movie clip.

A button, as anyone who has ever visited a Web site knows (and who hasn't?), can have different appearances and perform different types of actions. A button can, for example, appear one way when it is static, and then look different in response to a mouse action, such as the movement of the pointer over the button, and then look different again in response to a button click. Similarly, a button can initiate different actions in response to different mouse movements.

We'll look at many of the available types of interactivity in this group of tips (we looked at some of the forms actions in Chapter 8, and we'll check out ways to make a PDF containing multimedia interactive in Chapter 16). Whether you want to link different views in a document or add buttons to open other documents, you've come to the right place.

TIP
96

Linking Content in a Document

Which is better? A link or a button? The truth is that you often use them in much the same way. The fundamental difference is related to appearance and the extent of the actions you can apply (**Figure 96a**).

| Home | Products | Catalog |

Figure 96a Are these links or buttons? For simple navigation processes, you can choose either method.

Whether you use links or buttons depends on how you have constructed your source document and what types of navigation you need. For example, if you are building a large report, you can easily link accessory material to any part of the document using a link from some of the text in the document, in which case you don't need to do any advanced preparation.

Follow these steps to add a link to your document:

1. Choose Tools > Advanced Editing > Show Advanced Editing Toolbar to display the tools. You can certainly just click the tool on the menu, but it's simpler to open the toolbar if you are working with several editing functions.

2. Click the Link tool to select it 🔗 and then drag a marquee around the text you want to associate with the link. The Create Link dialog opens (**Figure 96b**).

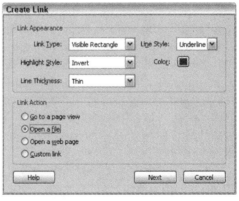

Figure 96b Choose settings for the link's appearance and common actions from the Create Link dialog.

Revisiting a Link's Properties

Once you add a link (or a bookmark or button) you can change the settings easily. Double-click the object with either the appropriate tool or the Select Object tool to open the Link Properties dialog. In the case of the Link Properties dialog, when you reopen it, the Actions tab is automatically shown as well as the Appearance tab, and the radio button options for common link actions, shown in the Create Link dialog when you start a new link, aren't shown on the Appearance tab.

3. Choose whether you want the link to be visible or invisible, and specify characteristics for the link's frame. You can draw a dashed or solid box around the text, as in Figure 96a, or underline the text.

4. Choose an action by clicking one of the radio buttons at the bottom of the dialog and click Next. The next dialog that appears depends on the option you choose:

- Go to a page view opens the Create Go to View dialog in place of the Create Link dialog, instructing you to set the target view, which is the magnification, page, and location you want using the scroll bars and Zoom tools. Once you have the view set, click Set Link to close the dialog and finish the link.

- Open a file replaces the Create Link dialog with a browse dialog for you to select the file you want to display. If you choose a PDF document, the dialog closes and another one opens for you to choose a window open preference (see the sidebar). Click OK to close the dialog and finish the link. If you choose a file that is not a PDF document, when you click Select the dialog closes and the link is finished.

- Open a web page replaces the Create Link dialog with the Edit URL dialog. Type the Web address you want to open from the link and click OK to close the dialog and finish the link.

(Continued)

The Perfect Link

You can apply Acrobat's Link tool function to a feature that serves as a button in another program to produce a custom appearance. For example, you may have converted a PowerPoint presentation to a PDF and want to use the controls in the presentation as links in Acrobat. Draw the link boxes over the button images. In the Create Link dialog, click the Link Type pull-down arrow and choose Invisible Rectangle. You then get the link action without any lines or frames distracting from the beauty of your button.

TIP 96: Linking Content in a Document

Keep an Eye on Your Properties

Don't waste time opening menus and choosing items or switching tools when you are in the midst of a big project. Open the toolbars you need and arrange them in the toolbar well at the top of the program window. One toolbar I rely heavily on is the Properties toolbar. Its content changes according to the selected object on the page, and you can use the same toolbar to modify links, buttons, drawings, and many other objects. Right-click in the toolbar well and choose Properties Bar to display the toolbar; drag it to dock it with your other toolbars and you are ready to go. You can also open the toolbar by pressing Ctrl+E/Command+E, or by choosing View > Toolbars > Properties Bar.

• Custom link replaces the Create Link dialog with the two-tab Link Properties dialog. Click Actions to display the tab, and choose an option from the Select Action pull-down list (**Figure 96c**). Configure the action, which is displayed in the bottom area of the dialog. Links have only one state—that is, the action occurs when the link is clicked. Read about actions in Tip 99.

Figure 96c You can choose from a wide range of actions to apply to a link.

5. Click the Hand tool on the Basic toolbar to deselect the Link tool—you can't see your link in action as long as the tool is selected. Test the link.

TIP 97 Drawing a Button

A button is a form element, and as such has more complex properties than a link. However, adding a simple button is almost as easy as creating a link.

Choose Tools > Advanced Editing > Forms > Button Tool. Or click the Button tool 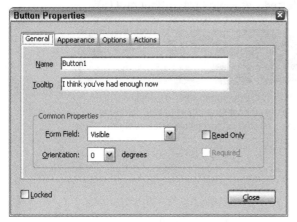 on the Advanced Editing toolbar; it is the Forms tool shown by default on the toolbar. Drag a marquee on the page where you want to place the button.

The Button Properties dialog opens to the General tab (**Figure 97a**). A button is named "Button1" by default; other buttons you add without customizing the name are numbered in sequence. To set the properties for a basic button:

Figure 97a Set characteristics for your buttons in the Button Properties dialog.

1. Name the button if you like. You can also add a tool tip that appears when the user moves the pointer over the button's area on the page.

2. Click the Appearance tab and define how the button will look by choosing background and text color, borders, font, and line styles. Read about building custom buttons in the next tip.

(Continued)

Mouse Actions

Buttons can cause different actions depending on where your pointer is in relation to the button, as well as the mouse action itself. These mouse movements are called triggers.

You can choose from a number of different triggers in the Options panel of the Button Properties dialog. Click the Trigger pull-down menu and then choose one of these triggers:

- Mouse Down—The mouse button is depressed.
- Mouse Up—The mouse button has been depressed and released.
- Mouse Enter—The pointer moves over the button.
- Mouse Exit—The pointer moves away from the button area.

There are several other triggers as well used specifically for forms and media, such as the on Blur and on Focus triggers for form fields, and Page Visible/Invisible for media clips. Refer to Chapter 8 for information on form fields, and Chapter 16 for tips on using multimedia.

And the Winner Is...

The most common trigger is the Mouse Up trigger. The user clicks a button with the mouse, and when the mouse button is released the action is initiated. It is good design etiquette to use the Mouse Up trigger rather than the Mouse Down trigger. Then, if the user decides not to select the button, the user can drag the pointer off the button and cancel the action.

3. Click the Options tab and define how the content on the button should look. You can use labels and icons for a button and customize it to your heart's content.

4. Click the Actions tab and specify both triggers and actions that you want to associate with the button. Triggers are described in the sidebar on the previous page.

Note

If you want to use separate actions for separate triggers, repeat the process and choose the appropriate trigger from the Triggers pull-down list. See how to use multiple triggers in Tip 103.

5. Click Close to dismiss the dialog and complete the button.

6. Click the Hand tool on the Basic toolbar to deselect the Button tool—you can't see your button in action as long as the tool is selected. Test your button (**Figure 97b**).

Figure 97b Test your button when it is finished. In this example, taken from an exotic vacation slideshow, the user is treated to tool tip messages as well as images.

TIP 98 Customizing a Button's Appearance

You aren't restricted to drawing and using buttons that are simple colored and bordered rectangles displaying a scintillating piece of text such as "Click Here." In Acrobat you can customize buttons using different layouts and appearances for different button states.

Buttons commonly change appearance when you move the pointer over them, and they may change yet again when you click them. These changes are called *button states*. Acrobat offers four different button behaviors, and one behavior, Push, allows you to configure different states for the buttons. In this tip you see how to add labels and icons to a three-state button; the same process applies if you are using a single-state button, of course.

1. Draw a button on the page or double-click an existing button to open the Button Properties dialog. Click the Options tab to display layout settings you can use to customize your button (**Figure 98a**).

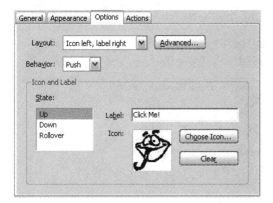

Figure 98a Add text and images to a button on the Options tab of the dialog.

Tip
If you have the Properties Bar open, it displays the Button properties when you click the button; click More on the toolbar to open the Button Properties dialog.

(Continued)

Button States

You don't have to use a push button to create a sense of interactivity in your document. The default button behavior is None, which, let's face it, can be pretty boring as the button stays the same regardless of your mouse actions. On the other hand, if you want a little something without having to do a lot of work, try one of the other options. The Outline behavior highlights the button's border when it is clicked; the Invert behavior reverses the dark and light colors in the button when it is clicked.

2. Click the Layout pull-down arrow to display a list of layout options (**Figure 98b**). Select an option from the list. If you choose any options that include labels, the Label field is active; if you choose any options that include an image, the Icon fields are active.

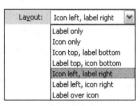

Figure 98b Choose from one of several layouts that use combinations of icons and labels.

3. Click the Behavior pull-down arrow and choose Push from the list. You see the State list change to include Down and Rollover along with Up, the only state available for the other behavior options.

4. For each button state, click the state in the list at the left of the dialog and then type text in the Label field. To add an icon, which can be an image or a PDF file, click Choose Icon to open a browser dialog. Locate the file and select it. A thumbnail appears in the Button Properties dialog.

5. Click Close to dismiss the Button Properties dialog, and then test your button (**Figure 98c**).

Figure 98c This three-state button includes labels on two states as well as a tool tip that appears when the pointer is over the button, known as the Mouse Enter state.

TIP 99 Editing Actions

Using buttons and links is a rather pointless exercise unless something happens when the user clicks the object. In Tips 96 and 97, we briefly mentioned actions when we discussed building links or buttons. In this tip, you learn about editing actions. By the way, actions are also used with bookmarks, which are described in the following chapter.

From either the Link Properties or the Button Properties dialog, click Actions to display the options you can choose and customize.

You can add any number of actions you like to a link, button, or bookmark. But be careful—you probably don't want an action that plays a sound to follow an action that opens another document, for example.

When you are editing link actions, click the action itself, not the details (such as a filename) that are listed for some actions (**Figure 99**). If you are editing a button action, also click the action itself, not the trigger or the details.

Figure 99 Select the name of the action on the Actions tab to edit or change it.

You don't have to plan a sequence of actions ahead of time, however. Add the actions you want to use, and then select an action you want to reorder and click Up or Down to move it in the execution list.

If you change your mind about using an action, select it on the Actions area of the dialog and click Delete.

Play a Sound

One of the actions in the example in this tip is the Play a sound action. Notice in Figure 99 that there is no file listed along with the name of the action in the Action dialog. Acrobat embeds the sound in the PDF document in a format that plays in both Windows and Mac.

Setting an Open Window Preference

How do you want a page in another document to be displayed when you click a link or button—in a new window or replacing the content in the current window? You can set a preference.

Choose Edit > Preferences (in Mac, Acrobat > Preferences) and click General in the list at the left of the dialog. Click Open Cross-Document Links in Same Window. When you view linked documents, the open document is replaced by the linked document in the same window. If you uncheck this option, each time you click a link or button to a different document, a new window opens.

TIP 100 Activating Menu Items

Did you know that you can control a program's function through a link? It sounds complicated, and you may wonder why you would do something like that. Here's a good example, and a terrific way to make a good impression on your readers: Provide a link that automatically prints your document. This tip shows you how to use a button; you can do the same thing using some text or an image and a link.

1. Draw the button on the page using the Button tool on the Advanced Editing toolbar's Forms subtoolbar. The Button Properties dialog opens.

2. Configure the button's appearance in the Appearance tab, and add a text label in the Options tab.

3. Click the Actions tab. From the Select Action pull-down list, choose Execute a menu item (**Figure 100a**). Click Add to open the Menu Item Selection dialog.

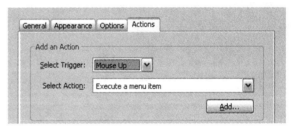

Figure 100a Choose Execute a menu item to add actions that use program commands.

Selecting an Object

Rather than changing among tools such as Link and Button tools, use the Select Object tool on the Advanced Editing toolbar. Double-click an object to open its Properties dialog. If the Properties bar is displayed in the toolbar well, clicking the object with the Select Object tool displays the appropriate tool options.

If you want to select multiple objects, press Control as you drag, and all objects of the same type within the marquee are selected. This feature is handy if you want to make a global change to a set of buttons or links, such as their color. However, you can't change the actions globally; you have to select each object and then change its actions in the Properties dialog.

4. Choose File > Print. The dialog displays the command (**Figure 100b**). Click OK to close the dialog and return to the Actions tab of the Link Properties dialog.

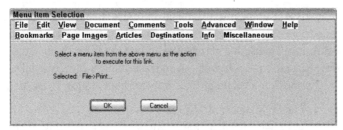

Figure 100b Select a command from the menu items.

5. The action now appears in the Actions window. Click Close to dismiss the Button Properties dialog and complete the button.

6. Click the Hand tool on the Basic toolbar and click the button to test it.

7. The Print dialog opens, which is the action you wanted. Close the dialog or click Print to print a copy of the document.

Jump into Action

Experiment with the options available in the Execute a menu item action. You may be surprised how interesting and functional your documents become. Here are a few of the things you can do:

- Send a document directly to a reviewer.
- Save the document as a certified or signed document.
- Open other documents or digital media.
- Zoom to various magnifications.
- Import or export forms data.

Positioning a Series of Links on a Page

Many documents use a series of headings laid out in a table as a means of navigating. Adding the links and then positioning them evenly can be quite a chore. Fortunately, Acrobat's align/distribute tools, designed to make the positioning process simple, are at your fingertips. Our sample document contains a table with links to six pages. To show you how the link alignment and distribution process works, we are using a narrow line around the links; in an actual document using a table layout, we suggest you use invisible links.

To position a group of links on your page, follow these steps:

1. Click the Link tool and draw the first link. The Create Link dialog opens. Set the characteristics for the first link, such as the appearance and its action, and close the dialog.

2. Ctrl-click/Option-click the link to copy it and drag the copy to the next text label. Click to deselect the new link box, and then Ctrl-drag/Option-drag the original link box again for the third text label. Continue until you've created the whole set of links (**Figure 101a**).

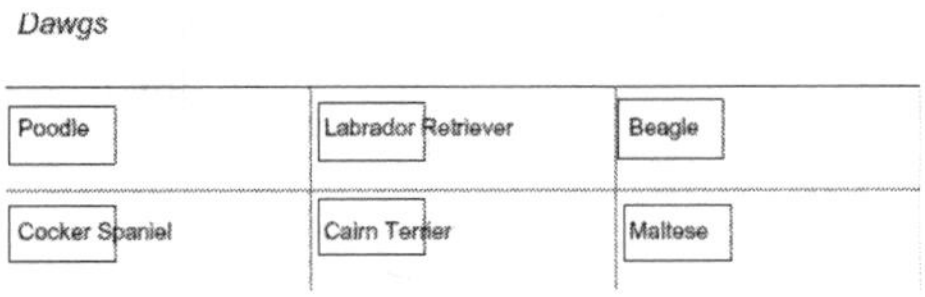

Dawgs

| Poodle | Labrador Retriever | Beagle |
| Cocker Spaniel | Cairn Terrier | Maltese |

Figure 101a All of the text labels have links pasted onto them.

3. Resize the links as necessary to fit over the text labels. You'll notice in Figure 101a that three of the links are narrower than the text labels. Drag a resize handle to increase the width of the link for the longest text label.

4. Leave the link around the longest text label selected—in the example, the Labrador Retriever link—and Ctrl-click/Command-click the other links on the table to select them. Right-click/Control-click to open the shortcut menu; choose Size > Width (**Figure 101b**).

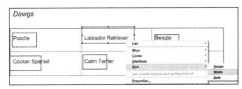

Figure 101b Use the shortcut menu to resize all the links.

Acrobat sizes the link boxes according to the first box you selected. The set of links are now wide enough to cover the text (**Figure 101c**).

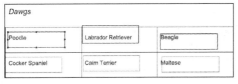

Figure 101c The links are all the same size, which is dictated by the selected link.

5. The boxes aren't aligned vertically or horizontally; that's next. Select the link that is in the correct position; in Figure 101c, the top left link is correctly placed, but we want to adjust the vertical position of the other two links in the top row. Ctrl-click/ Command-click the top links in the middle and right columns.

6. Right-click/Control-click to open the shortcut menu, then choose Align and an alignment option. You can choose from left, right, center, vertical, and horizontal alignment.

7. Repeat the selections horizontally and vertically until your set of links is distributed and aligned correctly (**Figure 101d**).

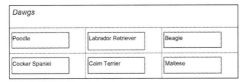

Figure 101d Align and distribute the set of links evenly on the page.

8. Now that your links are positioned properly, double-click each link to open the Link Properties dialog and set the page location as described in Tip 96.

Those Annoying Mistakes

Suppose you have created a set of links as described in this tip. Then you click the Hand tool and realize you left a border when you intended to have the links invisible. Not only that, but now the whole set of links use the wrong appearance. Not to worry. Select all the links and then change the appearance on the Properties bar. The changes are applied to all selected links.

Creating Batches of Buttons

Buttons have some common uses that Acrobat can handle with ease. You typically use more than one button on a page, and Acrobat obliges with a process for creating multiple buttons. You often see buttons used across numerous pages of a document, such as a Back button that returns you to the start of the document. Acrobat has a Duplicate process you can use to quickly add a button to your document's pages.

In both of these examples, start by drawing the first button. Configure the button and its appearance. If you are using a Back button for the entire document, for example, set the action as well. That saves you a lot of time later.

Here's how to add a batch of buttons to a single page:

1. Select the button (or two buttons, named Button0 and Button1, as in the example used in this tip) and then right-click or Control-click to open the shortcut menu. Click Create Multiple Copies to open the dialog shown in **Figure 102a.**

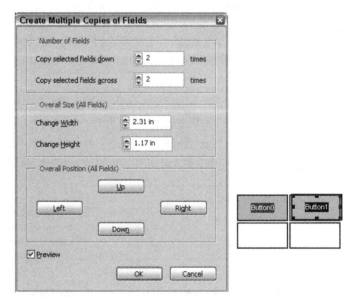

Figure 102a Draw the first buttons and then open the dialog to quickly create multiple copies.

2. In the dialog, define the numbers of rows of buttons you want to use in the document by clicking the arrow or typing a value in the fields. You can also resize the button in the dialog.

3. Finally, if you wish, use the positioning buttons to nudge the group of buttons on the page. As you make changes, the buttons are displayed on the document page.

4. Click OK to close the dialog.

The new buttons are named according to the names of the original buttons. In the example, the names of the two original buttons were changed to Button0.0 and Button1.0; the new buttons are named Button0.1 and Button1.1 (**Figure 102b**). Any additional buttons added to the collection continue the numbering sequence.

Figure 102b The button copies are named based on the original buttons' names.

Do you want a Back button that appears on every page of your document? That is even easier to create:

1. Build your button and add the appropriate action. For example, to use a Back button applied to the document's pages, draw the first button and in the Button Properties dialog set an action to go to a page view, in this case to page 1.

2. Set the view you want the button to initiate, and click Close to dismiss the Button Properties dialog.

3. Move the button to the correct location on the page.

(Continued)

Form Fields for All Seasons

A button is a type of form field, just as items like text boxes and radio buttons are form fields. The actions you use with buttons can be applied to any other type of form field you add in Acrobat. Read about working with forms in Chapter 8.

TIP 102: Creating Batches of Buttons

Reading Articles

You can also use a link or button (or a bookmark) to "shortcut" your readers directly to a series of articles in a document. Add the articles to the document first. Then add a link or a button and in the Actions tab choose Read an article from the Select Action pull-down menu. A Select Article dialog opens. Select the article you want to link and click OK to close the dialog; click Close to dismiss the Properties dialog. Read about articles in Chapter 7.

4. When the button is finished, right-click or Control-click and choose Duplicate from the shortcut menu. The Duplicate Field dialog opens (**Figure 102c**).

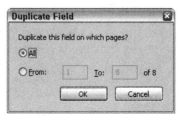

Figure 102c You can duplicate a button from one page across a whole document; each button maintains the actions, name, and appearance of the original.

5. The default selection is All pages; you can click From and type the range to use instead if you prefer.

6. Click OK and the buttons are added. Just like that. When you duplicate the button, it is merely a copy of the original—the buttons' names aren't changed.

TIP 103 Fun with Buttons

Who said buttons have to be boring! In Tip 97, you saw how to construct a basic button, and in Tip 98, you learned how to customize the button's appearance. You can also use buttons for visual effects such as showing and hiding content in a document. For example, you may have a street map, and when the user moves the pointer over certain areas on the map an image of a landmark pops up, as in the example in this tip. When the pointer is moved away from the button area, the image disappears. It isn't magic—it's interesting programming using a push-button process.

Here's how you do it:

1. Select the Button tool in the Advanced Editing toolbar and drag a marquee over the area where you want the image to be responsive to a user's pointer movement. Release the mouse when you have drawn the marquee and the Button Properties dialog opens.

2. Click the Appearance tab and set the fill and stroke to none.

3. Click the Options tab, and then click the Layout pull-down arrow and choose Icon Only from the list.

4. Click the Behavior pull-down arrow and choose Push as the button type. The three states for the push button appear in the State list on the dialog; select Rollover (**Figure 103a**).

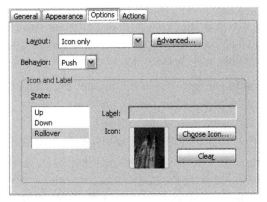

Figure 103a Choose a push button type and select an image to use as the button's icon.

(Continued)

Rollover Image Tips

Using buttons in the way described in this tip can greatly enhance a visual document. Keep these things in mind:

- When you are building several buttons, complete one pair and then use the Create Multiple Copies method described in Tip 102 to quickly build the remaining pairs. You then can customize each pair as required.

- Changing the size of the image button changes the size of the image. In the first example, the image used as a rollover is small; the one used in the second example is much larger since the button is sized much larger.

The Name of The Game

If you are using a large number of buttons, be sure to use a naming system that is logical for you. For example, if you are building six pop-ups, you can name the buttons button1 through button6 for the pop-ups, and image1 through image6 for the image buttons.

5. Click Choose Icon, and then click Browse in the Select Icon dialog. When the File of Type dialog opens, locate and select the file you want to use for the effect, and then click OK to close the Preview Icon dialog and return to the Button Properties dialog. In my example, I have an image of St. Louis Cathedral in New Orleans.

6. Click Close to close the Button Properties dialog.

7. Click the Hand tool on the Basic toolbar and move the pointer over the button's area. You see the image displayed over the map (**Figure 103b**).

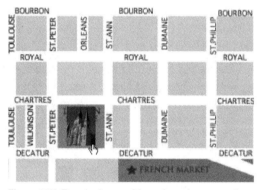

Figure 103b Test the button. Move the pointer over the button area to display the image; move the pointer away from the button area to hide the image.

Let's take it one step further. Suppose you want the image to appear in a different location on the page, and at a different size than the original map. No problem. You need two buttons, and actions attached to one button you use as a "hotspot" to make it happen:

1. Create a button as described in the previous steps but place the button on the page location where you want it to pop up—for example, the upper right of the map. In this example, my button that contains the image is called *image*. That's hard to forget!

2. Now add a second button over the area that you want to react to the user's mouse. In the Button Properties dialog, make sure the background and stroke are clear in the Appearance tab.

3. Click the Actions tab. You add two actions to make this effect work:

- First, click the Select Trigger pull-down arrow and choose Mouse Enter, and then click the Select Action pull-down arrow and choose Show/Hide Field. Click Add and the Show/Hide Field dialog shown in **Figure 103c** appears. Click the image field in the list (see how useful naming a field can be?) and then click the Show radio button. Click OK to close the dialog and return to the Button Properties dialog.

Figure 103c Choose the button containing the image and specify whether to show or hide the field.

- Repeat the process again, this time choosing the Mouse Exit trigger, and in the Show/Hide Field dialog, select the image field again and click Hide. Click OK to close the Show/Hide Field dialog, and click Close to dismiss the Button Properties dialog.

4. Click the Hand tool on the Basic toolbar and move the pointer over the "hotspot" button to show the content of the second button (**Figure 103d**).

Figure 103d Move the pointer over the hotspot to display the image button.

TIP 103: Fun with Buttons

CHAPTER THIRTEEN

Bookmarking a Document

Bookmarks—text links arranged in a list in the Bookmarks pane—are one of Acrobat's most powerful features for creating user-centric documents. If your documents will be used electronically (that is, read using Adobe Reader or Acrobat), use bookmarks as a table of contents for your document. That way, your reader can see at a glance what is in your document by viewing the Bookmarks pane. Simply clicking a bookmark takes the reader to the bookmarked location in the document.

Bookmarks provide orientation for your document, and they are invaluable for large and complex documents. For any type of document that uses headings, from a resumé to a user's manual, bookmarks add a professional touch.

Acrobat lets you create bookmarks in a variety of ways. Typically, you add them when you're converting a document using the PDF-Maker in a source program. But you can also add bookmarks to any document from within Acrobat itself. And you can configure, modify, and customize your bookmarks in Acrobat as well.

TIP 104 Creating Bookmarks in a Source Document

The PDFMaker lets you assign bookmarks in Microsoft Office programs quickly and easily if the source document is constructed properly using styles or headings. However, if you aren't that well versed in the source document's program, you may find the process of converting headings or styles to bookmarks a bit confusing—and your results will be less than optimal.

Figure 104a shows the first page of a document in Acrobat, created using all the wrong settings. It was produced in Word 2003 and uses columns and sections as well as headings. For a printed document, the example is fine as is. To use it interactively, however, users would benefit from some bookmarks for navigation.

Figure 104a Organize your source document if you need to convert the document with bookmarks.

The bookmarks in the document converted to Acrobat PDF are shown in **Figure 104b**. You can see that there are many, many bookmarks, they are too long, and their organization is rather chaotic—the sample uses every option available in the PDFMaker, the document uses too many styles and headings, and heading styles were even used to create blank lines.

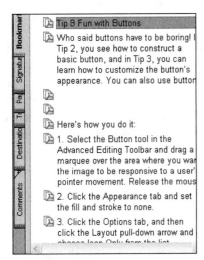

Figure 104b Many people use heading styles to add blank space in a document. This is a bookmarking no-no, and is one reason why some documents' bookmarks look so chaotic.

What Are Little Bookmarks Made Of?

Decide when you're designing the source document how you want to convert it. The PDFMaker lets you convert Word headings or Word styles to bookmarks, or both. You may want to use both styles and headings depending on the structure of your document. For example, if you use the default headings in the document and create a style for a specific type of information (such as a text box), you may want to convert both the headings and your custom style to bookmarks.

To convert a document so that the result is logical bookmarks, keep these points in mind:

- Choose the option that is most convenient for your purposes (**Figure 104c**). If you have a corporate template, for example, you can't arbitrarily assign headings to use for bookmarks; in many cases you have specific styles for your corporate template instead of generic headings. In that case, use the styles conversion option.

Figure 104c Choose either bookmarks or styles as the source for creating PDF bookmarks.

(Continued)

TIP 104: Creating Bookmarks in a Source Document

- If you aren't constrained by policy or other business-related issues, and you aren't an advanced user of Office products, use the Word headings conversion option. It is simple to attach a Heading1 style to major document headings, a Heading2 style to subheadings, a Heading3 to lower-level headings, and so on.

- In the document, don't use headings or styles for any text but the text you intend to use for bookmarks. Anything on the page that uses the heading or style is converted to a bookmark regardless of whether it contains any text. You will run into problems if you use headings to create blank space on your page. Assigning a heading to a blank line adds extra space, and that line becomes the dreaded blank bookmark in your table of contents.

1. When your source document is complete, choose Adobe PDF > Change Conversion Settings. The Change Conversion Settings dialog opens; click the Bookmarks tab.

   Don't simply click the Word styles conversion option. Unless you deselect the headings option, you get both types of content converted to bookmarks. Remember Figure 104b? It isn't a pretty sight.

2. Choose the settings you need and then click OK to close the dialog:

   - To use the headings as bookmarks, leave the default selections and click OK to close the dialog.

   - To use styles as bookmarks, deselect the Convert Word Headings to Bookmarks option and click Convert Word Styles to Bookmarks. Scroll through the list and click the styles you don't want to use for conversion, leaving selected only the styles you do want to use.

   Note
   You can convert the document using neither styles nor headings, and then wait until you get the document into Acrobat to choose the specific options you want to use for bookmarks as long as you use tagged bookmarks. See Tips 108 and 109.

3. Click Adobe PDF > Convert to Adobe PDF or click Convert to PDF on the Adobe PDF toolbar. The document is converted to a PDF document with your chosen bookmarks nestled inside it.

   In Tip 108, the same document is shown again, this time using an appropriate list of bookmarks.

TIP 105 Adding Bookmarks in Acrobat

You can create, configure, and customize bookmarks from within Acrobat. Acrobat lets you add new bookmarks to a document using one of two methods: You can either add blank bookmarks and fill them in manually, or you can use selected text from the document to create your bookmarks. The approach you use depends on how many bookmarks you have to add—if you want only four bookmarks, for instance, you can easily type in the text, but if you want 104, that's another story. How you prefer to work is a factor as well. Some people like to complete their work in one area—that is, they want to add the list of bookmarks in the Bookmarks pane and then add the actual text—whereas others prefer to complete one bookmark at a time and make their way through the document from start to finish. For either method, you need to start with the document and the Bookmarks pane open in Acrobat.

To add a blank bookmark, click Create New Bookmark on the Bookmarks pane toolbar to add a blank bookmark to the Bookmarks pane (**Figure 105a**). Or add a new bookmark even faster by using the Ctrl+B/Command+B shortcut keys when the Bookmarks pane is active. Click the selected Untitled text in the new bookmark and type a label for your bookmark.

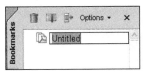

Figure 105a A new bookmark is named Untitled.

To create a bookmark label using your document's text, click the Select tool on the Basic toolbar and then click and drag with the tool to select the text that you want to use for the bookmark label (**Figure 105b**). Then, click Create New Bookmark ![icon] on the Bookmarks pane toolbar to add a bookmark using the selected text, also shown in Figure 105b.

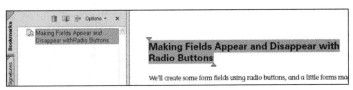

Figure 105b Select text on the document to use for a bookmark and convert the selected text to a bookmark label.

(Continued)

TIP 105: Adding Bookmarks in Acrobat

Bookmarks in a Hurry

Speed up the bookmarking process. Click the existing bookmark in the list above where you want to add a new bookmark, and click the Create New Bookmark icon. The new bookmark appears below the selected bookmark.

Jumping Bookmarks

Be sure to click the bookmark's name in the Bookmarks pane to activate it before setting the destination view. If you position the document in the desired location and set the magnification, as soon as you click the bookmark you want to change, Acrobat jumps to the original view—which means you have to start all over again.

Using Destination Options Correctly

As with many other settings, a magnification option applies until you change it, which means every time you add a new bookmark, it inherits the destination or magnification last specified. Suppose you add a couple of new bookmarks to a document that already contains bookmarks. If the settings you use for the new bookmarks are different from the settings used with the other bookmarks, readers will find the progress through your document jumpy and distracting.

On the other hand, the inherited magnification options can streamline your bookmarking processes. Select the first bookmark and set the magnification options as desired. To set all subsequent bookmarks, select a bookmark, which moves the document to the appropriate location in your document; right-click and select Set Destination. Click OK to confirm the destination, and the magnifications will be uniform.

Note:

Add correct spacing to your bookmark manually if the selected text on the document extends for more than one line—see the example in Figure 105b.

When you add a bookmark in either a source program or in Acrobat, the bookmark is usable as soon as it's deselected. Once you click the bookmark, the destination appears in the Document pane. The Document pane displays only the part of the document visible when you created the bookmark, called the destination, which may not be the ideal view (**Figure 105c**).

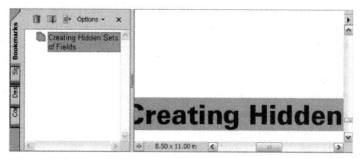

Figure 105c A new bookmark displays the part of the document that was visible when you created the bookmark. It's not always what you want to display.

Select the bookmark in the Bookmarks pane, and then use the zoom tools and scroll bars to place the document as you'd like to see it when the bookmark is clicked. Right-click/Control-click the bookmark to display the shortcut menu and select Set Destination. In the resulting confirmation dialog, click Yes to set the destination and dismiss the dialog.

TIP 106 Organizing a Bookmark Hierarchy

Bookmarks form an interactive table of contents that lets your readers quickly see an outline of the contents of your document. For your readers' convenience, it makes sense to organize your list of bookmarks into a logical hierarchy. That is, the main headings expand to display lower-level headings, which in turn expand to display another heading level. From a technical standpoint, there's no limit to the number of levels you can use—but from a functional perspective, you probably shouldn't use more than three levels. More than three levels makes your list confusing, as you can see in the example shown in **Figure 106a.** The more nested levels you have, the more screen space is required to display them, which decreases the size of the Document pane and ultimately reduces the value of using bookmarks at all. What good is an interactive table of contents if the entire screen is filled with the table and you can't see the contents?

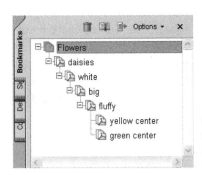

Figure 106a Bookmarks can be nested in an infinite number of levels, but the content may be difficult to see and work with.

You can create parent and child relationships between entries in your document's Bookmarks list. If you have a complex document with dozens of headings, create several main headings and then nest child headings for each main heading. That way, your readers can scan the main headings, and when they see a topic of interest, they can click the heading to open the nested list displaying the child bookmarks. Nesting bookmarks decreases clutter and makes it easier for your reader to see what's in the document.

(Continued)

Everything in Its Right Place

Before you start organizing the contents of your bookmark list into a hierarchy, make sure the heading levels are in the right order. Depending on how methodical you were when you created the bookmarks, they might not accurately reflect the order of the contents. To fix the sequence, first select the bookmark you want to move. Drag it up or down in the list to position it in its proper place. You'll see a dotted indicator line with a small black arrow below or above each title as you drag the bookmark up or down the list. The indicator shows where Acrobat will drop the bookmark. When you have the bookmark in the right location, just release the mouse. Reordering the list of bookmarks doesn't change the heading levels in any way.

If you prefer, you can also cut and paste bookmarks. Click the bookmark you want to remove, and then choose Cut from the Bookmarks pane's Options menu. Then click the bookmark preceding the location where you want the bookmark moved, and choose Paste After Selected Bookmark.

1. Click the bookmark to select it. Drag up or down with the pointer positioned over the bookmark's icon. You'll see a horizontal black line below the icon (**Figure 106b**).

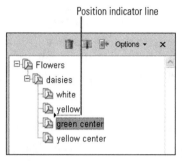

Position indicator line

Figure 106b Move a bookmark to a nesting position indicated by the horizontal line.

Note

Don't select and drag the bookmark label— you'll just move the bookmark in the list, not change its hierarchy. Make sure you're moving the icon.

2. When you see the horizontal bar below the bookmark you want to use as a parent, release the mouse. The bookmark moves into a nested position below the parent bookmark. A level indicator—either a minus or plus sign within a small box—appears to the left of the parent bookmark. Continue to move other bookmarks into the desired nesting locations (**Figure 106c**).

Figure 106c The child bookmarks settle in beneath the parent.

3. Click to expand and collapse the bookmark. When you move the parent bookmark, Acrobat includes any child bookmarks and levels in the move. Not only do child bookmarks move if you move the parent bookmark, but if you delete a parent bookmark, all levels of bookmarks nested within it are deleted as well.

4. If you want to move a bookmark out of a nested position, drag the bookmark icon to a position below the parent bookmark. When you release the mouse, Acrobat moves the bookmark up the hierarchy.

TIP 107 Modifying Bookmark Appearance

We naturally see bold and colored text as more important than regular black text. You can use that natural tendency to make it easier for your readers to understand how your document is organized. This is a great strategy to apply in combination with a hierarchical listing. For example, use a bold, colored text for the first-level bookmark, a bold text for the second level, and regular black text for the third level.

Coordinating a bookmark list with the document's color scheme gives it a professional look, especially when you set the document's initial view to open displaying both the document and bookmarks.

Figure 107a shows the "before" look in an example project. The bookmark hierarchy is in place, but it is difficult to see what is really important in the list—all the bookmarks use the same weight and color of font and are differentiated only on the basis of their indentation.

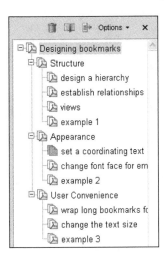

Figure 107a A document's bookmarks nested appropriately display the content in a hierarchy, but it's difficult to get a sense of more or less important headings.

(Continued)

This is my method of creating a set of bookmarks easily and accurately:

- Build the bookmark title list.
- Organize and arrange the hierarchy structure in the Bookmarks pane.
- Test and set destinations for the list.
- Modify the bookmarks' appearance.
- Test the Bookmarks list.
- Set the document properties to include the bookmarks in the initial view.
- Save the document.

Contrast that with the "after" look in **Figure 107b**. The bookmarks have the same structure, but you can easily see that the three section headings are the most dominant in appearance (after the title bookmark). The third-level bookmarks in italics are bookmarked images in the document.

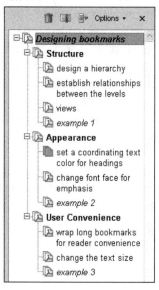

Figure 107b The modified set of bookmarks clearly shows the most dominant headings and makes the document's content easier to see at a glance. The bookmark labels are wrapped so they can be read regardless of the width of the Bookmarks pane.

Here are some tips on manipulating the appearance of bookmarks, including some shortcuts and timesaving methods:

- Before you start modifying, open the Bookmarks list and click a top-level bookmark. Click Expand Current Bookmark on the Bookmarks pane so that all lower-level bookmarks are visible.

- How you manipulate the bookmarks depends on the content and how you like to work. I prefer to use right-click or shortcut keys when practical. I also like to group items and work with them simultaneously. Open and close levels as needed to keep track of what you are doing.

- Another method that works well is to define an appearance for your bookmarks when you start. Add the first bookmark and then configure it using the Bookmark Properties toolbar (**Figure 107c**). Right-click the bookmark and choose Use Current Appearance as New Default.

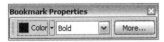

Figure 107c Use the Bookmark Properties toolbar to save time as you work. As you select a bookmark, the toolbar becomes active.

- Sometimes your bookmarks are quite lengthy. Although you should try to keep the titles short, sometimes that isn't possible. Right-click/Control-click any bookmark and choose Wrap Long Bookmarks from the shortcut menu. Regardless of the width of the Bookmarks pane, your reader can always read the bookmark label without scrolling; the wrapping feature is shown in Figure 107b.

- You can resize the text in the Bookmarks tab. Click the Options menu and choose Text Size > Small, Medium (default), or Large. Changing size has no effect on the other text characteristics, such as italic, that you set in the Bookmark Properties toolbar.

Belly Up to the Toolbar

All of the tools used for modifying bookmarks are in the Bookmark Properties toolbar. Open the toolbar to make configuration quicker (see Figure 107c). Right-click the toolbar well at the top of the program window and choose Properties Bar or use the shortcuts Ctrl+E/Command+E. If you are working with a large number of bookmarks, drag the toolbar into the toolbar well to dock it. When you click a bookmark in the list, the Bookmark Properties bar is active. Click More on the toolbar to open the Bookmark Properties dialog if you want to set actions for the selected bookmark.

TIP 107: Modifying Bookmark Appearance

108 Using Tagged Bookmarks

In the Bookmarks pane, an icon appears before the name of each bookmark. Bookmarks may be prefaced by the bookmark icon 🖻 or, in a converted and tagged document, by the tagged bookmark icon 🖻. (Converted Web pages display the Web bookmark icon; this type of bookmark is discussed in the sidebar in Tip 109.) Although you can configure the appearance of all types of bookmarks in the same way, functionally they are different.

Acrobat lets you add and delete bookmarks at will without affecting the content of your document. However, if you use tagged bookmarks you can modify the content of the document as well as provide navigation in the document. You can export a document from either Adobe InDesign or Microsoft Word as a tagged document. Don't bother to export styles or headings as bookmarks—you will build the bookmarks from the document tags rather than using styles or headings. Refer to the tips in Chapter 7 for more information on tagging documents.

So your first step is to open the PDF in Acrobat. Then:

1. Open the Bookmarks pane. Choose Options > New Bookmarks from Structure to open the Structure Elements dialog.

2. Scroll through the list in the Structure Elements dialog and select the tags you want to convert to bookmarks. The tags are based on the styles or headings used in the original Word XP document.

3. Ctrl-click/Command-click to select specific tags (**Figure 108a**). Choose tags according to the levels of headings you want in your Bookmarks list. In this sample document, I want to convert the heading 1 and heading 2 tags as well as the inline shape tags (to include bookmarks for the images) to a set of bookmarks. You might also want to convert other heading tags depending on the length and complexity of the document and how many bookmarks you need.

Figure 108a Select specific tags to convert to bookmarks.

Note
*If you click an element by mistake, click it again while pressing the Ctrl/
Command key to deselect it. You can choose Select All to select the entire
list. Click Clear All to deselect all the tags and start over.*

4. Click OK to close the dialog. Acrobat converts the selected tags
   to bookmarks and adds them to the Bookmarks pane in one
   collapsed basic bookmark named Untitled.

5. Click the plus sign to the left of the bookmark's name to open
   the list. As you can see, only the Untitled bookmark uses the
   basic bookmark icon; the others use the tagged bookmark icon,
   as shown in **Figure 108b**. The bookmarks are named using the
   content of the tag; in the case of the images, they are referred
   to as inline shapes.

Figure 108b The converted tags use
the tagged bookmark icon and the
content of the selected tags.

6. Modify the bookmarks' appearance and view as desired. If you
   add new bookmarks, they will use the basic bookmark icon
   because they are *added* bookmarks and not part of the document structure.

TIP 108: Using Tagged Bookmarks

Modifying Content with Tagged Bookmarks

Did you know you can modify the content of your document by using tagged bookmarks? Here's the scoop: First, select a bookmark or bookmarks from the list in the Bookmarks pane. Right-click/Control-click it to open a shortcut menu (or open the pane's Options menu); you see a number of document modification commands (**Figure 109**). Here's what you can do:

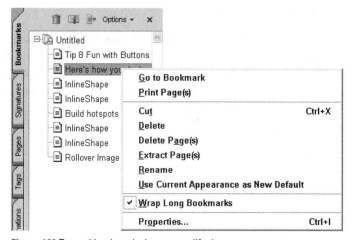

Figure 109 Tagged bookmarks let you modify document content.

- Click Print Page(s) to print the pages containing the selected tag(s).

- Click Delete Page(s) to delete the pages containing the selected tag(s). If you choose this command, you'll see a warning dialog telling you that you can't "undelete." Click OK to proceed.

  Note
  Even though Acrobat warns you that the action isn't reversible, it actually is. No, you can't choose Edit > Undo to undo the command. But you can choose File > Revert and revert to the last-saved version of the document (tricky, eh?). A good reason to save your documents regularly!

- Click Extract Page(s) to extract the information from the pages containing the selected tag(s) and to create a new PDF document.

Web Page Bookmarks

Tags are automatically created when you convert a Web page to a PDF document. The Web page-generated bookmark is indicated in the Bookmarks pane by its own icon. You can configure, rename, and modify Web bookmarks using the same methods you use for other bookmarks. In addition, you can open the link in a Web browser or append other Web pages from the converted Web page's site.

TIP 110: Applying Actions to Bookmarks

Bookmarks are used most often to control navigation in a document—they basically function as an interactive table of contents. But that's not all you can do with bookmarks. As with links and buttons, you can apply a wide variety of actions to bookmarks.

You can apply actions to any type of bookmark, whether it is generated within Acrobat, imported as a tagged bookmark, or from a converted Web page:

1. Select the bookmark you want to apply an action to in the Bookmarks pane. Then, open the bookmark's properties. You can choose Properties from the Bookmarks pane's Options menu, right-click/Control-click the selected bookmark, or click More on the Bookmark Properties toolbar.

2. The Bookmark Properties dialog has two tabs; the Appearance tab is used to set the font style and color. Click Actions to display the action options (**Figure 110**).

Figure 110 You can attach a range of actions to bookmarks.

(Continued)

Bookmarking an Image

You don't have to stick with boring old text to define a bookmark location—you can use an image as a bookmark location instead. Click the Select tool on the Basic toolbar. Then, click an image or draw a marquee around a portion of an image on your document. Right-click/Control-click the image and choose Add Bookmark. A new bookmark named Untitled appears at the bottom of the list (or below a selected bookmark). The "Untitled" label is active; click to delete the label and type a name for the bookmark.

3. The default action for bookmarks is the Go to a page view action, which you set when the bookmark is created. As with other objects, such as links and buttons, click the Select Action pull-down arrow and choose an action from the list.

4. Click Add to open the dialog specific to the type of action and configure its settings. Close the dialog and the action is added in the Actions list on the Bookmark Properties dialog.

5. Click Close to dismiss the dialog and apply the action.

Note
For more specific information on using some of Acrobat's actions see Chapter 12; bookmarking a layered document is described in Chapter 11.

CHAPTER FOURTEEN

Commenting and Marking Up Documents

Acrobat 7 lets you add a wide variety of comments to PDF documents and then share the comments with your workgroup. Unlike manual paper-based commenting, Acrobat's tools include many types of text comment and edit tools; you can attach other documents and sound files to a document, and even integrate your comments directly into their source documents in some programs.

Specific types of comments are described in other chapters. You can read about drawing tools in Chapter 11, and attaching files in Chapter 4. You can initiate workflows for routing and managing comments generated by a number of users; managing these workflows is the subject of Chapter 15.

The goal of the tips in this chapter is to help simplify your workload—with so many tools at your disposal, it's important to understand the reasons why you choose one type of tool versus another, and how to maximize your efficient use of the tools. You will also see how to manage comments.

By the way, all the commenting types and Comment tools can also be accessed from the Comments menu on the main program menu; throughout these tips I have referred to working from the Commenting toolbar, which is a good way to save yourself a couple of mouse clicks.

TIP 111 Using the Commenting Toolbar

Acrobat 7 has a range of commenting options you can access from the Commenting menu, the Comment & Markup task button , the Comments pane, and the Commenting toolbar: in the Commenting toolbar you'll find pull-down menus and subtoolbars for tool groups, such as text edits and stamps.

Click the pull-down arrow on the task button to open a list of options, which includes the Commenting toolbar (**Figure 111a**). From this task button menu, you can also access other toolbars such as the Drawing Markups and its subtoolbars, described in Chapter 11, as well as different workflows.

Figure 111a Choose from a range of options such as toolbars and processes from the Comment & Markup task button's pull-down menu.

To quickly open the Commenting toolbar (**Figure 111b**), click the Review & Comment task button itself, not the pull-down arrow. Click the task button again to close the toolbar.

Figure 111b The Commenting toolbar consists of several commands and pull-down menus.

The best way to understand how to use the toolbar is to examine its contents. Table 14.1 explains what each item is used for and what the pull-down menus contain.

Table 14.1 The Commenting Toolbar

Toolbar icon	Contains...
Note Tool	The Note tool lets you add notes to the document (indicated by an icon).
Text Edits ▾	The Text Edit tools let you indicate text edits on a document.
Stamp Tool ▾	The Stamp tool allows you to add a variety of stamps to a document. You can also use dynamic stamps and create custom stamps.
▾	The Highlighter tools are electronic versions of traditional highlighter, cross-out, and underline text edits.
▾	The Attach File tools let you attach either a file or a voice comment. (See Tip 36 in Chapter 4 to learn about attachments).
Show ▾	The Show tools let you access comments sorted in various ways, view the Comments list, and view the content of comments.

Using the Properties Bar to Modify Comments

If you're working with a number of comments using various icons, colors, text, and so on, you may find it easier to use the Properties bar than the comment's Properties dialog to modify comments' properties. Click the note icon, and the Note Properties options display in the toolbar. The bar switches from the note options to the text options if you click within the note's text area or select some text in the note.

TIP 111: Using the Commenting Toolbar

Adding Notes and Highlighting Comments

Finding Properties

To access the Properties Bar choose View > Toolbars > Properties Bar (Ctrl+E/Command+E). Or right-click/Control-click anywhere in the toolbar well at the top of the program window. The list of toolbars appears; choose Properties Bar.

Of all the comment tools, you'll probably use the note comment most frequently. Select the Note tool on the Commenting toolbar and then click the document where you want to place the note. You can also drag with the tool to create a marquee. A pop-up window opens (**Figure 112a**) showing an active cursor. Type the text for your note; if you enter more text than fits the size of the pop-up window, the text scrolls. When you have the Properties Bar open, also shown in Figure 112a, you can select text in the note and customize its color, font, and so on directly from the toolbar.

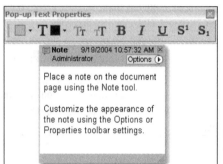

Figure 112a Type your note's text in the pop-up window. You can customize the text easily using the Properties Bar.

To tidy up the page, click the close box in the pop-up window. You can still read the content of your note; just move the pointer over the note's icon on the page and Acrobat displays its contents in a tool tip box (**Figure 112b**).

Administrator
Place a note on the document page using the Note tool.

Figure 112b Save space on your document by closing the note. Move your pointer over the note's icon to display its text in a tool tip.

Once the note is added to your document, you can change its appearance and characteristics beyond the options available from the Properties Bar. Click Options on the Note box to open the Note Properties dialog (**Figure 112c**), or right-click/Control-click to open the shortcut menu and choose Properties. When the Properties bar is displayed, it shows the Note Properties as well, also shown in Figure 112c:

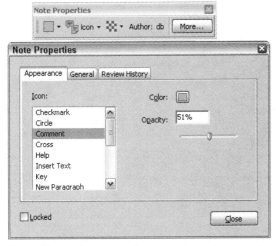

Figure 112c Configure a note's appearance and name and read its history in the Note Properties dialog.

- Choose an icon for the note, as well as color and opacity, on the Appearance tab.

- Specify a name for the comment author and a subject on the General tab.

- View the Review history and/or Migration history on the Review History tab.

Click Close to dismiss the Note Properties dialog and apply the changes.

Note
Once a note has been added, you can double-click its icon to open the text box. To delete a note, click the note icon with the Hand tool to select it. Then press Delete on the keyboard.

(Continued)

The Same—But Different

The Highlighting toolbar contains three tools that you can use to draw attention to content in your document. There are also three text edit tools that appear to do the same things. However, the Highlighting tools are used within Acrobat only, unlike their text edit counterparts, which can be exported from the document into a source Word or AutoCAD document (Windows).

The Highlighting tools are used to add visual comments to the text of your document. You can use an underline, highlight, or strikethrough. Choose Tools > Commenting > Show Highlighting Toolbar to open the toolbar (**Figure 112d**). Select a tool from the toolbar and then drag across the text you want to identify with the tool. An example of each tool's use is shown in Figure 112d. As with the Note tool, you can modify the appearance of the Highlighting tools either on the Properties bar or by selecting Properties from the shortcut menu.

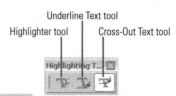

Figure 112d Use the Highlighting tools to point out content in a document's text.

TIP 113 Setting Commenting Preferences

One you've been working with comments in Acrobat for a while, you should evaluate how you use them and how you modify them. Ask yourself:

- Do I change the name on the comment box regularly?
- Do I change the font or size of the comment regularly?
- Am I repeatedly dragging comments out of the way to see other content on the page?
- Do I prefer the comments aligned along the side of the page or overlaying the document's contents?
- Do I find it difficult to keep track of which comment box belongs to which comment?

If you find you make the same modifications repeatedly, it's a good idea to modify the preferences. Begin by choosing Edit > Preferences (or Acrobat > Preferences on the Mac) and click Commenting in the left column to display the Commenting Preferences dialog (**Figure 113a**).

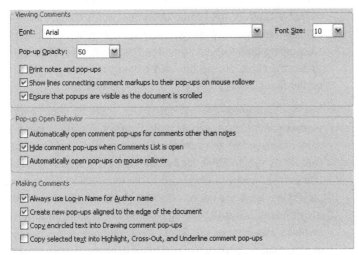

Figure 113a Choose preferences for configuring how you view comments, how they behave, and how they look.

(Continued)

Personal Preferences

Sometimes it's a good idea to modify Commenting preferences, either your own or those of a larger group:

- Color-code members of a workgroup who use commenting regularly. Each person uses a different color for his or her comments. That way, you can see at a glance who added comments. In an office environment, consider color-coding departments. Many documents and processes require input from a variety of departments; if each has its own color for commenting, it is easier to see where a document is in the commenting and reviewing cycle.

- Increase the font size if you are working with someone who reads comments on the page. I work on projects with a person who likes to read the comments as is (without opening the Comments list). If I use a large font size, he can clearly see my comments on the page.

- In a graphics layout review (a magazine, for example) decrease the opacity of the comments. That way, other members in the group can read the comments in place on the page and still see the graphics content underneath.

- Show lines connecting comment markups to their pop-ups on mouse rollover, as shown in Figure 113b.

The preferences are set in three categories:

- Viewing Comments—Choose options in this section to specify how comments are seen in the document. Arial font at 10 points is the default for comments. If you want, click the pull-down list and choose another font, type a different point size, and choose the opacity percentage for the pop-up box. Also in this section of the dialog you can choose to show connecting lines from the comment box to the comment location (**Figure 113b**).

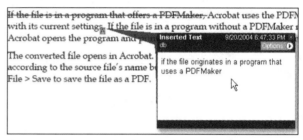

Figure 113b Use connecting lines to pair text and the comment icon.

- Pop-up Open Behavior—Choose options to define how the comments display in response to other document actions, such as opening the Comments pane or in response to mouse rollovers. The default setting for the Pop-up Open Behavior is to open a pop-up box when the comment is selected. Leave the setting selected if you are working on documents from the Document pane. If you prefer to see the entire pop-up box rather than the tool tip, choose the option Automatically open pop-ups on mouse rollover.

- Making Comments—Choose options to apply to your comment process consistently, such as their alignment on the page or the name displayed at the top of the pop-up box. The first option (Always use Login Name for Author name) is selected by default. If the only name you work with is the login name for your computer, then leave the option selected. If you use another name, or use different names depending on the work or workgroup you are involved with, deselect it. Select the Create new pop-ups aligned to the edge of the document option if neatness is your passion.

  Click the final option to copy the content of selected text into comment pop-ups for Highlight, Cross-Out, and Underline text comments.

TIP 114 Working with Text Edit Comments

The text edit tools let you edit a PDF document the same way you would with a printed page and a red pencil, but much more efficiently. Instead of having to print a document, add comments and edits by hand, and then deliver the document to someone who will make the changes, you can do it all from within Acrobat.

You'll find the text edit tools on the Commenting toolbar. Click the Text Edits pull-down arrow to display the list of tools (**Figure 114a**). If you have selected text on the page, the tools are all active, as shown in the figure. If you haven't selected any text and click the Text Edits pull-down arrow, click Indicate Text Edits Tool [T] to activate the Text Select tool. Use this option if you need to insert, delete, or replace text.

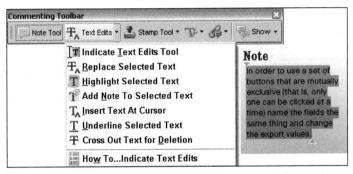

Figure 114a Most of the Text Edit comments are unavailable until you select some text on the page.

When you select Indicate Text Edits Tool from the pull-down menu, the Indicating Text Edits information dialog shown in **Figure 114b** appears, explaining what some of the editing options are and how to use keyboard shortcuts. Click OK to close the dialog.

(Continued)

278

See Attachments

The File toolbar includes a pair of tools for attaching other content to the document, including the Attach a File as a Comment tool 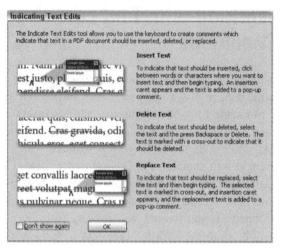. This tool is available on both the File and Commenting toolbars. Tip 36 in Chapter 4 describes attaching files.

Adding Comments to Your Edits

Need to explain why you deleted a specific paragraph in a document, or just want to leave a note to verify that your changes are correct? Acrobat makes it easy. Once you've added an edit with any of the text edit tools, you can also add a comment. Simply double-click the edit to open a note box, and then type your comment.

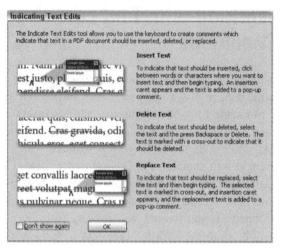

Figure 114b Learn about common types of text edits in the Indicating Text Edits dialog.

Here's how you work with the Text Select tool and keyboard, bypassing the commands in the pull-down menu:

- To insert text, click in the text of the document and type. On the document you see an insertion caret icon Λ, and the text appears in a pop-up comment box.

- To delete text, select the text to delete using the tool and press Delete or Backspace on your keyboard. The text is crossed out on the document.

- To replace content in the document, select the text and type new text. The replacement text is added to a Replacement Text pop-up comment box, the selected text displays a strikethrough, and an insertion caret is shown at the end of the string of text you selected with the tool (**Figure 114c**).

Figure 114c Acrobat adds indicator icons on the document to show you the location and content of your edits.

A comment added to an edit is indicated by a small "A" above the selected text Th.

Rather than using the Indicate Text Edits tool, you can select text using the Select tool and then choose any of the editing options from the pull-down menu; the tools and their purpose are described in Table 14.2.

Table 14.2 The Text Edit Commenting Tools

Use this tool...	For this purpose...
T̶A̶	Replace the selected text with text you type; the text is displayed in a pop-up comment box.
T	The selected text is highlighted.
T	A pop-up comment box opens for you to type notes about the selected text, which is highlighted in the document.
T_A	Type to insert new text in a pop-up comment box.
T	The selected text is shown with an underline.
T	The selected text is shown with strikethrough; no replacement text appears.

If you select text using the Select tool on the Basic toolbar, the Select icon appears on the page over the selected text. When you click the icon, the menu appears (**Figure 114d**). You can choose a number of different comment types from the menu. Note that the menu doesn't contain the entire list of comment types; for some text edit comments, such as cross out for deletion, you have to use the Text Edits pull-down menu option.

Figure 114d Some types of text edits can be selected from the pop-up menu that appears when you select text using the Select tool.

Which Method Is Best?

You can find some or all of the comment tool options using three or four different methods. For example, if you want to insert text, you can:

- Select the Text Edit tool from the Commenting toolbar, click the document with the tool, and then use the keyboard.

- Select the text using the Select tool on the Basic toolbar, wait for the Select icon to appear, and then click the icon to open a list of editing options.

- Select the text using the Select tool on the Basic toolbar, and then choose another tool from the Text Edits pull-down menu.

- Select the text using the Select tool on the Basic toolbar, and then right-click/Control-click to open the shortcut menu and choose a tool.

Which is best? It depends on how you like to work. Try them all—you're sure to find a favorite method.

115 Using the Stamp Tools

The Stamp tools are like the old-fashioned ink stamps you apply to a document (such as Draft, Approved, or Confidential). Unlike ink stamps, some of the Acrobat stamps are dynamic in that they automatically add the time or date when you apply the stamp to the document—you can even create your own custom stamps. Stamps are a central part of an approval workflow, described in Chapter 15. The Stamp tools are located on the Commenting toolbar.

1. To locate a stamp, on the Commenting toolbar click the Stamp Tool's pull-down arrow to open the menu shown in **Figure 115a**.

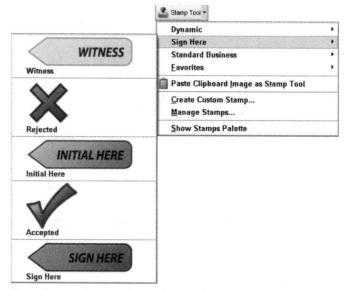

Figure 115a Acrobat provides a collection of stamps you can use on your documents.

The first three commands on the menu have submenus containing the stamp choices (the figure shows the Sign Here options at the left); the fourth option contains stamps you define as favorites.

2. Click a stamp to select it. The pointer changes to resemble the comment's icon.

Who Are You?

The Identity Setup dialog doesn't allow you to change the log-in name used for stamps or other types of comments. To revise the name:

1. Choose Edit > Preferences/ Acrobat > Preferences, and click Commenting in the column at the left of the Preferences dialog.

2. Deselect the option Always use Log-in Name for Author name in the Making Comments section of the dialog. Click OK to close the preferences.

3. Right-click/Control-click a comment on your document to open the shortcut menu and choose Properties to open the Properties dialog. Click the General tab, type a new name in the Author field, and click Close to dismiss the dialog.

4. Open the shortcut menu again and choose Make Current Properties Default. Any subsequent stamps or other processes using the Identity Setup information now use the new author (login) name.

3. Click the document where you want to apply the stamp. An Identity Setup dialog opens if you haven't already specified an identity as part of a commenting, review, or digital signature setup (**Figure 115b**).

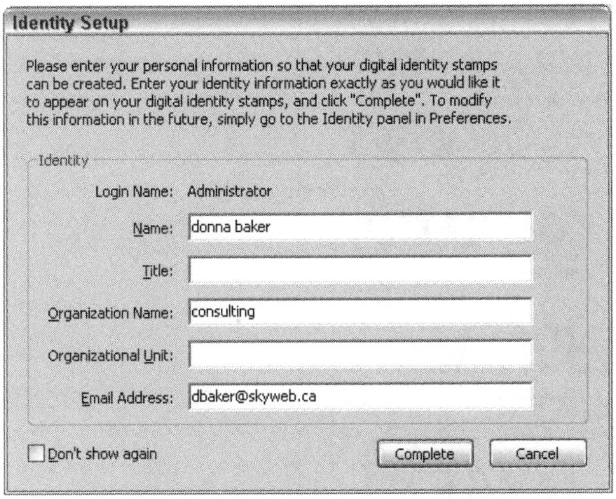

Figure 115b Acrobat needs to know who you are—define an identity in this dialog for use in a number of processes.

4. Add identity information and click Complete to close the dialog and apply the stamp.

5. If you want to change the identity information, choose Edit > Preferences/Acrobat > Preferences and click Identity in the left column of the dialog, and then modify the information in the identity fields, such as your name or organization.

The Dynamic stamps include the username as well as the date and time the stamp was applied. The Sign Here stamps are specific formats used for common communications, and the Standard Business stamps are a collection of labels you commonly use with many office documents (**Figure 115c**). You can use these stamps to indicate a document's status, such as a confidential or preliminary document, instead of adding note comments or a watermark.

(Continued)

Get It Together

Many stamps are available in the Acrobat stamp collection. You can add an infinite number of stamps as well. Use the Stamps palette to keep them straight. Click the Stamp Tool's pull-down menu and choose Show Stamps Palette to open the Stamps dialog. Click the pull-down arrow and choose a category of stamps to display the contents of the collection as thumbnails. For the program's stamps, right-click/Control-click to open a shortcut menu and select either to choose that stamp as the current stamp or add it to your favorites. In a custom stamp category, right-click/Control-click a stamp to open a shortcut menu and either choose to select the stamp or remove it from the favorites list. If you decide to add more stamps, click Import to open the Select Image for Custom Stamp dialog; follow the steps in Tip 116 to create a new stamp.

TIP 115: Using the Stamp Tools

Snap a Stamp

Here's a terrific tip (if I do say so myself!) for using a stamp to show exactly what you mean. Suppose you have a multipage document and think an image should be located elsewhere. Click the Snapshot tool on the Basic toolbar and snap the image on the page. Now move the document to display the location where you think the image should be placed. Click the Stamp Tool's pull-down arrow to display its menu and choose Paste Clipboard Image as Stamp Tool. Then click the page with the Stamp tool. The image is pasted as a stamp. To make your point, double-click the image (now a stamp comment) to open a comment text box and describe your idea.

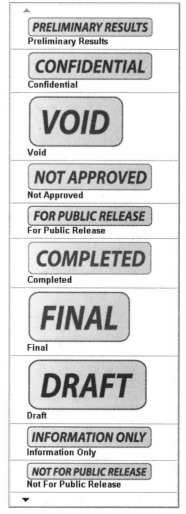

Figure 115c Look for a stamp in the Standard Business collection to apply to a range of common business purposes.

Note

If you move your pointer over the Stamp tool on the Commenting toolbar (not over the pull-down arrow), the last stamp you selected during a session is displayed; click the Stamp tool and the displayed stamp is active.

For some people, stamps are the perfect way to comment on a document. If you add similar types of comments repeatedly, consider constructing your own custom stamp. For example, you may have stamps bearing your business logo that you would like to use. You can create one using the method described in Tip 116.

TIP 116 Creating and Managing Stamps

If you can imagine it, you can use it in a stamp. You can easily add a custom stamp to Acrobat:

1. Click the Stamp Tool's pull-down menu and choose Create Custom Stamp. The Select Image for Custom Stamp dialog opens.

   ### Note
   You can also create custom stamps through the Manage Stamps command on the Stamp Tool's pull-down menu. Click Manage Stamps to open the Manage Custom Stamps dialog, click Create, and the Select Image for Custom Stamp dialog opens. Proceed with the remaining steps.

2. Click Browse to find the file you want to use for the stamp. You can use a range of graphic formats, as well as PDF and Word files. The Select dialog opens and displays the chosen file. Click OK to close the browse dialog and return to the Select Image for Custom Stamp dialog, which shows a preview of the chosen stamp (**Figure 116a**).Click OK to dismiss the dialog and open the Create Custom Stamp dialog.

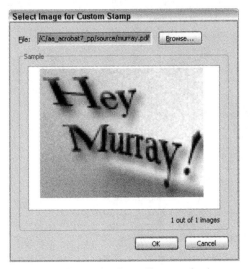

Figure 116a When you select a file to use for the stamp, you see its preview in this dialog.

(Continued)

A Few of My Favorite Stamps

If you use a stamp and then choose Add Current Stamp to Favorites, that stamp will appear at the top of the Stamp Tool submenu, so you can quickly use it again without having to navigate the system of submenus. If you find you are using another stamp regularly, choose Add Current Stamp to Favorites and it joins the list. If you find that you no longer use an old favorite, you can just as easily delete it. Select the stamp from the Favorites list on the submenu and then choose Favorites > Remove Current Stamp from Favorites.

3. Click the Category field and type a name for a new stamp category or choose one of the existing categories; then type a
name for the stamp (**Figure 116b**). Click OK.

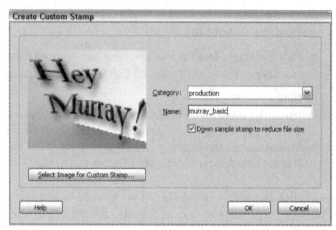

Figure 116b Select a file to use for the stamp, name it, and specify its category.

4. To use your new stamp, first click the Stamp Tool's pull-down
arrow. Your custom stamp category now appears along with
any other custom stamps you have added to your system. The
contents of your custom stamp category display thumbnails,
just like the program's stamp collections (**Figure 116c**).

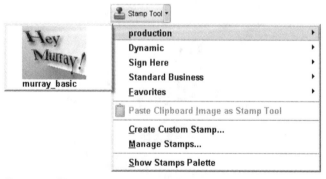

Figure 116c Choose your custom stamp from the pull-down menus.

5. Click the stamp in the menu to select it, and then click the
document page to apply the stamp.

6. If you want to add more information, double-click the stamp to open a comment text box and type the information you want to attach (**Figure 116d**).

Figure 116d You can add note comments to a stamp as well.

You can easily remove or edit a custom stamp from Acrobat:

1. Open the Stamp Tool's pull-down menu and choose Manage Stamps to open the Manage Custom Stamps dialog.

2. To remove a stamp, select the stamp (**Figure 116e**) and click Delete; to edit a stamp, click Edit to reopen the Create Custom Stamp dialog (use this dialog if you want to rename the stamp, for example); to start building another custom stamp, click Create. Click Close to dismiss the dialog.

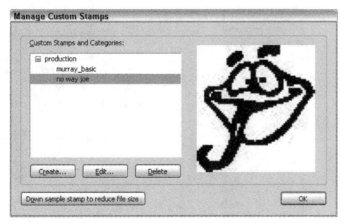

Figure 116e You can add, edit, and delete stamps using the Manage Custom Stamps dialog.

Use a Custom Stamp When...

Here are some circumstances where it makes sense to take a few minutes to build a custom stamp:

- You write the same comment repeatedly. You may be a department head who needs a date and time stamp as well as a department information stamp. Build a stamp that asks for the information; you can now use a dynamic date/time stamp, and your new custom stamp.

- Your work includes different roles. You may be a designer and also a supervisor. You can build separate stamps defining your role in different situations.

- Your work includes the same role and different moods. Use your imagination and create a suite of expressive stamps. A smiley face can be worth a thousand words—and so can a bolt of lightning.

<table>
<tr><td>TIP
117</td><td># Exporting Comments to a Word Document (Windows)</td></tr>
</table>

If you're working with a tagged PDF that was originally built in Microsoft Word 2000, 2002, or 2003 (Windows) or Microsoft Word X (SR-1) or 2004 (Mac), and then converted to PDF using the PDFMaker, you can export the PDF directly from Acrobat back into Word and make the corrections there. Rather than having to work with both the PDF document and the original source document open side by side, while making corrections manually, you can have your comments exported directly from the PDF document back into the original document and have the changes made automatically.

To export comments to a Word document:

1. Click the Comment & Markup task button's pull-down arrow to display its menu and choose Export Comments to Word, or click Comments on the menu and choose Export > Comments to Word. Microsoft Word opens, and a dialog describes the process (**Figure 117a**).

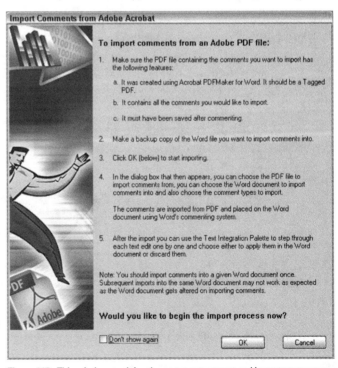

Figure 117a This window explains the comments export and import processes.

2. Once you are familiar with the process, click Don't show again at the bottom left of the dialog. Then click OK to close the dialog and start the import process. The Import Comments from Adobe Acrobat dialog opens (**Figure 117b**). The name of the PDF file from which you are exporting appears in the top field.

Figure 117b Specify the file that contains the comments, and then specify the file in which you want to insert them.

3. Click the top Browse button and locate the source Word document used to generate the PDF.

4. Choose from the various comment-import options. Read Tip 118 for more information. Click the Turn Track Changes On Before Importing Comments option if you are involved in an editing or review process and are using several versions of the document.

5. Click Continue. Acrobat processes the comments and adds them to the Word document. Acrobat displays the Successful Import dialog once it processes the comments (**Figure 117c**). The dialog summarizes the activity and describes how text edits can be integrated. Click Integrate Text Edits to start the process.

(Continued)

Copy That

You can import comments only once; if you are working on several versions of a document, save copies and number them sequentially. That way, each time you send comments for a round of reviews you have a copy of the document that can accept comments. Alternatively, you can choose to Migrate comments, described in Tip 119.

TIP 117: Exporting Comments to a Word Document (Windows)

Is That Confirmed?

Sometimes the placement of text edit comments can't be confirmed in a source Word document; this occurs when Acrobat can't precisely decipher the structure of the source document's tags. Unconfirmed placements are available in a list from the Successful Import dialog, shown in Figure 117c. Click the View List button to see a list of the comments that have unconfirmed placements. On the document, if you have the tracking feature active, you see comments added where Acrobat thinks the comment belongs. You can transfer the information from these comments to the document and delete the Word comments.

Figure 117c Acrobat tells you when it has finished integrating the comments into the document.

Note
Any formatting of text you add to the comments in Acrobat, such as font or bold text, isn't transferred to the Word document.

6. The Adobe Acrobat Comments dialog opens, displaying the number of comments available for converting. The dialog identifies the first comment in the document and displays the action (**Figure 117d**). Click Apply to make the edit. The text is modified in the Word document (using colored or underlined text if changes are being tracked).

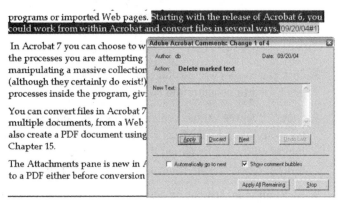

Figure 117d The Adobe Acrobat Comments dialog displays the first comment you can integrate.

7. Click Next in the Adobe Acrobat Comments dialog to continue with the next edit; repeat until you've finished all the edits. If you don't want to use the edit, click Discard.

8. You'll see the Text Integration Summary dialog when all the comments are processed (**Figure 117e**). After you've reviewed the summary, click Done. Depending on the options you chose in the Import Comments from Adobe Acrobat dialog (described in step 4) you may have instructions for cleaning up the document, such as accepting changes if you have the tracking feature active, or deleting comment bubbles.

Figure 117e The Text Integration Summary dialog appears when all comments are processed.

9. Check the document. You'll see that the edits are applied and that basic note comments are attached to the document as well (**Figure 117f**). Save the corrected Word document.

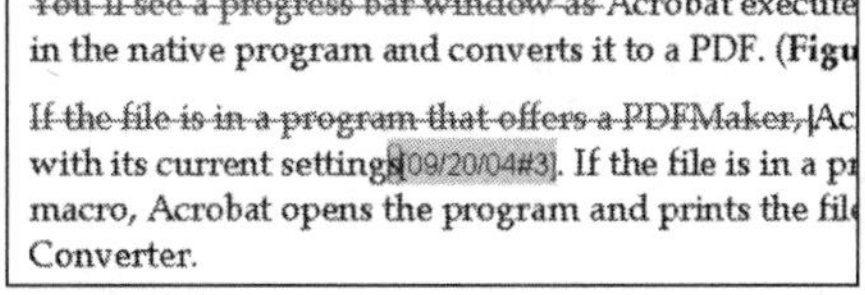

> You'll see a progress bar window as Acrobat executes in the native program and converts it to a PDF. (Figu
>
> If the file is in a program that offers a PDFMaker, Ac with its current settings 09/20/04#3]. If the file is in a pr macro, Acrobat opens the program and prints the file Converter.

Figure 117f Both text changes and comments are applied to the document.

What happens next with the Word document depends on its purpose. If you originally created the PDF to circulate it and collect comments, you've finished, and can print or email the document. If you need a second review, create another PDF document and start over.

TIP 117: Exporting Comments to a Word Document (Windows)

Choosing Which Comments to Export

Back and Forth

You can either work from Acrobat and export the comments using the Comment menu's commands, or you can work from Word and import the comments using the commands on the Acrobat Comments menu. Which is better? Your choice depends on where you are in a particular workflow. If you have finished working with a group of comments, work from within Acrobat; if you have the source document open in Word, work from within Word.

If you have the document open in Word, choose Acrobat Comments > Import Comments from Acrobat. You use the same dialogs and options from within Word as you do from Acrobat, as described in the previous tip. If you want to read the instructions for comment imports again, you can access them by choosing Acrobat Comments > Show Instructions.

You can choose certain groups of comments to export in the Import Comments from Adobe Acrobat dialog. First decide how much you want to edit the Word document, and then choose a type of export accordingly. You don't want to import all the comments into the document if your intention is to simply correct the content of the document. For example, you might not want to deal with comments that address responsibility for actions, office politics, and so on. By the same token, you might not want to make corrections without having supporting comments from the person who suggested the changes.

- If you have set up a personal commenting system using checkmarks, you can select the option All Comments with Checkmarks under Choose Comment Types to Import (read about checkmarks in Tip 123 in Chapter 15). You'll import only those comments marked with checkmarks (**Figure 118**).

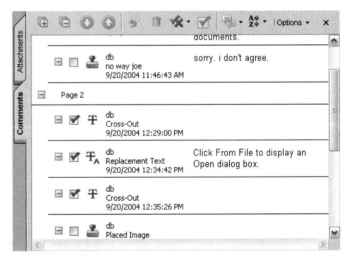

Figure 118 Decide which comments to work with in an exported document; one way of sorting a large list of comments is by using checkmarks.

- If you are editing the document's content using the text edit tools, select the Text Edits only: Insertions, Deletions, and Replaces option. That way, only the comments pertaining to the document's content and structure are transferred. This option is especially useful for large reviews where you're dealing with many comments, not all of which actually apply to modifying the document.

- Often you develop commenting systems, particularly in large organizations. Acrobat lets you design a custom set of comment-conversion options. Choose Custom Set and then filter the comments you want to export to Word. The filter can be based on the author, status, or checkmark. (Learn more about filtering in Chapter 15.)

TIP
119 Migrating Comments

Birds migrate, so why not comments? Suppose you have created a document and then added comments to it. Then suppose you either exported text edits and other comments from Acrobat and integrated them into the source Word document, or revised the source document and then generated a new PDF document. New in Acrobat 7 is the ability to add comments to a document after it has been revised. The migration process searches a document and tries to place additional comments in the correct locations.

Make sure the documents are tagged before migrating comments; the feature uses the tags to find word groupings and elements in the document to place the comments. You can read about tagging and using tagged documents in Chapter 7.

Open the revised document in Acrobat, and then:

1. Choose Comments > Migrate Comments to open the Migrate Comments dialog (**Figure 119a**).

Figure 119a Migrate comments from one document into a revised PDF document to save time.

2. Click the pull-down arrow and choose a filename (if you have used the function before), or click Choose to locate and select the file you want to use from your system. The name of the file displays in the From field.

3. Click the Review migrated comments in the Comments List check box to display the comments in the document after migration. This option is selected by default.

4. Click OK. The comments are imported into the PDF document and placed in the same locations as those in the document you are exporting from. (Read about managing migrated comments in Chapter 15).

The comments may or may not appear in the same location in both documents (**Figure 119b**). In the figure, the modified PDF document is shown in the top image; a portion of the PDF document from which the comments are migrated is shown in the bottom figure. You can see there are some matching comments (in terms of location on the page) while others don't seem to coordinate very well. The key is the document tags.

Comment seems to move on the page   Comment stays in the same position   Comments migrated from this document   Into this document

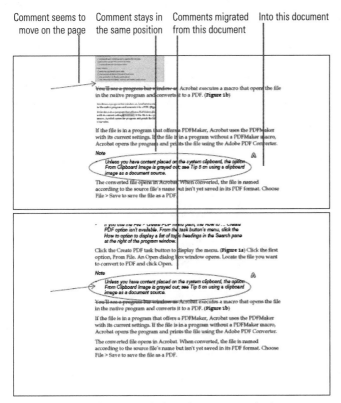

Figure 119b Check the locations of migrated comments on the document—they may be in different locations depending on the two documents' structures.

(Continued)

Migration Road Rules

What you see when you migrate comments depends on a few factors. Acrobat uses these concepts to place comments in a revised document:

- Text comments that apply to selected words are displayed within the same words, if they exist in the revised document.

- Stamps, notes, and drawing markups are placed according to the original document's structure (for example, the arrow in the sample document described in this tip)

- If you delete the words or tags where a comment was originally placed, it is placed on either the first or last page of the document.

- If you delete text that originally had text edits, the edits are converted to a note.

- Drawing markups or stamps are placed on the same page as the original document regardless of position—unless the page is deleted, in which case the comment is placed on the last page of the revised document.

TIP 119: Migrating Comments

For example, the note on the page enclosed by a circle comment is the same on both documents—because the note uses a specific tag in the document. However, the arrow is in different locations—again because of the tags. The revised document shown at the top of the figure shows the arrow placed just below the image, and above a paragraph of text. The source document from which the comments were migrated also has the arrow just above a paragraph of text. Why does it look different? The paragraph has been moved.

Once the comments have been migrated into a document, they are included in the Comments list using the default Migration options (**Figure 119c**). Comments that have been migrated show the Migration status message, and you see a message about the applied filter at the top of the Comments list as well.

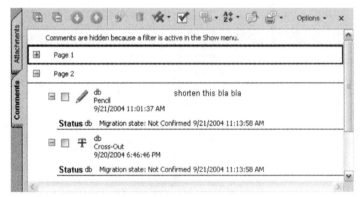

Figure 119c Comments migrated into a document show a notation in the Comments list, and a filter is applied automatically.

CHAPTER FIFTEEN

Reviewing and Collaboration

One of Acrobat's strongest features (among a collection of strong features!) is the ability to communicate with others using a single document. In the old days, you could share a document with others, but it wasn't as easy.

Here's a scenario: You're writing a draft of a procedure that requires input from several people. Once you finish the draft, you start it on its route, either as a single or multiple copies, depending on your standard practice. Eventually you receive your original document back from your reviewers, laboriously interpret the comments and notes scribbled on the margins and backs of pages, and generate a second draft. The second draft is circulated; repeat endlessly.

You don't have to do that. Acrobat's reviewing features allow you to distribute content by email or Web browser, and then collect and collate the comments—much faster than interoffice mail! If you are working with Acrobat 7 Professional, you can even enable a document's commenting features for users working with Adobe Reader 7.

Keep Your Sources Safe

It's a good idea to save a copy of the document prior to incorporating reviewers' comments. Edit the document using the copy to preserve the layout and structure. This way, imported comments are in the correct locations on the document. Acrobat reminds you about document versions. If you open a copy of a document that is part of an active review, a message window appears asking if you want to open the copy or incorporate any returned comments. A handy feature!

TIP 120 Starting a Review Process

In Acrobat 5 you could share comments with others and then incorporate all the comments into the original PDF document. Acrobat 6 made the process simpler, managing it through wizards and prompts. Now in Acrobat 7, you work with a separate Review window to control and manage your reviews. If you initiate the review process using Acrobat 7 Professional, you can enable the documents to be used by recipients working with Adobe Reader 7 as well. When you do this, some functions are restricted in Acrobat 7, such as inserting and deleting pages or editing content, signing the document, and filling in form fields.

The process involves several steps—the review is initiated and copies are sent to those you want to include in the process; the recipients add their comments and return them to you, at which time you integrate them into the original document and process them.

Let's say you have a document that you want to share with a colleague for commenting. Follow these steps to set up an email review from within Acrobat:

1. Choose Comments > Send for Review > Send by Email for Review to open the Send by Email for Review dialog, or click the Send for Review task button's pull-down arrow (on either the program's or the Organizer's toolbar) and choose Send by Email for Review from the menu (**Figure 120a**). Alternatively, in any program containing a PDFMaker, you can choose Adobe PDF > Convert to Adobe PDF and Send for Review or click the button on the PDFMaker's toolbar ▣.

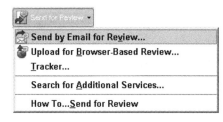

Figure 120a Choose a command from the task button's menu or the program menu.

2. The Send by Email for Review wizard opens. There are three steps in the wizard. Here's what you do in each pane:

- Click the pull-down arrow on the Step 1 pane and choose an open document, or click Browse and locate the document you want to send. Click Next.

- On the Step 2 pane, click Address Book to open your Outlook address book and select email addresses (if Outlook is your email program), or click the Address list and type addresses. You can customize the review options as well—see the sidebar "Customizing the Review Options" in this tip. Click Next.

- On the Step 3 pane, preview the contents of the invitation (**Figure 120b**). Then click Send Invitation.

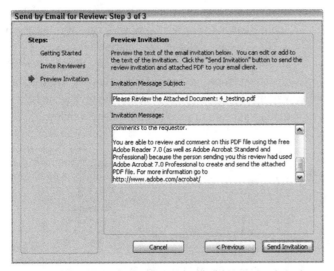

Figure 120b Follow the instructions in the wizard's dialog to set up the review.

3. An Outgoing Message Notification information dialog opens, explaining what happens next. Depending on your security settings, the email may be sent automatically, or you may need to move through dialogs approving the mail process. Click OK to dismiss the dialog.

(Continued)

TIP 120: Starting a Review Process

Customizing the Review Options

When you are setting up an email review, you can customize the options available for your reviewers. On the second pane of the Send by Email for Review wizard, click Customize Review Options to open the Review Options dialog. You can:

- Specify that the comments are sent to an email address other than yours.

- Display Drawing Markup tools for your reviewers to use.

- Allow reviewers using Adobe Reader 7 to participate.

You can also choose Comments > Enable for Tracking in Adobe Reader from the program menu to allow Adobe Reader 7 users to comment on a document; to include the feature automatically, you must resave the document.

That's it for the first part. You've added comments to a document, assigned a recipient, and emailed it. Next it lands in the recipient's email inbox. Here's what the recipient needs to do:

1. Open the email message (**Figure 120c**). Read the instructions. You can see that the PDF document is attached to the email.

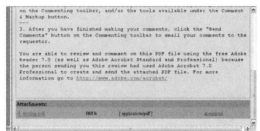

Figure 120c
The instructions are emailed to the recipient and the document is shown as an attachment.

2. Double-click the email attachment to open it in Acrobat or Adobe Reader.

3. Make comments and review the comments sent from the initiator. **Figure 120d** shows the sample document as it appears in Adobe Reader 7. You see the How To pane displayed at the right of the window; it shows information on how to participate in an email review. A Document Message Bar appears above the document showing basic instructions. I chose the Drawing Markups option as I constructed the review, and therefore the toolbar appears in the Adobe Reader 7 window.

Document Message Bar

Toolbars enabled in the email review setup

How To pane showing information on doing a review

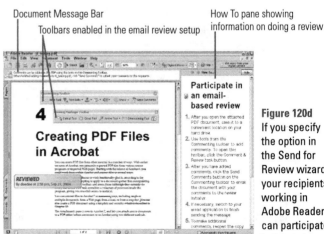

Figure 120d
If you specify the option in the Send for Review wizard, your recipients working in Adobe Reader 7 can participate in the review.

4. When you have finished, choose File > Send Comments or click Send Comments [Send Comments] on the Commenting toolbar. A dialog opens explaining that the comments are being sent back to the initiator, and shows the email address specified by the originator of the review. You can type a different email address or choose one from the Outlook Address Book, just as you can when designing the review.

Once the comments return to you (the initiator), they are integrated into the PDF as soon as you double-click the email attachment to open the document in Acrobat. If you open a document that is being tracked, a message window appears asking if you want to open the copy or incorporate returned comments (**Figure 120e**). You can then review the contents of the Comments list and finish the document's processing.

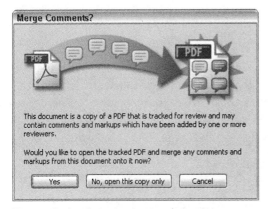

Figure 120e Acrobat prompts you to integrate a received document containing additional comments into the original document being circulated for review.

Using a Browser-Based Review

The beauty of a browser-based review is that you can keep working regardless of where you are—on vacation or at home on the weekend—as long as you have an Internet connection and your documents are uploaded to a server folder that you can access online. This feature can be awfully handy if you're caught away from the office and need to make last-minute changes to that critical report.

You can coordinate and participate in document reviews with a browser and Web server. Browser-based review can be used in Windows, and is supported on the Mac using Safari 1.2.3 or later and Mac OS 10.3. You can choose and configure a server for conducting the review either through the program's preferences or on a file-by-file basis. If you work with the same online locations, it's simpler to set the preference.

Follow these steps:

1. Choose Edit > Preferences (or Acrobat > Preferences) and click Reviewing in the left column on the Preferences dialog to display the Online Comments Repository options. Choose a server from the pull-down list (**Figure 121a**). Specify the folder or URL for the chosen server type. Click OK to close the dialog.

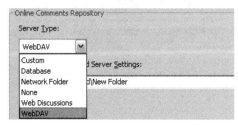

Figure 121a Choose a server type for reviewing online.

2. Open the document; click the Send for Review task button's pull-down arrow and choose Upload for Browser-Based Review, or choose Send for Review > Upload for Browser-Based Review from either the File or Comments menu. The four-step Initiate an Online Review dialog opens.

3. Follow through the wizard's panes:

- Click the pull-down arrow on the Step 1 pane and choose an open document or click Browse/Choose and locate the document you want to send. Click Next.

- On the Step 2 pane, define the location where you want to store the PDF file for your reviewers' use. Click Browse and locate the network or server location you specified in the Review preferences (**Figure 121b**). The file is saved to the folder location. Click Next.

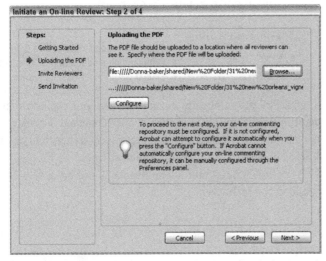

Figure 121b Specify a server folder to use for the review in the second pane of the Review setup process.

(Continued)

TIP 121: Using a Browser-Based Review

- On the Step 3 pane, click Address Book to open your Outlook address book and select email addresses (if Outlook is your email program), or click the Address list and type addresses. Click Next.

- On the Step 4 pane, preview the contents of the invitation. Click Send Invitation. An Outgoing Mail Notification dialog opens explaining the invitation will be sent by email. Click OK to close the dialog.

When your review recipients receive the invitation, it lists instructions similar to those for the email review except that the PDF document opens in a Web browser.

When the recipient has finished reviewing the document, he or she uses the Send and Receive Comments tools on the browser-based Commenting toolbar (**Figure 121c**).

Figure 121c Send and Receive Comments commands are added to the Commenting toolbar for browser-based reviews.

If a PDF file is already on your server, you can open the document in a Web browser, and then choose Comment & Markup > Invite Additional Reviewers to add other reviewers rather than opening the Tracker in Acrobat 7 covered in the next tip.

In both Acrobat 7 and Adobe Reader 7, the browser-based review is added to the Tracker.

TIP 122 Tracking a Review

It's easy to keep track of a simple two-person document review cycle. But many business and professional processes require several participants and numerous rounds of reviewing—tracking a beast like that isn't so easy. Fortunately, Acrobat's Tracker helps you keep tabs on the process.

Click the pull-down arrow on the Send for Review task button and choose Tracker to open the Tracker window (you can also choose Comments > Tracker). All your current reviews, both those you have initiated and others you are participating in, are listed in the left column of the window.

Click the plus sign indicator at the left of the My Reviews name to open the list of reviews (**Figure 122a**) and display the contents. In the example, we are using a number of reviews, including email and browser-based, as well as an offline browser-based document. In the Tracker you can do the following:

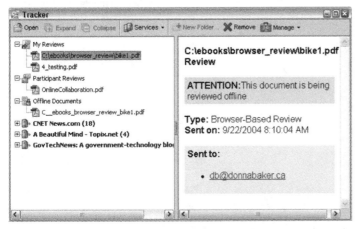

Figure 122a Manage email reviews, browser-based reviews, both online and offline, as well as news trackers and other subscriptions in the Tracker.

- Click a document in the list to display information about it in the right pane of the window. As shown in Figure 122a, the type and information about the review are listed along with the name and a hyperlink to the document.

(Continued)

Tracker on the Web

You can use the Tracker as a news reader or for accessing other broadcast services such as music channels. The Tracker subscribes to Web content that uses the Really Simple Syndication (RSS) format. Click the Services [Services ▾] pull-down arrow on the Tracker window to open a menu and choose Subscribe. In the Add Subscription dialog, type the URL for the service location and click OK. The Tracker shown in Figure 122a lists three RSS feeds, identified by the Services icon [] below the Reviews and Offline Document listings in the Tracker listing.

- Click a review's link in the right pane to open the document in Acrobat 7, or in Adobe Reader 7 if you open the Tracker within Adobe Reader 7.

- Click the name of a review listing and click Remove [✗ Remove] to remove a selected document from the Tracker (this option removes the document only from the Tracker listing; it has no effect on the file itself).

When you initiate a review, a listing of those you have invited is shown; each is an active link. You can also manage the list. Select a review, and then click Manage [Manage ▾] to open a set of options that allow you to send reminders and emails and invite others to participate in the review (**Figure 122b**). When you have finished, close the Tracker.

Figure 122b You can send reminders, emails, and invite others to participate by using the Manage options in the Review Tracker.

TIP 123 Working with the Comments List

Each comment added to a document is stored in the Comments list, which is one of the panes displayed in Acrobat 7 by default. If you have closed the pane, choose View > Navigation Tabs > Comments. Click the Comments tab at the left margin of the program window to open it. Unlike the other panels that open to the left of the Document pane, the Comments list is displayed horizontally below the document (**Figure 123a**).

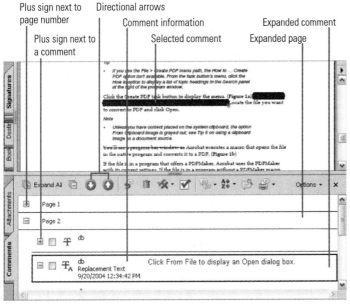

Figure 123a The Comments list appears horizontally below the document. Both the document's pages have been commented on. Click the plus sign (+) to reveal the page's comments, and the comments' information.

As you can see in Figure 123a, both Page 1 and Page 2 appear in the Comments list, meaning that our two-page sample document contains comments on both pages. The plus sign (+) to the left of a page number indicates that the page contains comments. Click a comment in the list. If the comment is located on the portion of the document that is displayed in the Document pane, it is highlighted.

(Continued)

Check That

One of the simplest methods of organizing your work is to add checkmarks to selected comments. Click the comment to select it, and then click the Checkmark tool ✓ Checkmark, or right-click/Control-click the comment in the Comments list or on the document and choose Mark with Checkmark from the shortcut menu. Checkmarks aren't shared with other people as part of a review; you use them to organize your own work. For example, add checkmarks as you finish a correction.

Get It Together

As you will find when you work with a large number of comments, it is quite easy to get confused. If you have a large number of comments addressing the same thing, you can group them together as one comment. For example, the sample document used in Tip 119 contains an arrow and two circles identifying a desired correction on a table. Each of these comments is a separate object. By grouping them together, they appear as one entry in the Comments list—much simpler to work with.

Click the Hand tool on the Basic toolbar and click the first comment; press Shift+click to select the others you want to include in the group. Then right-click/Control-click and choose Group. The comment displays the grouped icon on the Comments pane's listing. To ungroup the comments, right-click/ Control-click any of the comments in the group and choose Ungroup. Each then becomes a separate item in the Comments list.

In a grouped comment, the comment's status, text you add in notes, and any replies to the comments are shown only for the first comment you select. The remaining content exists for all comments—it is merely hidden in a grouped comment.

Comments are organized in levels within the Comments list. Here are some tips for viewing comments:

- Click each page's plus icon (+) to open the page and display the comments—a comment on Page 2 in the sample document in Figure 123a is shown in its expanded state. Once the page is open, you can see the list of comments. You also see an additional plus sign to the left of the comment; click it to open the comment and read details such as the author and the time the comment was added.

- Clicking plus signs can get tiresome. To quickly open all the pages and all the comments, click Expand All Expand All on the Comments list toolbar. You can close the page and comment contents just as quickly; click Collapse All on the Comments list toolbar.

- You can position the comment in the Document pane and highlight it using the directional arrows on the Comments toolbar. The downward-pointing arrow moves the view to the next comment in the list; the upward-pointing arrow goes to the previous comment.

Working on a long document can involve dozens or even hundreds of comments. That's a lot of information to keep track of. Here are a few tips for working with comments:

- Sometimes you want to reply to a comment rather than adding one of your own. First, click the comment to select it in the Comments list. Then click the Reply button Reply on the toolbar. Type the reply in the text field (**Figure 123b**). Acrobat places the Reply icon before your text. After you deselect the reply, the row stays colored to distinguish replies from comments.

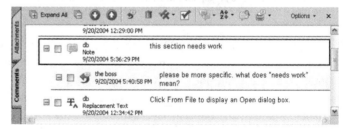

Figure 123b Reply to comments rather than adding new comments to stay organized.

- You can click anywhere on a comment's listing in the Comments list (on the name or on the comment text) to display a text field, which is used to add a note to an existing comment. It isn't the same as adding a reply because it originates with the person creating the original comment. Sometimes you need to add information to a comment, such as explaining why you want to make a change in the document (**Figure 123c**). Such notes appear in a tool tip when the pointer moves over the comment on the document page.

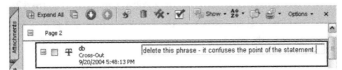

Figure 123c Add a note to an existing comment if you are the original comment author.

- Delete comments you don't want to maintain. Click the comment to select it and then simply click the Delete icon on the Comments list toolbar.

TIP 124 Organizing Comments in the Comments List

You can organize the comments in your document in a number of ways. By default, comments are listed as they appear in the document from start to end. Here are a few tips:

- If you are working on a large document, or if you want to check what you have added to a document, sort the comments. Click the Sort By icon to open a pull-down menu (**Figure 124a**). For example, click Sort By Author to reorganize the comments in the Comments list according to the names of each comment author.

Figure 124a Choose a method for sorting a list of comments.

- If you want to see some of the comments, you can filter them. Click the Show icon to open a pull-down menu. Select a filtering option, and then a specific type of filter (**Figure 124b**). For example, if you choose Show by Type, a submenu opens to select a type of comment to display. When you apply a filter, the Comments list shows the message "Comments are hidden because a filter is active in the Show menu".

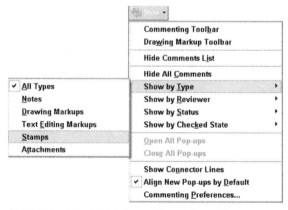

Figure 124b Use a filter to view only a portion of the comments in a document.

- If you migrate comments into a document, a migration filter is automatically applied (see Tip 119 in Chapter 14). For reference, the message "Comments are hidden because a filter is active in the Show menu" appears below the Comments list toolbar. The message is a good reminder for you to check whether you have addressed all the comments in the document or whether a certain reviewer has seen and commented on the document.

Note

Filtering does not apply to the comment replies. If you have added a series of comments and replied to other comments as well, sorting the comments by author displays only your original comments.

- In the Comments list, sorting according to the Checkmark Status reduces the list to two categories: Marked and Unmarked (**Figure 124c**). The categories are closed initially; expand a category to reveal its contents.

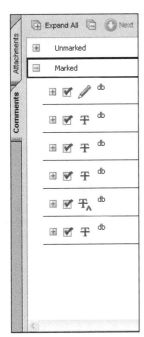

Figure 124c Checkmarks provide a handy way for you to keep track of comments in your copy of the document.

TIP 124: Organizing Comments in the Comments List

TIP 125
Setting Comment Status and Creating Summaries

Once a document has been through a review cycle or two, it's time to take care of some last-minute issues. These include defining a status for the comments (both those generated by reviews and migrated comments), creating summaries, and printing comments and comment summaries for reference or archiving.

First select a comment on the Comments list. Then click the Set Status ![Set Status] pull-down arrow on the Comments list toolbar and click Review to display a list of options (**Figure 125a**). Unlike the checkmark, which is used only on your copy of the document, you can set a status for a comment that can be shared with other reviewers.

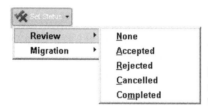

Figure 125a Set a status for comments that can be shared with other reviewers.

You can work with both comments received in a review and those migrated into a document. Click Status > Migrate and choose an option from the menu (**Figure 125b**). If you choose Confirmed, the comment's migration notation is removed from the Comments list; if you choose Not Confirmed, the migrated comment is removed from the Comments list; the None option leaves the migration notation as it appears when the comments are migrated into the document. **Figure 125c** shows the various status options for a list of comments.

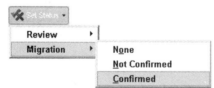

Figure 125b Manage migrated comments using the same methods as those you use for comments received in a review.

Comment with a status applied
Migrated comment with statuses applied

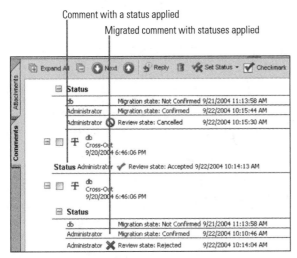

Figure 125c You can assign a status to comments that is displayed with the other comment information.

Note
For both integrated comments and migrated comments, you can also right-click/Control-click a comment in the Comments list and choose Set Status and the options described in this tip.

When you're collecting feedback from reviewers, or when a project is coming to a close, creating a comment summary is a good idea—that way, all the comments are organized and collated in one handy place for easy reference.

Follow these steps:

1. On the Comments list toolbar, click Options to open a pull-down menu (**Figure 125d**).

Figure 125d Choose one of several options for managing a document's comments.

(Continued)

TIP 125: Setting Comment Status and Creating Summaries

Choosing a Comment Summary Layout

You can generate a summary of comments in one of several ways using the Summarize Options dialog. Choose an option depending on the characteristics of the document and its comments, how you like to work, and what you intend to do with the summary:

- Choosing the Document and comments with connector lines on separate pages option is a good idea if you have very long comments. This summary type is complicated when you're using a printed paper copy because you have to follow the lines across pages.

- In a short document or one with short comments, use the Document and comments with connector lines on single pages option.

- Use the Comments only option to print just the comments added to a document. This can be useful in some workflows. For example, if you are the originator of a document and have circulated it to a group for feedback, having a printed list of comments can serve as a "To Do" list.

- If you have finished a project and want a paper copy for archiving, or you want to work on a document away from your computer (does that really happen?), use Documents and comments with sequence numbers on separate pages.

2. Choose Summarize Comments to open the dialog shown in **Figure 125e**. Choose layout options (see the sidebar "Choosing a Comment Summary Layout"), paper size, a sort option, which comments to include, and a font size. Click OK to generate the summary.

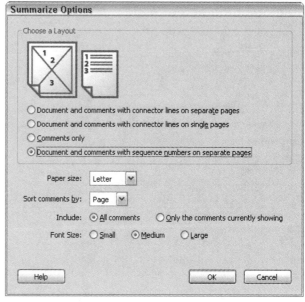

Figure 125e Define the options for a comment summary.

3. Acrobat opens the summary as a PDF file named Summary of Comments [*filename*] and lists all the comments information sorted according to the option you chose. Save this file for reference.

4. Finally, to print the comments and comment summaries, click the Print ⬚ Print Comments ▾ pull-down arrow and choose an option from the resulting menu. You can print the comments summary, generate a PDF document containing the document and its comments, or configure the comments using the same dialog and processes available from the Options pull-down menu. If you prefer, choose File > Print with Comments Summary; again the dialog for configuring the comments opens.

CHAPTER SIXTEEN

Working with Multimedia

Acrobat 7 continues the trend of integrating media in PDF documents, making them a richer viewing experience.

As in Acrobat 6, you can add different types of media, such as sound and movie files, Flash movies, and transitions to your PDF documents.

In Acrobat 7 Professional, you can customize the movies by providing different versions for users working with different players. For JPEG image PDFs created in some programs, such as Photoshop Album or Photoshop Elements, you can also work with an Acrobat 7 plug-in called Picture Tasks, which lets you save, edit, and print images using different layouts. PDF documents play any video and sound files that are compatible with the Windows Media Player, Apple QuickTime, Macromedia Flash Player, Windows Built-In Player, and RealOne players. You can play media files from links or bookmarks, form fields such as buttons, or page actions.

As in past versions, you can read and manage special types of PDF documents called eBooks, and in these tips you see how to work with eBooks and other digital editions.

TIP **126** Using Media in Documents

You can embed media files directly into PDF documents within Acrobat, or you can add the media to a source document—such as a Word document or a Web page—and then convert the file.

To set general multimedia preferences, begin by choosing Edit > Preferences or Acrobat > Preferences and click Multimedia in the left column to show the options.

In the Player Options at the upper section of the dialog, click the pull-down arrow and choose a player option (**Figure 126a**). The preferences do not identify the versions of the chosen players. For example, the latest Flash Player is version 7; if users choose Flash as their player option but have version 4 installed on their computers, they won't be able to see your work unless it is playable on a version 4 player.

Figure 126a Choose a player option you want Acrobat to use in the Multimedia preferences.

At the lower portion of the dialog are the Accessibility Options (**Figure 126b**). If you use assistive devices, enable the appropriate options.

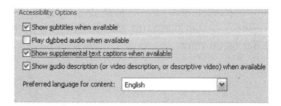

Figure 126b You can define accessible multimedia options in the preferences; the playback of multimedia using these options depends on how the material is authored.

In addition to choosing how to manage multimedia documents in Acrobat, you need to define permissions. Click Trust Manager in the column at the left of the Preferences dialog to display the Trust Manager settings (**Figure 126c**). At the top of the dialog, click the Change Permission for selected multimedia player to pull-down menu and choose an option. In the figure, the options for a trusted document are shown, as is the option to allow multimedia to be played.

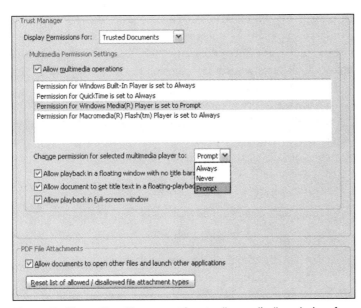

Figure 126c Choose Trust Manager settings to allow or disallow playing of multimedia content from different sources.

Note
A trusted document means it is included in your list of trusted documents and authors; see Chapter 18 for more information.

You can select different options for the listed players. Select a player from the list, and then click the Change permission for selected multimedia player to pull-down arrow and choose a permission level:

- **Always** plays content in the player at all times.

- **Never** prevents the player from being used.

- **Prompt** asks for a decision when a nontrusted document is open that contains media. You decide whether to add a nontrusted document to your list of trusted documents or authors.

You can also select various options for playback, such as floating windows or full-screen views; the options are shown in Figure 126c.

When you've selected the settings you want, click OK to close the Preferences dialog.

When working with multimedia in a project, you have to take your audience into account. If you're targeting the cutting-edge design crowd, you can safely work with the latest and greatest in terms of media formats. This group is likely to have the most recent version of the media player, and they're also more likely to have a high-bandwidth Internet connection. On the other hand, if you are designing for a much more generic audience, you shouldn't assume that they have, for example, the latest Flash player and design material specifically for that player. Some functionality requires Flash 7, but a simple animated logo, for instance, doesn't. If you want to cater to a wide audience, add renditions—that's coming up in Tip 128.

TIP 127 Adding Movies to a Document

In Acrobat 7 Professional you can add a movie to any document from within the program by embedding the movie or linking to it. An embedded movie is integrated into the PDF document itself, while a linked movie simply has a programmed link from the PDF document to the original movie, stored in its original location.

If you want to use actions to control the movie (described in the following tip), the movie must be embedded. The movie formats and other options you can use vary depending on whether you choose Acrobat 6 or Acrobat 5 compatibility. This tip shows how to work with Acrobat 6–compatible settings.

Follow these steps to add a movie:

1. Choose the Movie Tool ⊞ from the Advanced Editing toolbar, or you can select it by choosing Tools > Advanced Editing > Movie Tool.

2. Double-click the document page where you want the upper left of the movie to be placed, or drag a marquee. Regardless of the method you use, the inserted movie can be easily placed on the page. The Add Movie dialog opens (**Figure 127a**).

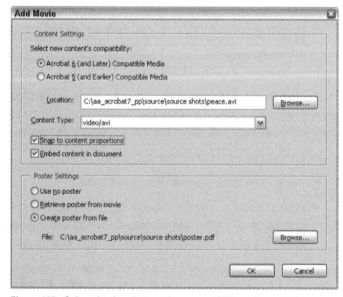

Figure 127a Select the Acrobat version compatibility option and then choose settings in the Add Movie dialog.

Working with Multimedia

3. Click Acrobat 6 (and Later) Compatible Media to access all the available options.

4. Click Browse/Choose to locate the movie and select it. The file's location displays in the dialog. When you select a file, Acrobat assigns a content type automatically that determines the player needed to view the movie. You can click the Content Type pull-down menu and select a different format—but be careful because you may have difficulties playing the movie.

5. Deselect either of the additional options (which are active by default) if you wish. Embed content in document includes the movie file in the PDF document; Snap to content proportions maintains the movie's size when it plays.

Tip

If the Embed content in document option isn't selected, the movie is linked to the document instead.

6. Choose a poster option; a poster is a placeholder image that is seen on the PDF document when the movie isn't playing:

- Use no poster shows the movie's background document.

- Retrieve poster from movie uses the movie's first frame as a static image.

- Create poster from file allows you to use a different image for a poster. Click Browse/Choose to open a dialog to select the image, then click Select; the file's location is listed on the dialog.

(Continued)

More Tips for Working with Movies

Movies can add a lot of interest to a document. Here are some more tips:

- If you see an alert dialog telling you that no media handler is available when you try to insert a movie, it means you are missing the required media players. Install the player (such as Windows Media or QuickTime) and try again.

- If you have designed a graphic background for the movie, consider creating a custom poster image as well, like that shown in Figure 127b, to complete the look.

- Be very aware of file sizes when embedding movies into a PDF document. A movie can add to a PDF file's size dramatically depending on the movie's frame rate and frame size.

- If you want to embed media clips, use renditions (see the following tip), use a different file as a poster, or use a range of content, you must choose the Acrobat 6–compatible option in the Add Movie dialog.

TIP 127: Adding Movies to a Document

Embed or Not?

First, think about what you plan to do with your document. If it is intended for distribution, then embedding is usually simpler since there's only one file to keep track of. If the document is playing on your own system, then linking may be better as the PDF document is smaller. However, if you move the linked movie, the link is broken and the movie won't play in the PDF document.

7. Click OK to close the dialog and insert the movie. As shown in **Figure 127b**, my sample movie uses another PDF document as its poster image. The movie is framed with a dashed line to show you its location on the document page. When the Movie Tool is active, you see the handles on the border as well.

Figure 127b A movie added to a PDF document can use a frame of the movie or another image as a poster image.

Note

You can customize the appearance of the movie on the document—that's coming up in the next tip.

8. Click the Hand Tool, and then click the movie on the screen to play it.

Adding a sound file to the movie is a very similar process. Choose the Sound Tool 🔊 from the Advanced Editing Toolbar and click the document where you want to place the file. For the most part, you leave the sound file invisible, unless you want to use a poster to identify a sound button. The Add Sound dialog opens and offers the same options as those shown for the Add Movie dialog, with the exception of the Snap to content proportions setting, which doesn't apply to a sound file. Choose your settings. Then click OK to close the dialog.

TIP 128 Tweaking a Movie

Once a movie is added to your document, as described in Tip 127, there are a number of ways you can customize it. This tip describes working with an Acrobat 6–compatible movie; the same dialogs and options are available for working with an embedded sound file as well.

You can use a number of versions of the movie, called *renditions*. Use alternate renditions when you are unsure which player your users have, or if you want to offer both high-quality and lower-quality versions of a movie.

With the Movie Tool, double-click the movie on the document to open the Multimedia Properties dialog. You configure renditions as well as other settings for the movie in this dialog.

First, let's look at renditions. The Multimedia Properties dialog opens to the Settings tab (**Figure 128a**). The Annotation Title is a name assigned by Acrobat to identify the object; click the field and change the name if you like. Type a description for an alternate text tag to assist in making the document accessible.

On the List

Renditions you want to include in your movie are listed on the Settings tab of the Multimedia Properties dialog. Consider what types of players your users are likely to have on their computers, and then reorder the list as necessary by clicking a rendition's name and then clicking the Up or Down arrow to the right of the list. On playback, Acrobat tries to play the first rendition in the list; if unsuccessful, it tries the second, and so on until the movie and player are compatible.

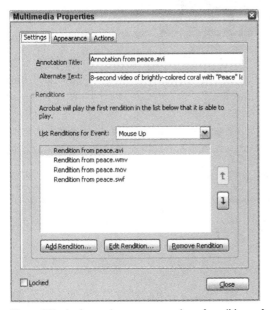

Figure 128a Assign and manage a number of renditions of your movie in the Multimedia Properties dialog.

(Continued)

Play It Again, Sam

You can modify the characteristics of any of the renditions you add to a movie. Click a rendition in the Multimedia Properties dialog and then click Edit Rendition to open the Rendition Settings dialog. This five-tab dialog can be used to tweak your movies as necessary:

- On the Media Settings tab, make a rendition accessible to JavaScript, as well as choosing options similar to those in the basic Add Movie dialog.

- On the Playback Settings tab, define looping, specify how long the player remains open, add controls, and specify players.

- On the Playback Location tab, choose to play your movie in a floating window or full-screen and select options.

- On the Systems Requirements tab, specify languages and playback requirements such as screen resolution and subtitles.

- On the Playback Requirements tab, review the settings chosen in other tabs.

The default action for playing a movie is a Mouse Up action, shown in the List Renditions for Event field. You can select other actions from the pull-down menu. See Tips 129 and 130 to learn how to use actions.

The movie you add to the document is shown as the first (and only) rendition. You can add more versions—click Add Rendition to locate and select additional versions; click Edit Rendition to open the Rendition Settings dialog, where you can select a wide range of customizations, such as placing the movie in a floating window and adding controls, as shown in **Figure 128b**. Read about further customizations in the sidebar "Play It Again, Sam" in this tip. Remove a rendition you don't want to keep by selecting its name in the list and clicking Remove Rendition.

Figure 128b Put your movie in a floating window and add playback controls using options in the Rendition Settings dialog.

To modify the border of your movie, click the Appearance tab of the Multimedia Properties dialog (**Figure 128c**). The default border for a movie is a thin black line. Click the Type pull-down arrow and choose Invisible Rectangle if you want to hide the border altogether, or choose color, thickness, and style from the appropriate options.

Figure 128c Customize the appearance of the movie using options in this dialog.

TIP 129 Controlling the Action

The default action to start playing a movie is a MouseUp event—when you double-click a movie you have added to a document using the Movie Tool or Select Object Tool to open the Multimedia Properties dialog, the default MouseUp trigger for playing a rendition is selected for you. In other words, when you or your user clicks the movie's poster image with the Hand Tool, the movie starts playing when the mouse is released.

Your use of multimedia in Acrobat can be much more creative, however. You can attach triggers to links, bookmarks, buttons, or other form fields, or even page actions. In this tip, I'll show you how to play a movie and a sound file using buttons.

There are three multimedia-specific actions in Acrobat:

- Play a Sound—Plays a specified sound file. The sound is embedded into the PDF document in a cross-platform format that plays in Microsoft Windows and the Mac OS.

- Play Media (Acrobat 5 Compatible)—Plays a specified Quick-Time or AVI movie that you created as Acrobat 5 compatible. A media object using Acrobat 5 Compatible options is automatically embedded in the PDF document.

- Play Media (Acrobat 6 and Later Compatible)—Plays a specified movie that you created as compatible with Acrobat 6 and Acrobat 7. Again, a media object must already be embedded in the PDF document for you to be able to select it.

Construct the buttons you want to use for the document. In the example, you see there are three buttons: play, stop, and rewind (**Figure 129a**). Select the Button Tool from the Advanced Editing toolbar or from the Forms toolbar if you have it open. Draw the buttons and set their properties (read about building buttons in Chapter 12).

Another Dimension

Acrobat 7 allows you to use 3D content exported from various 3D modeling programs in the U3D format in your PDF documents. You embed a 3D model in the same way as you embed movies or sounds. Click the 3D Tool on the Advanced Editing toolbar, and then double-click the page, or drag a marquee. The Add 3D Content dialog opens. Locate the file you want to embed, as well as any scripts you would like to run. You can choose poster options similar to those for movies. Click OK to close the dialog.

Figure 129a You can control movie and sound files in your document using several options, including buttons.

(Continued)

Sound Comment or Sound Action?

Sound attached to a file using the Sound Tool and controlled by actions is not the same as sound attached to a file using a Comment tool (see the sidebar "The Sound of Your Voice" for Tip 114 in Chapter 14). The sound comment is a file attachment; using a sound action actually embeds the sound into the document. Use a sound comment if you've dictated a message to accompany a document or other comment, for example. Your readers have to click the Sound Comment icon on the page to activate their computer's audio utility program to play the message. The sound action can be part of a multimedia presentation, such as a background score, music that plays as a page loads, or sounds you hear as a button is clicked.

To configure the playback action for a movie:

1. In the Button Properties dialog for the first button (the play button in the sample), click the Actions tab to display the settings.

2. Click the Select Action pull-down menu and choose Play Media (Acrobat 6 and Later Compatible), then click the Add button. The Play Media dialog opens.

3. The default action shown is Play. Click the Operation to Perform pull-down menu and choose an option (**Figure 129b**).

Figure 129b Choose a media-specific action to control a movie or sound file using Acrobat objects such as buttons.

4. Click the annotation for the media you want to apply the action to (**Figure 129c**). When you select a listing, the OK button is activated.

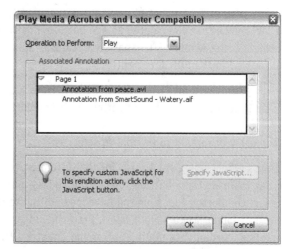

Figure 129c Select the embedded media file to which you want to apply the action.

5. Click OK to close the Play Media dialog, then click Close to dismiss the Button Properties dialog.

6. Click the Hand Tool on the Basic toolbar, and then click the button to test the action.

TIP 130 Making Your Document Responsive

Actions can be applied to individual elements of a document, or to the entire document. You can use actions applied to your document for a variety of purposes—for example, to display instructions or thank visitors for completing a form.

Document actions are set using Acrobat JavaScript, a relatively simple (read: not frightening!) scripting language.

1. To start a document action, choose Advanced > JavaScript > Document Actions. The Document Actions dialog opens (**Figure 130a**), showing a list of actions that refer to different states of a document. There are five states:

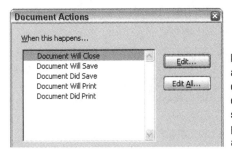

Figure 130a You can attach actions to different states of a document's activity, such as before or after printing, or before or after saving.

- Document Will Close—When a document closes

- Document Will Save—Before a document is saved

- Document Did Save—After a document is saved

- Document Will Print—Before a document is printed

- Document Did Print—After a document is printed

Take note of the different states. For example, an action used in the Document Will Save state takes place before the document is saved, whereas the Document Did Save action occurs after the document is saved.

2. Select an action from the list at the left of the dialog. Then click Edit to open the JavaScript Editor dialog.

(Continued)

Scripting Assistance

There are many resources available to help you learn to write JavaScript, including the form of JavaScript used in Acrobat. See, for example, Adobe's JavaScript Scripting Reference or the JavaScript Scripting Guide; both are available at http://partners.adobe.com/links/acrobat.

3. Type the text for your script in the JavaScript Editor dialog. Here's a sample script:

```
app.alert("For more movies, visit our Web site.
Come back again.",4);
```

4. Click OK to close the dialog. The script now appears in the Document Actions dialog (**Figure 130b**). The selected document action now has a green circle beside it, indicating that it has an active script.

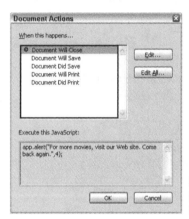

Figure 130b Type the JavaScript you want to run in the JavaScript Editor dialog.

5. Click OK to close the Document Actions dialog.

6. Save the document. To test the script, close the document. The sample uses a Document Will Close action, meaning the script is executed when you choose the command to close the document. Before it closes, the message appears, as shown in **Figure 130c.**

Figure 130c In this example, an alert message appears after the file is closed.

Creating a Presentation with Page Transitions

One of the strengths of presentation software is the ability to display content and control movement through a document. Using page transitions and page view settings, you can create a presentation of a PDF document in Acrobat. The material you use for a presentation can come from a number of sources. You can use files from a range of programs converted to a PDF (see tips in Chapter 3 for conversion information for various types of source materials), or assemble a binder using any number of file types (described in Chapter 4). If you use documents converted from Microsoft PowerPoint presentations (Windows), the transitions are preserved. Bullet fly-in animations are also transferred to the PDF document.

Acrobat provides a number of transition effects. You can apply them to selected pages or to all the pages in a document. In addition, you can configure the speed of the transition and specify whether the pages advance automatically or require keyboard or mouse actions.

Follow these steps to add transitions:

1. Choose Document > Pages > Set Page Transitions to open the Set Transitions dialog (**Figure 131a**).

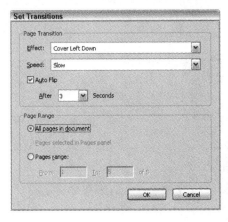

Figure 131a Select the type of transition and its characteristics, such as speed and how the pages advance.

2. In the Set Transitions dialog box, choose a transition effect from the Effect pull-down menu. You can choose among several dozen effects.

(Continued)

Varying Effects

Instead of applying the same transition throughout your presentation, you can quickly choose individual pages or groups of pages and apply a different effect to each group. Select the pages using the page thumbnail view in the Pages panel (Shift-click to select a group; Ctrl-click /Command-click to select pages in different locations in the document). From the Options menu, choose Set Page Transitions to open the Set Transitions dialog.

Use different transitions to identify different segments of a document. For example, I use a PDF presentation as a resume/portfolio. The document contains several pages of artwork samples. To differentiate the artwork from other elements of the document, the artwork pages use a different transition than the rest of the document.

Tips for Using Transitions

As anyone who has sat through a mind-numbing presentation can tell you, transitions can be overused, or used poorly. Although transitions are not the main part of your presentation, your audience receives visual cues from them, just as they will from other page elements like fonts and colors. Here are a couple of tips for using transitions in a document:

- Pick transitions that relate to the content. If the document is a collection of images set against a pale background, a glittery transition may look good. For a document discussing business losses over the past quarter, a somber transition is more appropriate.

- If you use the Auto Flip option, be sure to test the pages. The content determines how long a page should be visible. If the user has a lot of content to read, specify a longer display time.

Note

Choose Edit > Preferences > Full Screen to view the same effect options as those in the Set Transitions dialog. If you set a transition preference, it overrides any document's settings. Also, if you choose Ignore All Transitions, transitions added to a document aren't played.

3. Select a speed for the effect: Slow, Medium, or Fast.

4. Set the navigation method. To have Acrobat turn the pages automatically, select Auto Flip and choose the number of seconds between automatic page turning. You can choose a value in the range 1 to 30 seconds. If you leave the Auto Flip setting deselected, the user moves through the document using keyboard commands or mouse clicks.

5. Select the page range you want to apply the transitions to, or leave the default (which is the entire document).

6. Click OK to close the Set Transitions dialog.

7. You'll see the transitions only when the document uses Full Screen view. To set this view automatically, choose File > Document Properties > Initial View. Click Open in Full Screen mode in the Window Options section.

8. To test the presentation, click Full Screen View  on the status bar at the bottom of the program window, or save the file, close it, and reopen it to view your presentation (**Figure 131b**).

Figure 131b Test the slideshow using the Full Screen view.

TIP 132 Using Photoshop Album Slideshows and Picture Tasks

If you've forgotten to get a birthday card in the mail to your best friend, don't despair. You can use Adobe Photoshop Album (Windows), or other Photoshop products, to create interesting slideshows and email greetings called eCards. Content can be exported from Photoshop Album in PDF format. Once you open that PDF document in Acrobat, two plug-ins are activated, and Picture Tasks is added to the Task Button toolbar; the button is also available by choosing View > Task Buttons > Picture Tasks, although it isn't active unless the appropriate document is open in Acrobat. The Image Viewer plug-in displays the slideshow or eCard content; the Picture Tasks plug-in provides some new commands that let you work with the files' content. The first time you open a document created in Photoshop Album, you'll see a message dialog that tells you you can export, edit, and print the pictures embedded in the document, as well as send them to an online print shop for developing. Once you've read the message, click Don't show again at the bottom left of the dialog to hide it in future sessions.

With your file open, click the Picture Tasks button's pull-down arrow to display its menu. Then click the Picture Tasks task button to check out its How To pane (**Figure 132a**).

Take It for a Test Drive

Photoshop Album is a program that interacts seamlessly with Acrobat. You can try the program for yourself. On the Picture Tasks menu, click Get Adobe Photoshop Album to open an Online Services Wizard (Online Services Assistant). Follow the instructions on the wizard to buy Photoshop Album or download the free Photoshop Album 2.0 Starter Edition.

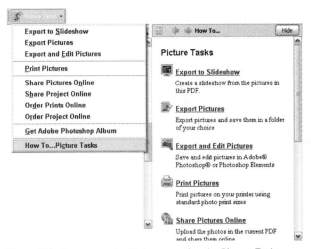

Figure 132a You can work with images using the Picture Tasks; open the How To pane to read about the different options.

(Continued)

TIP 132: Using Photoshop Album Slideshows and Picture Tasks

Modifying Photoshop Album Slideshows In Acrobat

Creating a slideshow using the Picture Tasks method is quick and simple.

Unlike presentations you create manually in Acrobat (described in Tip 131), those created using the Picture Tasks plug-in offer only limited customizations. Available settings are included in the Export to Slideshow dialog. If you need extra content, such as captions, additional text blocks, or custom text or backgrounds, you'll need to create your presentation from scratch, using the techniques described in the previous tip.

Picture Tasks offer you several options for using the content in your documents:

- You can export images to use in other documents. Click Export Pictures to open the dialog shown in **Figure 132b**. Select the images for export, and choose a folder for storage and a common name if you like. Just click Export to export the images from the document.

Figure 132b Export images from Acrobat using the Picture Tasks.

- You can export images and modify them before using them elsewhere. Click Export and Edit Pictures to open the Export and Edit dialog. It's the same as the Export Pictures dialog, with an additional option to open the images in your image-editing program.

Note
The Picture Tasks dialog uses the same image-editing program you specify in the TouchUp preferences. Choose Edit > Preferences or Acrobat > Preferences (Mac) to open the dialog, and click TouchUp in the left column to show the TouchUp preference options. Click Change to choose a different image-editing program if you so desire.

- Print the images in a wide variety of sizes and arrangements. Click Print Pictures to open the Select Picture dialog. Choose the images you want to print and click Next; the Print Pictures dialog then opens. Acrobat offers an interesting collection of printing options (**Figure 132c**). For example, you can print sets of wallet-sized images or larger portrait-sized images; you can even print multiple sizes of the same image using the Picture Package option. Be sure to specify the number of copies you want to print.

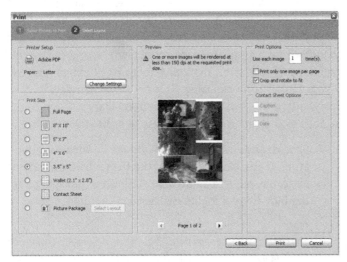

Figure 132c Select the images you want to print and choose size and layout options.

- You can order prints of your photos online. Click Order Prints Online to launch a dialog connecting you to an online printer. Follow the prompts in the Online Services Wizard (called an Online Services Assistant in Mac OS) and the specific upload and payment instructions for the online service.

- There's even an option for ordering projects from the Web. Click Order Project Online to connect to an online printing service to produce Photoshop Album template-based material, such as calendars and photobooks.

Storing eBooks and Other Digital Editions

To save time, store all of your eBooks in the same location. It makes it easier to find them to add to the collection, and it certainly makes it easier to delete eBooks from the collection.

Modifying eBooks and Other Digital Editions

eBooks are the same as other PDF files—you can add comments, links, export images, and so on, depending on the permissions granted in the security settings.

TIP 133 Downloading and Reading Digital Editions

A Digital Edition is a specially packaged PDF document that may contain copyright protection; eBooks are a common type of Digital Edition. Prior to Acrobat 6 and Adobe Reader 6, you viewed general PDFs using Acrobat Reader, and you used the Adobe eBook Reader when you wanted to view eBooks. Both Adobe Acrobat 6 and Adobe Reader 6 combined both viewers in one package, and eBooks and other Digital Editions were controlled through the My Bookshelf dialog. Now you can organize and control digital media, such as eBooks, reports, and magazines, through Acrobat 7 or through Adobe Reader 7's My Digital Editions dialog. This tip shows you how to download free digital editions and create your own library.

Let's look at the download process in Acrobat 7:

1. Choose Advanced > Digital Editions > Adobe Digital Media Store. If you have never used the Digital Editions options, you must first activate an account. Follow the prompts to activate the DRM (Digital Rights Management) account.

   Note
   You can also work through the dialog. Choose Advanced > Digital Editions > My Digital Editions to open the dialog and click Adobe Digital Media Store to go to the Web site.

2. The program's link leads you to Adobe's Digital Media Store. From the Web site, you can select a book to purchase, and follow the prompts for payment and download. You can also try a free eBook; click the *Try an eBook* or *Preview an eBook* link on the main page of the store's site to open the Try Adobe Editions Web page listing free content.

   Note
   You can find plenty of free eBooks in many online venues. For example, Planet PDF (www.planetpdf.com) offers dozens of classics you can download and read, and its library is growing. Search online for other great sources. In some cases, the eBook opens in your browser; simply click Save a Copy on the Adobe Reader 7 toolbar to save it to your digital editions collection.

Working with Multimedia

3. Click an eBook's link to select it, and follow the prompts for download. The file is downloaded and opens in Acrobat 7 or Adobe Reader 7. The file is stored on your hard drive. When you install Acrobat 7 or Adobe Reader 7, a folder named My Digital Editions is added to My Documents (Windows) or to Documents > My Digital Editions (Mac).

4. Close your browser when you have finished downloading your book(s).

In Acrobat 7, you can use the My Digital Editions dialog to organize your digital material:

1. Choose Advanced > Digital Editions > My Digital Editions to open the dialog (**Figure 133a**).

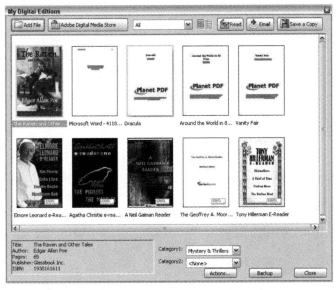

Figure 133a Your digital editions are collected in one location and displayed in this dialog.

(Continued)

TIP 133: Downloading and Reading Digital Editions

Where Did My eBooks Go?

If you worked with Acrobat 6 previously, you will have had access to a system similar to that in Acrobat 7. However, your eBooks and other digital editions are not automatically added to Acrobat 7's My Digital Editions dialog. The first time you open the Digital Editions dialog, a dialog opens offering you a variety of options. Each option provides prompts:

- Yes I Want To Activate Acrobat 7.0 Using My Passport Or Adobe ID—Use this option when you have recently installed Acrobat 7 and haven't activated the program yet (Windows).

- Yes, Migrate These Books To Acrobat 7.0 But Not With A Passport Or Adobe ID—Use this option to select files and migrate them to the My Digital Editions bookshelf.

- No I Don't Want To Migrate These Books—This choice is quite obvious. If you choose this option, you won't be able to migrate the books at a later time.

- Why Am I Being Asked This Question?—This option opens the Acrobat Help files.

- Don't Ask Me Again—Also an obvious choice. The dialog is closed permanently.

2. Click Add File [Add File] to open the Add File dialog.

3. Locate and select the book or books you want to add to the listing and click Add. The dialog closes. The selected books now appear in the My Digital Editions dialog. By default, books are organized using large thumbnails of their first page.

4. Click a thumbnail. At the bottom left of the dialog, you'll see information about the book, including its author, title, and filename. You can click the List toggle [icon] to display the book information in a list form instead of thumbnails (**Figure 133b**).

Title	Author	Date Last Accessed	Category
The Geoffrey A. Moore Reader	Geoffrey A. Moore	9/14/2004 10:46 AM	Business & Investing,None
Agatha Christie e-reader one	Agatha Christie	9/19/2004 9:26 AM	Literature & Fiction,None
Elmore Leonard e-Reader	Elmore Leonard	9/22/2004 6:36 PM	Literature & Fiction,None
Tony Hillerman E-Reader	Tony Hillerman	8/7/2004 6:15 AM	Literature & Fiction,None
The Raven and Other Tales	Edgar Allan Poe	9/24/2004 11:55 AM	Mystery & Thrillers,None
A Neil Gaiman Reader	Neil Gaiman	9/16/2004 11:10 AM	None,None
Around the World in 80 Days	Jules Verne	9/24/2004 10:55 AM	None,None
Dracula	Bram Stoker	9/24/2004 10:55 AM	None,None
Microsoft Word - 4118178B-6513-1822CF.doc	www	9/24/2004 10:55 AM	None,None
Vanity Fair	William Makepeace Thackeray	9/24/2004 10:55 AM	None,None

Figure 133b You can display the contents in either thumbnail view or a list view.

5. To read a book, double-click its name in the list or the thumbnail view, or select the book and click Read [Read] on the My Digital Editions toolbar.

TIP
134
Organizing and Managing Your Digital Editions Collection

The problem with digital editions is that, since they are so easy to get and to use, you can end up with dozens or even hundreds of files. Fortunately, the My Digital Editions dialog lets you classify your collection for easy access.

Organize your books by category. You can use combinations of two categories, both available from pull-down menus at the bottom of the My Digital Editions dialog. Each list contains the same categories.

Select a book in the list or click its thumbnail, and then click the Category 1 pull-down arrow to display the list (**Figure 134a**) and choose a category for the book. The categories include Romance, History, Reference, Travel, and so on. You can assign two categories to digital editions; choose a second category from the Category 2 pull-down list.

Figure 134a Categorize your digital editions for ease of access.

You can sort the collection using the list view. Simply switch to list view and click any of the list headings (Title, Author, Date Last Accessed, Categories) to sort the list alphabetically or by date.

Even if you download them for free, you may want to back up your eBooks. It may not be a problem if you lost your copy of *Wuthering Heights* to some sort of computer failure; however, if you are using it as part of a thesis and have added a huge number of comments and bookmarks to the document, losing the file could be frustrating.

(Continued)

Tips for eBook Creation

eBooks are a special hybrid of a traditional book and an online document. Here are some tips for building interesting and useful material:

- Set the Document properties before finishing the project. Set the initial view so that the document opens with both the bookmarks and the page showing, and set the magnification so that the entire first page is visible. When your readers open your book, they immediately see all of the first page and the bookmark list as well.

- Tag the document. Your viewers read digital editions on a wide range of devices, ranging from computer screens to handheld devices. If a document is tagged, readers can use a reflow view if necessary for clear viewing. Refer to Tip 62 in Chapter 7 to learn about reflow.

Follow these steps to back up your Digital Editions:

1. At the bottom of the My Digital Editions dialog, click Backup Backup.

2. When the Backup and Restore Digital Editions dialog opens, choose the content you want to back up from the pull-down list, which includes all types of digital content such as categories of eBooks, subscriptions, and other PDF documents stored in the Digital Editions bookshelf (**Figure 134b**). The option to back up comments and markup is selected by default.

Figure 134b Use this dialog to back up some or all of your collection, and to restore your collection in case of computer problems.

3. Click OK.

4. The Browse For Folder dialog opens; select the folder you want to use to store the backup.

5. Click OK and then Close to close dialogs and store copies of the digital editions in your backup folder.

If something corrupts your original file, you can use your backup file by following these steps:

1. In the My Digital Editions dialog, click Backup to open the Backup and Restore Digital Editions dialog.

2. Click Restore and then OK.

3. Locate the backup file in the Browse For Folder dialog, and then click OK. The files will be restored to your collection.

If you want to remove a listing from your collection follow these steps:

1. Select the eBook or Digital Edition in the My Digital Editions dialog.

2. Click Actions [Actions...] at the bottom of the My Digital Editions dialog to open a menu (**Figure 134c**).

Read
Remove
Email
Save a Copy
Check for New Issues
Subscription Preferences...
Visit Subscription Website
Send to Mobile Device
Return to Lender

[Actions...]

Figure 134c You can update subscriptions, send content to a mobile device, and implement other commands using the Actions menu.

3. Click Remove, and then click OK in the confirmation dialog.

The document is removed from the listing in the dialog, but is not removed from your computer. You have to remove it manually from the My Digital Editions folder in My Documents (Windows) or Documents (Mac).

Creating eBooks

Is an eBook really just a PDF in fancy literary clothes? Aside from the name, what differentiates an eBook from a regular PDF document is primarily related to layout—eBooks are designed for onscreen use.

Consider these factors when planning your own eBooks and other digital editions:

- Use a smaller page size, approximately 5 or 6 inches by 7 or 8 inches, for a digital edition. The smaller page size makes it easier for the page to be viewed on a variety of screen sizes and still lets the viewer print on a standard-sized page.

- Leave the margins at approximately 1 inch all around. The content is clearly displayed, and there is still enough room for header and footer material.

- Use a clear font that will work well for online use. A simple serif font such as Times or Palatino looks good. Don't use a heavy or bolded font. The added weight doesn't contribute to a clearer page. Make sure you embed the fonts used in your eBook project (refer to Tip 48 in Chapter 6 to learn about embedding fonts).

- Don't use too large a font; it wastes screen and page space. I usually use a 12-point font. That is large enough for the reader to see the content clearly in a full-width page view.

- Don't use a colored background for an eBook. The color is very distracting, and extremely difficult for your viewers using screen readers or other assistive devices. For a shot of color, consider a colored logo, horizontal line, or other small graphic.

- Bookmark chapter headings, and use descriptive names when necessary, such as in technical material.

- Provide navigational cues in the document itself such as page numbers and headers or footers containing the chapter number and name.

- Take advantage of the power of Acrobat when designing a digital edition by including links to additional sources of information, Web sites, and so on.

- An interesting cover image can add a lot of character to your book. When the digital edition appears in your bookshelf, you see a thumbnail of the first page.

CHAPTER SEVENTEEN

Becoming an Acrobat Power User

This entire book is devoted to giving you tips and tricks to make your work with Acrobat faster and more efficient. This chapter takes you one step further. It shows you how to use some of Acrobat's advanced functions to help you become an Acrobat power user.

Have you ever noticed how some of your actions are repetitious? If you are working on a big project you may have to repeat the same processes, such as adding page numbers, over and over. Rather than opening dialogs and choosing the same settings repeatedly, you can use a batch sequence to do the job for you. Can't find the precise process you want to use? You can write one of your own. Acrobat includes a specialized type of batch process for print production as well as a method for processing files in Distiller using a watched folder system.

Acrobat also contains some specialized tools for evaluating your document's content and decreasing file size, helping you create files that are quicker and easier to use.

Another timesaving feature Acrobat offers is the ability to capture the content from a scanned document and convert it into words and images, so you don't have to rebuild the source documents manually. You'll learn how to use this feature, too.

A Batch for Every Reason

Acrobat includes several default batch processes, and offers a wide range of options for writing custom batch sequences. Are there times when you would like to perform any of these actions on a number of files? Instead of repeating the same actions over and over, consider building a custom batch sequence that allows you to:

- Delete or summarize comments
- Check for Accessibility status or make the document's content accessible
- Add elements like headers and footers, watermarks, and backgrounds
- Add descriptions to documents
- Export images in a wide range of formats
- Define how a document opens, and how its thumbnails are used
- Print
- Add or change security settings
- Add printer marks; manipulate pages (such as cropping, numbering, rotating, adding transitions)
- Run a Preflight check
- Run a JavaScript

TIP 135 Using a Batch Sequence

Suppose your usual workflow entails adding description details to your documents, then adding a header or footer, adding page numbers, and finally removing the comments before saving a copy of the document. And suppose you have to do this process over and over on a regular basis. Wouldn't it be nice to click a couple of buttons and have Acrobat do the work for you? Acrobat 7 Professional lets you take the ho-hum out of performing many repetitious tasks by using batch sequences.

Acrobat includes eight default batch processes, and you can easily write your own custom sequence, as you'll see in this tip. Unlike most things you do in Acrobat, you don't need to have documents open in Acrobat to apply a batch sequence. The beauty of using a sequence to perform a variety of tasks for you is that you can customize it to meet both your work requirements and your work habits.

Decide what you want the program to do for you, and assemble your own custom batch sequence—this tip shows how to build a batch process that modifies a document's description, adds a footer and page numbers, removes the comments, and then saves the file with a unique name separate from the original file. You must make four decisions when building your own files: the commands you want to run, what files you want to use, where you want the finished files stored, and in what format.

Follow these steps:

1. Choose Advanced > Batch Processing to open the Batch Sequences dialog. Click New Sequence New Sequence.... A small dialog opens for you to name the sequence (**Figure 135a**). Type the name and click OK. Use a meaningful name for the sequence—the example is called mm_summary reports, which refers both to a specific project as well as the types of documents the batch process will be applied to.

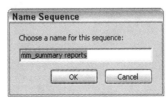

Figure 135a Name your custom batch sequences. If you use a lot of batch processes, make the names descriptive.

2. The Edit Batch Sequence [name] dialog opens. Click Select Commands [Select Commands...] to open the Edit Sequence dialog (**Figure 135b**).

Interactive mode active

Can be customized

Can't be customized

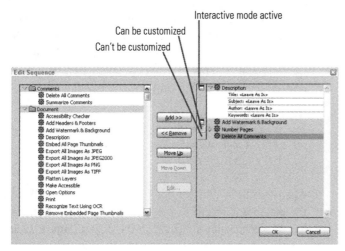

Figure 135b Add the commands in this dialog, and specify if you want to customize each document as a command is run.

3. Click an arrow to open the category of action, such as Document, in the column at the left of the dialog. Click to select an action, such as Description, and then click Add to move the action to the list at the right of the dialog.

4. Add other actions for your sequence. In the example, in addition to the Description action, I have used the Add Watermark & Background and Number Pages actions from the Document category, as well as the Delete All Comments action from the Comments category. You can reorder them by clicking the Move Up or Move Down button, or you can delete an action if you change your mind by clicking Remove.

(Continued)

TIP 135: Using a Batch Sequence

5. Assign an Interactive Mode to actions you want to control manually. In Figure 135b, the action for deleting comments has a solid gray box to the left of the command's name, which means this action has no configuration options—comments are either deleted or they aren't. The other three actions have a depressed gray box to the left of their names, which means they can be defined as Interactive. Click to toggle the Interactive Mode, which displays a gray and white icon in the gray box. When the batch script is run, Acrobat will prompt you for decisions about these actions. In the example, the Number Pages action will occur automatically, while both the Description and Add Watermark & Background actions will pause and wait for my input before continuing the sequence.

Note

You can see the characteristics of the action as well. Click the arrow to the left of the command's icon to display the contents. In Figure 135b, the Description details are shown.

6. When you have finished adding commands, click OK to close the dialog and return to the Edit Batch Sequence [name] dialog. The commands are listed in the dialog (**Figure 135c**).

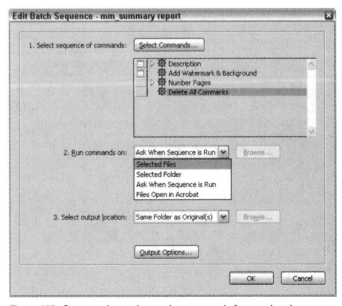

Figure 135c Once you have chosen the commands for your batch sequence, choose the files to process and where to store them.

7. Click the pull-down arrow and choose an option for running the command based on the requirements of your project. If you are building a sequence for a specific project and have stored the files in one folder location, choose that option; if you have files in several folders, choose Selected Files, as shown in the figure. The option you choose determines the other selections that are available. For example, if you choose Files Open in Acrobat, the rest of the dialog is dimmed.

8. Click the pull-down arrow and choose an option for storing the processed files according to your project's needs (**Figure 135d**). If you think you might use the sequence repeatedly, choose Ask when Sequence is Run, or if the files are intended for the same output folder, choose Specific Folder and select the folder.

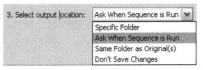

Figure 135d Decide where you want to store the files according to your workflow.

9. Click Output Options to open the Output Options dialog so you can configure the processed files further (**Figure 135e**).

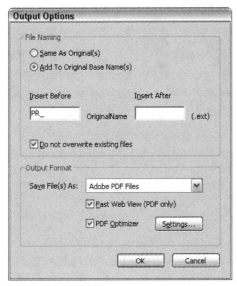

Figure 135e You can choose additional options for the finished files, such as modified names and file formats.

(Continued)

TIP 135: Using a Batch Sequence

10. Select custom options for your project. For example, you can append or prepend characters to the original files' names, choose to overwrite the original files or not, choose an output format from the pull-down menu (you can save the processed files as Web pages, Word documents, text, and so on), or select fast Web save or PDF Optimizer options. (Read about the PDF Optimizer in Tip 138.) In the example, the files prepared by this batch process will all have the prefix PR_ attached to their names, will be saved as PDF documents, will be optimized, and will be separate from the original documents.

11. Click OK to close the Output Options dialog, and then click OK again to close the Edit Batch Sequence [name] dialog, returning you to the original Batch Sequences dialog. Your new sequence is included in the dialog's list (**Figure 135f**).

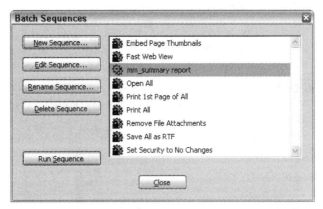

Figure 135f Your custom batch sequence is listed in the dialog in alphabetical order and ready for use.

12. If you are ready to use the process (either a custom sequence or one of the defaults), click Run Sequence. You can also rename it, edit it, and delete it by clicking the appropriate buttons.

As the process is applied, you may see dialogs, depending on the commands you added to your sequence. In the example, since I specified an Interactive Mode for both the Description and the Add Watermark & Background commands, when each document is processed the two dialogs open for custom settings.

Plan Ahead

To get you into the batch sequence mindset, here are a few ideas to consider:

- Plan ahead. As you start working on a project, consider tasks that are likely to be repetitious and plan to use a batch sequence before you start the project. That way, you won't waste time making simple changes in some of the documents in a project that could easily be handled with a batch sequence applied to the whole project.

- Put the files you plan to batch into a separate folder. It's easier to keep track of where you are in your workflow. You can include other files in your batch sequence besides PDF documents. (See the sidebar "But What About…?").

- Configure and tweak a sample file. If you want headers and footers on 50 documents, for example, test and apply them to one document. When you are satisfied with the appearance, you are ready to build and use a batch sequence for the rest.

- Write and test your batch sequence at any time. You don't need to be working with a project's files to write the sequence.

- Consider writing a group of batch sequences. In a large project, you may need several sequences for different purposes. Set aside some time to construct and test them.

- Pay attention to how you like to work. As you construct a batch, you can allow for prompts that let you check documents. Some people like to see each document as it is changed; others prefer to let Acrobat do its thing independently.

TIP
136

Creating and Using a Printing Droplet

It's Raining Droplets

If your specialty is print production, you will often find you have a series of preflight tests you have to run depending on your client. Take a few minutes and build droplets and storage folders for each of your regular jobs. You can store the droplets on the desktop or in any folder on your hard drive. Why not a folder on the desktop for easy access? Need to check a file for Client A? Open your folder and drag the file to the appropriate droplet. Acrobat opens and runs the preflight process, storing the document and reports according to the droplet's settings.

In Windows, you can add the droplet right to the system's Start menu if it is on your desktop. Right-click the droplet to open the shortcut menu and choose Pin to Start menu. Then drag your document for testing to the Start button and hold it for a second or two until the Start menu opens; then simply drop the file on the Droplet item.

A Preflight Droplet is a special application you build to process documents in preparation for printing that you can store on your desktop. With a droplet on your desktop, you don't even have to open Acrobat dialogs to test a file! In addition to using droplets to evaluate files, you can use them to separate your files by their results and create reports automatically. Build the droplet in Acrobat through the Preflight dialog. Construct and name your Preflight profile and include it in the Preflight dialog's listing. (Find out about creating and using Preflight profiles in Chapter 6.)

> **Note**
> *If you intend to create folders to store files that have been processed both successfully and those that generate errors, add and name the folders before building the droplet to save time.*

Follow these steps to construct the droplet:

1. Choose Tools > Print Production > Preflight from the menu to open the Preflight dialog.

2. Click Options on the Preflight dialog and choose Create Preflight Droplet. The Preflight: Droplet Setup dialog opens (**Figure 136a**).

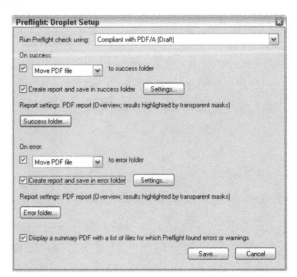

Figure 136a Use this dialog to set the type of evaluation, how you want to handle the files, and whether you want reports.

3. If you selected a profile before opening the dialog, the profile is automatically selected; otherwise, choose the profile from the Run Preflight check using pull-down menu.

4. Choose options for a successful test. You can move, copy, or create an alias of the document in a specified folder. Click the Success folder button to choose a folder to hold the successfully processed files.

5. Click Settings to open the Preflight: Report Settings dialog (**Figure 136b**). You can specify the type of report as well as its level of detail. Click OK to close the dialog and return to the Droplet Setup dialog. The report settings now appear on the dialog.

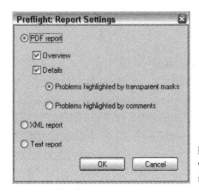

Figure 136b Define what you want to see in a report using these settings.

6. Choose options for a test that generates errors. Again, you can move, copy, or create an alias, as well as generate reports. Click Settings to choose options for the error report, using the same dialog shown in Figure 136b. In the Preflight: Droplet Setup dialog, click the Error folder button to choose a folder to store the output.

7. Click Save. The Save Droplet as dialog opens; choose a location to store the droplet and click Save to close the dialog and create the droplet.

When you want to test a file, locate and select the file on your computer. Then drag it to the Droplet icon ⬇. Acrobat starts and tests the file. Depending on the outcome and your settings, the file is processed and saved, and reports are generated.

Modifying Droplets

Can't be done. A droplet is an executable file, which is in essence a separate application. You won't find droplets listed in the Preflight Profiles, and you can't reopen one to change the options. Plan carefully. Of course, since it only takes a few minutes to construct one, you can start again if necessary.

TIP 136: Creating and Using a Printing Droplet

TIP 137 Watching Folders

Another Acrobat tool for enhancing productivity is Acrobat Distiller 7, which lets you create a special folder system of "watched" folders and then have Acrobat look for and process files in these folders automatically. You don't have to install Distiller—it is installed as part of the overall Acrobat 7 installation process.

How would you like Acrobat Distiller to automatically look for PostScript files in an In folder, convert them to PDF according to specified settings, and send the finished documents to an Out folder? In some workflows, an automated process like this could save you a lot of time.

Add a folder you want to use as a watched folder to your hard drive. Then open Distiller and follow these steps to set up watched folders:

1. Choose Settings > Watched Folders to open the Watched Folders dialog (**Figure 137a**).

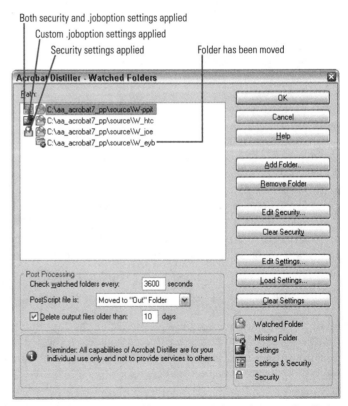

Figure 137a Configure a set of folders to watch for and process PostScript files automatically.

2. Click Add Folder; locate and select the folder you want to use (you can't create a new folder through this dialog). Distiller adds In and Out subfolders automatically.

3. You can add security, custom settings, or both to a folder. Distiller adds an icon to the left of folders you have customized, as shown in Figure 137a. Select the folder and then:

- Click Edit Settings to open the Settings dialog (**Figure 137b**). Modify the settings and click OK; Acrobat saves the file to the individual folder as folder.joboptions.

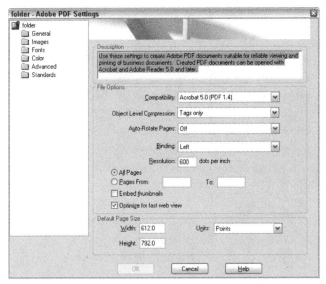

Figure 137b Configure custom settings that are applied to the contents in the watched folder.

- Back in the Watched Folders dialog, click Edit Security to add password protection to the folder; if you change your mind, click Clear Security.

- Click Load Settings to locate and attach .joboptions files from your system.

(Continued)

It Isn't Polite to Share

Don't set up watched folders to act as a service for other users on your system. Everyone who creates Adobe PDF documents needs a separate Acrobat license.

Develop a System

You can create up to 100 watched folders. If you have different conversion settings, instead of generating PDF files on a file-by-file basis—very time-consuming when you work with a large number of files—set up a folder for each .joboptions file you need to use. As you finish working with a file, drop it in the appropriate watched folder. According to your specified time settings, Distiller checks the folder and processes the files. Make sure the folder names are descriptive to prevent adding files to the wrong folders. For example, instead of naming a file *watched_5*, name it *W_Bob_Menu* if you use the folder to process documents for Bob's Pizza Emporium.

TIP 137: Watching Folders

Which Is More Secure?

Be aware of the settings applied to a folder and the settings used in Distiller. If you specify security in Distiller's settings, the settings may or may not be the same after the file is processed. In fact, the file may not be processed at all. If a folder's .joboptions file is read-only, Distiller won't convert the file. If Distiller's settings include security options and the watched folder doesn't, the file is processed and the security settings are in place.

Note
You can delete a folder from the Watched Folders list by clicking Delete on the Watched Folders dialog. Deleting a watched folder does not delete the In and Out folders, contents, and the folder's .joboptions files from your computer; you'll need to remove them manually. If you delete or move a folder from your computer that you have designated as a watched folder in Distiller, the next time you open the dialog, you see the Missing Folder icon to the left of the folder's name.

4. Choose options to manage your set of watched folders:

- Specify how often to check the folders in seconds. You can check every 1 to 9999 seconds; 1 hour is 3600 seconds.

- Specify what to do with the original PostScript file—it can be moved to the Out folder with the PDF document or deleted; log files are copied to the Out folder.

- Specify how long to keep the PDF documents in the folder in days, up to 999 days. You can also specify to delete the PostScript and log files.

5. Click OK to close the dialog.

TIP 138 Optimizing Your PDF Documents

Some projects are quite involved. You may have had a few rounds of reviewing, and dozens of comments have been applied. You may have received a document from a user less skillful in the construction of source documents and the resolutions of images may be too high for your intended use of the document. You may have embedded a movie in several renditions and then changed your mind and deleted most of them... the list can be almost endless.

You don't have to try to remember all the different elements that can bloat your files' size and then manually clean them up. Instead, use two tools in Acrobat to take care of the problem areas for you. The PDF Optimizer (which you can customize) checks all aspects of a document for unnecessary content, and then removes it. Beware: Optimizing a signed document will invalidate the signature. (Read about signatures in Chapter 18.)

First, analyze the document. Choose Advanced > PDF Optimizer to open the dialog. Click Audit space usage Audit space usage... at the upper right of the dialog. Acrobat examines the document and displays a report (**Figure 138a**). Depending on the type of contents in the document, you see listings for such elements as fonts, comments, and images; each is defined both in percentages of the entire document size and in bytes. Click OK to close the audit report.

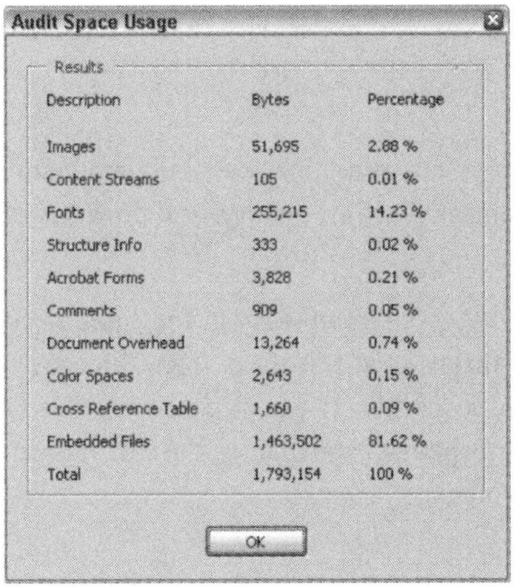

Save It Again

One of the simplest ways to reduce file size is to save a file as itself. If you have been working with a document—for example, adding and removing pages—the file is saved on top of itself each time you save it, and these iterations can really add up to a huge file size. Choose File > Save As. In the Save As dialog, leave the name as is and click Save. A prompt asks if you want to overwrite the file; click Yes. The file is resaved, and content is consolidated. You may be surprised how much smaller the file becomes!

Description	Bytes	Percentage
Images	51,695	2.88 %
Content Streams	105	0.01 %
Fonts	255,215	14.23 %
Structure Info	333	0.02 %
Acrobat Forms	3,828	0.21 %
Comments	909	0.05 %
Document Overhead	13,264	0.74 %
Color Spaces	2,643	0.15 %
Cross Reference Table	1,660	0.09 %
Embedded Files	1,463,502	81.62 %
Total	1,793,154	100 %

Figure 138a Test your document first to see how its elements contribute to the file size.

(Continued)

Easy Optimizing

Do you need to apply the same optimization settings to a number of files? Once in a while or on a regular basis? Do you have a number of files that need optimizing right now? Customize a collection of settings in the PDF Optimizer and click Save on the dialog to name and save the settings. The next time you need to optimize a file using the same settings, click the Preset pull-down menu, and your custom settings are included in the list for you to select. You can remove your custom settings as well—select the settings' name from the Preset pull-down menu, and click Delete.

If you find you are optimizing files on a regular basis, include Output Options in a batch sequence instead. Read about batch sequences in Tip 135.

The default settings in the PDF Optimizer are for Acrobat 5.0 compatibility. If you click the Make compatible with pull-down arrow and choose another program version, the Preset in the upper left of the dialog changes from Standard to Custom. The options available in the different panes of the dialog vary according to the selected program version.

Click a label in the left column on the dialog to display settings (**Figure 138b**). As you look through the list, deselect items that you don't want to optimize; look for optimizing in these areas:

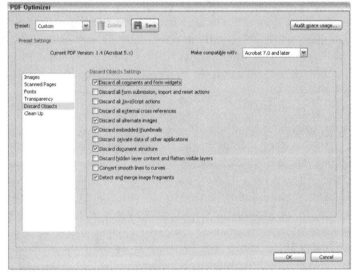

Figure 138b You can customize dozens of settings in the PDF Optimizer to precisely balance the quality of the document against the file's size.

- Images—Define settings for color, grayscale, and monochrome images. Choose compression types, quality, and downsampling values.

- Scanned Pages—Activate the compression and quality check box and then apply filters to clean up a scan, such as halo removal, descreen, or despeckle. If you choose Adaptive Compression options on this pane of the dialog, the settings on the Images pane are disabled.

- Fonts—The fonts in the document are listed in the dialog; unembed those you don't need, such as system fonts or common fonts. If a document is intended for departmental circulation, for example, and you know everyone viewing it uses the same set of fonts, you can delete those from the list.

- Transparency—Choose transparency flattening and settings such as resolutions for text, line art, and gradients.

- Discard Objects—Decide what objects can be removed from the document, such as layers, form content, cross-references, and comments.

- Clean Up—Choose other cleanup details, such as removal of invalid links or bookmarks, encoding options, and a method of compressing the document's structure.

Click Save to name and save the settings if you plan to reuse them at a later time. If optimizing is a one-time thing, click OK to close the dialog. The Save Optimized As dialog opens. Click Save to overwrite the original file; to be on the safe side, save the document with another name instead. Once you check the results and are satisfied, delete the original.

Creating Editable Text from an Image PDF

Ways and Means

You can convert an image to captured text in three ways, and choose from four different image options. The sample document in this tip shows the worst possible outcomes. The text uses a wide range of fonts, some of the text isn't recognized at all, and the background graphic's gradient is strongly banded.

In the Recognize Text - Settings dialog, click the PDF Output Style pull-down menu and choose from three options:

- Searchable Image (Exact) keeps the foreground of the page intact and places the searchable text behind the image.

- Searchable Image (Compact) compresses the foreground and places the searchable text behind the image; compressing affects the image quality.

- Formatted Text & Graphics rebuilds the entire page, converting the content into text, fonts, and graphics.

As well as choosing a conversion, choose an Image Downsampling option. Click the Downsample Image pull-down arrow and choose from four options—anywhere from 600 down to 72 dpi. Downsampling will reduce file size, but can result in unusable images.

A scanned or image PDF is only an image of a page, and you can't manipulate its content by extracting images or modifying the text. However, Acrobat can convert the image of the document into actual text or add a text layer to the document using optical character recognition (OCR). Be sure to evaluate the captured document when the OCR process is complete to make sure Acrobat interpreted the content correctly. It is easy to confuse a bitmap that may be the letter I with the number 1, for example.

To capture the content of a scanned document:

1. Choose Document > Recognize Text Using OCR > Start. The Recognize Text dialog opens (**Figure 139a**). Specify whether you want to capture the current page, or an entire document, or specified pages in a multipage document.

Figure 139a Choose settings for working with OCR in the Recognize dialog.

2. Click the Edit button to open the Recognize Text - Settings dialog (**Figure 139b**). Choose a language, PDF Output Style, and Downsample Image setting, and then click OK to return to the Recognize Text dialog. (See the sidebar "Ways and Means" for more information about the choices).

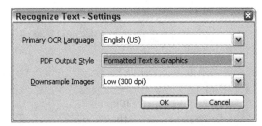

Figure 139b You can convert the content in different ways.

3. Click OK to start the capture process. Be patient. Depending on the size and complexity of the document, the process can take a minute or two. When it is complete, the dialog closes.

Converting a bitmap of letters and numbers into actual letters and numbers may result in items that can't be definitively identified, known as *suspects*. First take a quick look at the job ahead. Choose Document > Recognize Text Using OCR > Find All OCR Suspects. All content on the page that needs confirmation is outlined with red boxes (**Figure 139c**). The sample document was captured using the Formatted Text & Graphics option.

Figure 139c Show all the capture suspects to evaluate the conversion.

(Continued)

Do You Have to Convert a Page?

The answer is: it depends. Why are you scanning the page into Acrobat in the first place? Do you need a visual image of a document to put into storage, or to use as part of your customer service information package? For either of these purposes, you probably don't have to convert the content. Here are some reasons you'd need to convert content from an image PDF to text and images:

- You need to be able to search the text, as within a document collection.
- You want to make the content available to people using a screen reader or other assistive device.
- You want to repurpose the content for different output, such as a Web page or a text document.
- You want to reuse or change the content, such as moving paragraphs or extracting tables.

Scan and Convert

If you are scanning a document, you can convert it to searchable text as part of the scan. Choose Create PDF > From Scanner to open the dialog. Select Recognize Text Using OCR, and click Settings to open the Recognize Text - Settings dialog shown in Figure 139b.

TIP 139: Creating Editable Text from an Image PDF

The Usual Suspects

Here are some tips for working with scanned or image documents with a minimum of suspects:

- Evaluate the content of the document. Determine whether you can simply scan or create an image PDF (such as those you create in Photoshop), or whether you must scan and capture the document, creating editable, searchable text.

- If you plan to capture the content, scan using specific resolutions—scan black and white at 200–600 dpi, with 300 dpi an optimal resolution, and scan at 200–400 for grayscale or color. Acrobat requires a minimum of 144 dpi to perform OCR; otherwise you see a warning message and have to rescan or reconvert the image.

- Not all fonts and colors scan well. In the sample document, the decorative "T" wasn't recognized as a letter, and much of the font information is lost when converting to letters. The word "before" isn't captured at all since it overlays the background graphic.

- Use OCR fonts if possible, or any clear font at about 12 points. Black text on a white background scans and converts the best while colored or decorative fonts are the most difficult.

Select the TouchUp Text tool on the Advanced Editing toolbar and click a suspect on the document to open the Find Element dialog (you can also select Document > Recognize Text Using OCR > Find First OCR Suspect).

In **Figure 139d**, the word "the" is suspect. Acrobat's interpretation of the word is spelled "tlie" because of the shape of the font's letters. Click the text in the Suspect field and type the correct letters. If the suspect isn't a word at all, click Not Text. Click Find Next to go to the next suspect, click Accept and Find to confirm the interpretation, and go to the next suspect, or click Close to end the process.

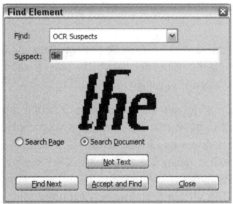

Figure 139d Confirm or modify suspect entries in this dialog.

Depending on the characteristics of the document's text, you may have to modify some conversion results, such as the font or character spacing (**Figure 139e**). Use the TouchUp text tool. When you are pleased with the results, save the document; if you want to start again, choose File > Revert or save the document with an alternate name.

Figure 139e Depending on the characteristics of the document and the conversion settings you choose, the results can be dreadful.

CHAPTER EIGHTEEN

Making Your Documents Secure

In many cases, once you've finished tweaking, modifying, and perfecting your document, there remains one important final step: guaranteeing your document's security. It isn't necessary to secure every document you create. I don't bother with security for any material I use and store on my own computers. On the other hand, if I want to have someone review my work, or am putting documents on a Web site for general distribution, I usually protect the document's content in some way.

As you'll learn in this set of tips, you can add security to your documents in several ways. Which option you choose depends on the material involved, as well as on your intended audience; you can:

- Restrict opening of your document with a password, and further restrict any types of changes with another password.

- Digitally sign your document, which restricts editing of the document's contents.

- Restrict access to your document to a specific user list, based on digital signatures, and assign different rights to different users.

- Encrypt the content and attachments in a document for secure distribution.

There are many security functions and activities you can perform in Acrobat—anything from adding a password to encrypting a document, as you will see in this chapter. The option you choose depends both on the level of security you need for a document as well as its intended recipients. Most of Acrobat's security policies are controlled through one central dialog, the Managing Security Policies dialog (**Figure 140**).

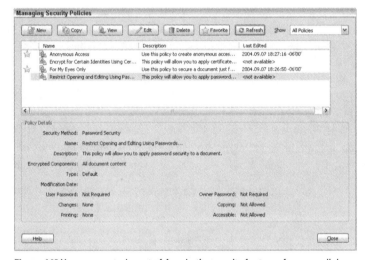

Figure 140 You can control most of Acrobat's security features from one dialog.

In Acrobat 7 you can choose the following types of security processes:

- **Password Protection.** Use passwords to prevent unauthorized users from opening documents. You can also specify whether to allow users to copy, print, or extract content from a document.

- **Document Certification.** Certify documents to define the content of a document and show any changes. You can restrict access to a document to specified users using this method.

- **Digital Signatures.** Use Digital Signatures to approve a form or other PDF document. You can also approve a document or form by a number of users all using signatures.

- eEnvelopes. Use secure document transmission, called eEnvelopes to protect a document during email distribution. You can also protect attachments using the same type of security.

- User Security Policies. Apply security policies to a number of documents at the same time. You can use server systems to add special security features such as controlling access, setting expiry dates, etc.

Checking Security Status

Depending on the security settings applied to a document, you see different icons at the lower left of the program window. Hold your pointer over an icon to see basic information in a tool tip; hold the pointer over the icon for a few seconds or double-click the icon to open a larger dialog with more information.

Choose Document > Security > Show Security Settings For This Document or click the Secure task button and choose the command from its menu to open the Document Properties displaying the Security tab. You can choose File > Document Properties > Security to show the Security tab as well.

If you want to check the status of a document through a Web browser, choose Document Properties from the arrow icon above the vertical scroll bar on the right side of the document. Then click Security.

TIP 140: Choosing a Security Method

TIP
141

Using Security Levels and Passwords for a Document

Some Words About Passwords

Here are a few things to remember about Acrobat passwords:

- A PDF file with both Document Open and Permissions passwords can be opened by using either password.

- Passwords can use any characters, but they are case sensitive.

- You can't use the same characters for both Document Open and Permissions passwords.

You can add password security to a document in source programs that use a PDFMaker, from programs such as Photoshop CS or InDesign CS, or set the options in Distiller. In Acrobat, you add the security through the Document Properties or Security Policies dialog. Add passwords if you intend to convert and email a document from your source program; if you plan to work with the document in Acrobat, or want to set specific encryption options, wait until the work is complete and then add passwords. Otherwise, each time you open the document you have to reenter your passwords.

The default setting is a high level of security compatible with Acrobat versions 5 and 6. When you open Distiller or a PDFMaker, you see the Compatibility level listed on the dialog below the Default Settings box (**Figure 141a**). To change to a lower level of security to share documents with readers using older versions of Acrobat, or a higher level of security to use more features, you have to first modify the Compatibility level.

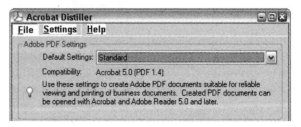

Figure 141a The Acrobat version displayed defines the available security characteristics.

In Distiller, choose Settings > Edit PDF Settings to open the Adobe PDF Settings dialog with the General tab displayed. Then, choose a version option from the Compatibility pull-down list (**Figure 141b**).

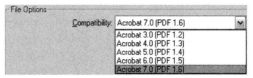

Figure 141b Select an alternate Compatibility version from the pull-down list.

Click Save As and save the settings as a custom .joboptions file. In a program using a PDFMaker, choose Adobe PDF > Change Conversion Settings > Advanced Settings. The same dialog shown in Figure 141b opens, and you can select a compatibility level. The level you choose defines what options are available when you're setting passwords.

You can use two levels of passwords. The user level, or Document Open password, is a traditional type of password that requires the user to type the correct characters in order to open the file. The master-level password, or Permissions password, allows you to modify the document restrictions. You can use one or both of the password options in the same document.

In Distiller, choose Settings > Security; in a program using a PDF-Maker, choose Adobe PDF > Change Conversion Settings > Security. You see the encryption level at the top of the dialog (**Figure 141c**). You can add one or two passwords:

About Metadata

Metadata is descriptive information about a file that can be searched and processed by a computer. Adobe's eXtensible Metadata Platform (XMP) lets you embed metadata into a file to provide information about the contents of a document. Applications that support XMP can read, edit, and share this information across databases, file formats, and platforms. If you use Acrobat version 6 or 7 compatibility options, you can choose to enable Metadata in the security settings.

Figure 141c Set Document Open, Permissions, or both levels of password in this dialog.

(Continued)

TIP 141: Using Security Levels and Passwords for a Document

Check Your Settings

Unless you choose Acrobat 6 or 7 in the Advanced Settings dialog, the Enable Plaintext Metadata option isn't available.

- Click the "Require a password to open the document" check box to activate the field. Type in the password.

- Click the "Use a password to restrict printing and editing of the document and its security settings" check box. Type in the password. Then specify the restrictions you want to add to the document.

When you add one or both passwords and click OK to close the Security dialog, you see a confirmation dialog; retype the password and click OK, and then click OK again to dismiss the encryption information dialog. When you set both passwords, you must confirm both in separate dialogs.

After you convert the document to a PDF, you must enter the password to open it in Acrobat (**Figure 141d**). Type the password and click OK to open the document.

Figure 141d Type the password you saved in the Security dialog to open the document.

When the document opens, you see a security icon at the bottom left of the Document pane. Click the icon to open the Document Status dialog, which explains that the document has been encrypted and has attached security features (**Figure 141e**). Click Close to dismiss the dialog.

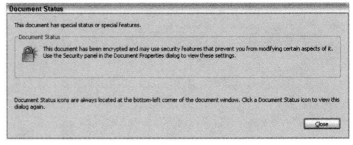

Figure 141e Read about the document's security in the Document Status dialog.

You can change, add, and remove security in Acrobat as part of the security policy process, described in Tips 147 and 148.

TIP 142 Creating a Digital ID Profile

The key to document security (pun intended) is a *key encryption* process. In order for you to share secure documents with others, and for others to share secure documents with you, you need to use digital signatures. A digital signature is based on a digital ID, just as your handwritten signature represents you. A digital signature, digital ID, and digital profile are the same thing.

The visual signature applied to a document, either a default or custom signature, is referred to as an *appearance*. The appearance can be composed of a combination of information fields (such as dates or text), the Acrobat logo, or imported graphics.

You can either create default signatures or design custom signatures. To create a new signature:

1. Choose Advanced > Security Settings to open the Security Settings dialog. Click to open the Digital IDs list in the left frame of the dialog; existing ID files display in the upper-right frame of the dialog (**Figure 142a**).

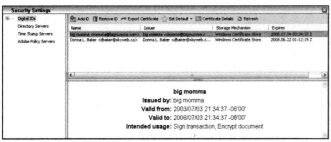

Figure 142a The Security Settings dialog contains lists of Digital IDs and security servers.

2. To build a new signature, click Add ID [Add ID] on the dialog's toolbar. The Add Digital ID dialog opens. You can choose three options: find an existing ID on your system, create a new one, or retrieve one from a third-party source. Click Create a Self-Signed Digital ID and then click Next at the bottom of the dialog.

(Continued)

Signature Preferences

There are many ways to customize signatures. Click Advanced Preferences on the Security pane of the Preferences dialog, shown in Figure 142c, to open the Advanced Preferences dialog. Select verification methods and time options, and whether to use Windows Certificate Store root certificates. Verification can be document-specific, or based on a default method. Time options include the current time, the time the stamp was created, or a secure timestamp from a server.

3. A disclaimer dialog appears telling you that with this type of security, you have to exchange certificates with others. Click Next at the bottom of the dialog.

4. The next dialog asks where you want to store the Digital ID. You have two choices: create a new PKCS#12 Digital ID file, which is the default selection, or add the Digital ID to your Windows Certificate Store (Windows). Click an option, and then click Next. The sample certificate creates a new PKCS#12 Digital ID file.

5. In the next dialog, add the information you want to include in the certificate (**Figure 142b**). Add a name for the certificate as well as other identifying information. Choose a Key Algorithm from the pull-down list, and define how you want to use the Digital ID. As shown in the figure, you can use it for either digital signatures, data encryption, or both. Click Next.

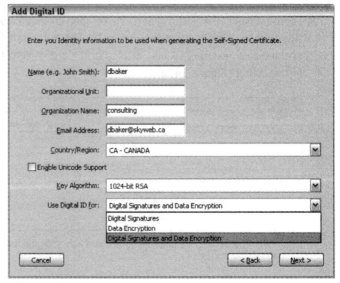

Figure 142b Type the information for your new certificate, and specify how you want to use the Digital ID.

6. In the final pane of the dialog, click Browse to set a storage location for the certificate. It's safer to use the default location in the Security subfolder of the Acrobat program's installation folders so you don't lose track of your certificates. Type a password and a confirmation of the password and click Finish.

You can sparkle up the appearance of a Digital ID using an image rather than using the default appearance:

1. Choose Edit > Preferences (on the Mac, Acrobat > Preferences) to open the Preferences dialog; then choose Security from the list on the left. The Appearance window lists existing signature appearances (**Figure 142c**). Click New.

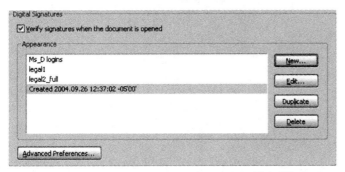

Figure 142c You can select and create appearances for Digital IDs in the Security pane of the Preferences dialog.

Note

If you want to modify a signature's appearance, select it in the list and click Edit; click Delete to remove a particular signature appearance; click Duplicate to create another copy you can use with alternate information blocks or security settings.

(Continued)

Which System Is For You?

If you are designing digital signatures to use for sharing secure material with a workgroup, for instance, a self-sign security system is appropriate. Each person who wants to access a secure document using a self-sign security option has to contact you directly for permission to use the document. If you want to share material at an enterprise or public level, use a third-party security system.

2. The Configure Signature dialog opens (**Figure 142d**). Enter the new signature's description and information:

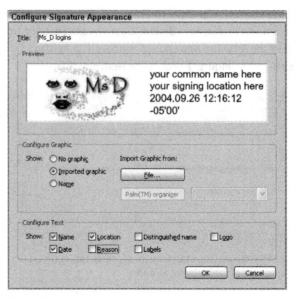

Figure 142d Name a custom signature appearance, and choose its text and image characteristics.

- Type a name for the appearance. Use a descriptive name so you can easily identify the signature appearance. In Figure 142c, a number of custom appearances have been created—it is much simpler to identify a signature with an actual name than one that uses a default creation date and time name.

- Select a Configure Graphic option. You can choose to use no graphic, an image from a file, or your default name. To use an image, click Imported Graphic and then File to open a Select Picture dialog. Locate the file and click OK to close the dialog. You'll return to the Configure Signature Appearance dialog.

- Specify the text options you want to display in the Configure Text section of the dialog. All options are selected by default.

3. Click OK to close the Configure Signature Appearance dialog. The new signature appearance is added to the Appearance list. Click OK to close the Preferences dialog.

When you apply a digital signature (coming up in Tip 144), you can specify a particular appearance, or create a new one.

TIP 143 Certifying a Document

One way to maintain a PDF document as a legally correct document is to certify it. When you certify a PDF document, you're certifying the contents and specifying the types of changes allowed that maintain the certification. For example, a form may be certified and allow the user to fill in the fields; however, if the user tries to delete or replace pages, the document will no longer be certified. Certification is one way of using Digital IDs. Make sure you have finished modifying your document before certifying it. Otherwise, changes you make may corrupt the signature.

Choose File > Save as Certified Document and follow the wizard-like screens, starting with the introduction. To use a third-party security company, click Get Digital ID from Adobe Partner on the introductory screen; otherwise, proceed through the dialogs defining the type of certification and what actions you want to allow your users to take. You also define the visual characteristics of the signature, including its location on the page, and whether or not it is visible.

Here are some tips for making the certification process smoother:

- In the Choose Allowable Actions dialog (**Figure 143a**), specify the rights you want to grant the user. The pull-down list offers three options: you can prevent any changes from being made, allow users to fill out forms, or allow users to both comment and fill out forms. Also specify if you want to lock the certifying signature.

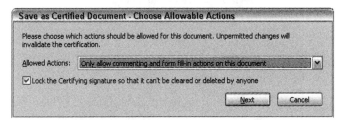

Figure 143a Decide what actions you want your readers to access when certifying a document.

- The Warnings dialog describes document features that may compromise the integrity of the document. In **Figure 143b**, for example, the warning mentions the use of comments, which were allowed in the previous dialog.

(Continued)

Signing and Saving

Here are some tips to keep in mind as you incorporate digital signatures as part of your Acrobat workflow:

- If you aren't completely sure the document is finished, don't click Sign and Save; instead, click Sign and Save As. Save the document with another name, and preserve the original unsigned in case you decide to make changes before distributing the document.

- Don't try to save the document with another name after the certification is complete. Saving is not allowed at this point.

- You cannot encrypt a document if it already contains signatures. If you want to share a document that has been signed, either use an unsigned copy or remove the signatures. To delete the signatures, click the Options menu in the Signatures pane and click Clear All Signature Fields.

- In order to use a document in a review process, you should certify the document to allow commenting and form fill-in.

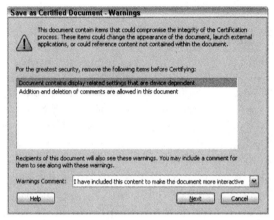

Figure 143b Acrobat informs you of any potential issues that can occur as a result of the rights you grant to your users.

- In the Save as Certified Document dialog, choose options for the actual signature used in the certification process (**Figure 143c**). Click Show/Hide Options `Show Options >>` to toggle additional options on the dialog so you can choose the signature appearance, reason for signing, and other options (see the previous tip). If you wish, you can click New on this dialog and create a new appearance.

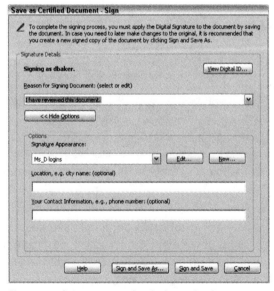

Figure 143c Select a reason for signing and a signature appearance to use for the certification process.

Once a document is certified, you can find out certification information from the document itself. When the document is opened, you'll see a Certified Document icon ⬛ at the left of the status bar. Hold your pointer over the icon, and a message appears telling you that the document is certified. Click the certified document icon to open a dialog that describes the document's status. The dialog explains that the document has special security features, and contains buttons for accessing legal and signature information.

You can also find information about the document's status in the Signature pane. Click the Signatures tab on the Navigation tabs to open the pane (**Figure 4d**). Information about the document, its status, signature dates, encryption method, and so on are listed in the pane.

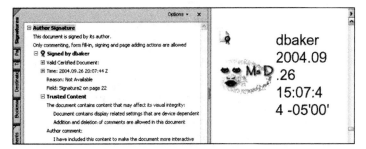

Figure 143d The Signatures pane describes all the information you selected in the certification process; the stamp applied to the document at the right of the figure shows the custom appearance, as well as the Certification symbol.

Certification Tips

The document certification process can be intricate. Smooth your way by keeping these ideas in mind:

- A document that can be modified is potentially dangerous. The document is said to have "malicious potential." In the Signatures pane, information about the potential problems is included with other signature information.

- Plan as you work your way through the Certification dialogs. You can't go back and change any options in previous dialogs. If you need to make changes before you have finished the certification process, click Cancel on any dialog and start over.

TIP 143: Certifying a Document

Adding a Signature Field and Signing a Document

If you are the creator of a document, you can certify it with a digital signature, as shown in the previous tip. You can also sign a document as part of a review process, specifying whether you are the author or have reviewed the document, and so on.

Instead of adding a single certifying signature, you add a blank signature field, which is a specialized type of form field. You can use the same field for collecting signatures from others.

To add a signature field, follow these steps:

1. Activate the Digital Signature Field tool. You can choose a menu option or select the tool directly:

   • Click the Sign task button **Sign ▾** to display its menu. (To display the Sign task button, choose View > Task Buttons > Sign.) Choose Create a Blank Signature Field from the menu, and Acrobat activates the Digital Signature Field tool.

2. Next, draw a signature field on your document (**Figure 144a**). The Digital Signature Properties dialog opens.

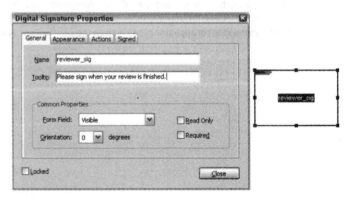

Figure 144a Draw a field for a signature on a document to open this dialog.

3. Type a name for your field in the Name text box on the General tab, also shown in Figure 143a, and then specify whether you want the field to be visible or invisible. Click Locked at the bottom left of the dialog if you want to lock the signature field to prevent changes after you sign the document.

Note
I always supply a tool tip as well. When recipients move their mouse over the field, they see a prompt to sign the document. Tool tips serve as good reminders.

4. Choose other characteristics for the signature field if required:

- On the Appearance tab, choose options for the field's display, such as color and line thickness.

- Choose a trigger and actions from the Actions tab.

- Click the Signed tab and select options for the document's function as the field is signed (**Figure 144b**). (Read the sidebar "More Digital Signatures Properties.")

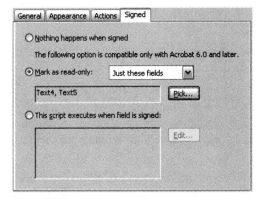

Figure 144b In addition to setting appearance and action options, you can specify how your document behaves once it is signed.

5. Click Close to dismiss the dialog and complete the signature field. The new signature field and its characteristics are listed in the Signature pane.

6. Save the document with its signature field.

(Continued)

More Digital Signatures Properties

The Digital Signatures Properties dialog includes two more tabs: Actions and Signed. The Actions tab lets you add mouse actions to the signature field. For example, you can set an action to have the user go to another page in the document when he or she clicks the signature field. (See Chapter 12 for tips on using triggers and actions.) The Signed tab includes options that let you reset fields as read-only or execute a custom JavaScript. The options on this tab are compatible with Acrobat 6 and 7 only.

TIP 144: Adding a Signature Field and Signing a Document

When you move the pointer over the field's location on the page, it changes to a pointing hand, and the tool tip added in the dialog appears (**Figure 144c**).

Please sign when your review is finished. (click to sign)

Figure 144c Add a tool tip to display information for your reviewers.

If you've created and originated the document, sign it as well. You can use a certification process (covered in Tip 142), or you can use the blank signature field and sign it. Click the field on the document and follow the signature prompts. When the process is complete, your signature appears in the field. Also, the information in the Signatures pane now includes the information about your signature (**Figure 144d**).

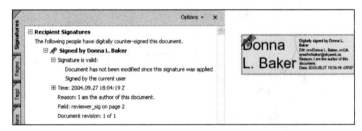

Figure 144d Read about the signature in the Signatures pane.

Notice the checkmark at the top left of the signature appearance. This checkmark indicates that the signature is valid. At the bottom left of the document status bar, you see a signed document icon ⬚. Hold the pointer over the icon to read the tool tips, and click the icon to read more information about the signature.

When you modify, close, and reopen the document, the signature information as well as its appearance will change, as you can see in **Figure 144e**. Instead of the checkmark at the upper left of the signature, you now see a question mark. In the Signatures pane, Acrobat tells you that the validity of the reviewer's signature is unknown. You may see the Modified Signature icon  overlaying the signature field after you validate the signature; in this case, the original signatory is still valid, but changes have been made since signing.

Figure 144e The question mark over the information means the validity of the signature has to be confirmed.

To check the validity of your signature (and that of others, coming up in the next tip):

1. Select a signature in the Signatures pane. Right-click/Control-click the signature or click the Signatures menu to open it.

2. Choose Validate Signature. The signature is tested, and Acrobat displays the results in a dialog (**Figure 144f**).

Signature Validation Status

Signature is VALID, signed by Donna L. Baker.
- The revision of the document that was covered by this signature has not been altered; however, there have been subsequent changes to the document.
- The document is signed by the current user.
- Click Signature Properties and then click View Signed Version to see what is covered by this signature.

[Legal Notice...] [Signature Properties...] [Close]

Figure 144f Acrobat displays the results of a signature validation in a dialog.

3. Click Close to dismiss the dialog, or click Legal Notice or Signature Properties to read more about the signature.

TIP 144: Adding a Signature Field and Signing a Document

Sending and Receiving Certificates

You can automatically include your certificates to add to your contact's list of trusted identities. Just click Include My Certificates. If you click this option, you have to choose a signature profile and enter your password in order to include the information in the email.

You can't open a document that has been signed by someone unless you have a copy of that individual's certificate. (Read about creating and customizing digital IDs in Tip 141.) Certificates you share with others are referred to as *trusted identities*. You can share your certificates with others working in a group or review process. Begin by choosing Advanced > Trusted Identities. The Manage Trusted Identities dialog opens.

Acrobat lets you display the contents of your identities list in one of two ways: by using contacts or by displaying certificates (**Figure 145a**). Contacts are formal FDF files you exchange with someone else. You request an FDF (signature) file by email, and your contact sends back his or her FDF file.

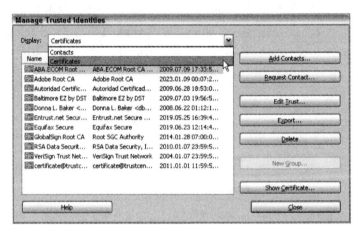

Figure 145a To create your Digital ID list, select either contacts or certificates to exchange with others.

A contact is secure as you go through a formal data exchange process, but an extracted certificate is much quicker. Rather than having to email people and request their certificate, you just extract it from a document they have sent to you.

1. Select a certificate or contact from the list to send that person your certificate information, or to save a copy of your certificate to your hard drive or other storage location, and then click Export. The Data Exchange File - Exporting Contact Information dialog opens (**Figure 145b**).

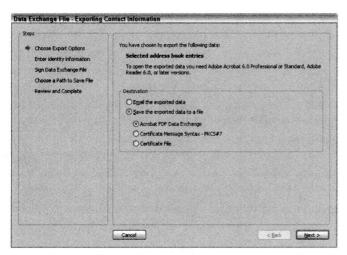

Figure 145b In this dialog, define how you want to export the certificate information.

2. Choose the email radio button to export the data file, or choose the Save the data to a file radio button and select a file type to export the information. In either case, a series of wizard screens will walk you through the process.

You can also ask others to share their certificates with you. Start the process in a similar way to the sharing process:

1. Choose Advanced > Trusted Identities. The Manage Trusted Identities dialog opens as shown in Figure 145a.

2. Click Request Contact. The Email a Request dialog opens.

3. Type your name and email address. You can choose to email the request or save it as a file to send later. Click Next and proceed through the wizard-like dialogs.

When you have assembled contacts and certificates, you can distribute a document to a restricted list of users. (Read about recipients in the sidebar "Naming Names" in Tip 147).

TIP 145: Sharing and Importing Digital IDs

Comparing Documents

What Are You Comparing?

Click the pull-down arrow and choose a level of Page by Page visual comparison. The default is the detailed analysis (shown in Figure 146b); choose Normal or Coarse. These alternate choices still display the same information but in less detail. For example, in the sample document, the extra signature fields are circled individually using a Detailed analysis, and circled as a group in a Coarse analysis. You can access these tools in the Compare Documents dialog, which is described on page 375.

What if you have had several signatures on a document and have granted users rights to change the content as the workflow progresses? How can you keep track of who has done what to your document? Simple. Acrobat includes a neat feature that allows you to compare documents based on signatures. Each time a document is signed by another person, a copy of the document as it exists when they signed it is appended to the original document, which allows you to view changes.

You can do a quick comparison from the Signatures pane. To quickly compare one version of a signed document to another, open the document and display the Signatures pane. Select a signature that you want to use as the basis for the comparison. Right-click/ Control-click to open the shortcut menu and choose Compare Signed Version to Current Version, choose the command from the pane's Options menu, or right-click/Control-click the signature field on the document to open the shortcut menu and choose the command.

Acrobat processes the document versions, and opens a new PDF document showing the results—save the document if you want to keep the comparison report for future reference. In the sample comparison report shown in **Figure 146a**, changes were made by three different people, who also signed the document. When the third version was compared to the original, the report document briefly defined the differences.

```
Page by Page Comparison


Documents Compared
  tip14b.pdf
   Current Version
  tip14b.pdf
   Signature1, Signed by Donna L. Baker, 2004.09.27 19:23:53 Z


Summary
  1 page(s) differ
  2 page(s) added
```

Figure 146a You can compare two versions of a signed document. The report document includes a summary of the changes.

Scrolling through the document shows the pages of the two signed versions side by side; differences are circled on each version (**Figure 146b**).

Signature version

Font changes identified

Comment changes identified

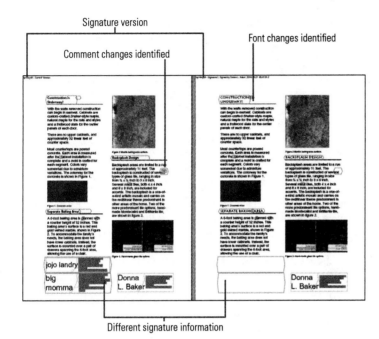

Different signature information

Figure 146b Scroll through the document to see the differences between the versions. The signature version information is shown at the top of each page.

If you want more control over the comparison report, or want to compare two documents regardless of they are signed, choose Document > Compare Documents to open the Compare Documents dialog (**Figure 146c**). In this dialog you can select the pair of documents from the Compare and To pull-down lists; use the same document and choose two versions from the Revision pull-down lists.

• Choose a page-by-page comparison type (described in the sidebar) or choose Textual differences if you want to see changes made in fonts or text; you can't use font information in a consolidated report.

(Continued)

TIP 146: Comparing Documents

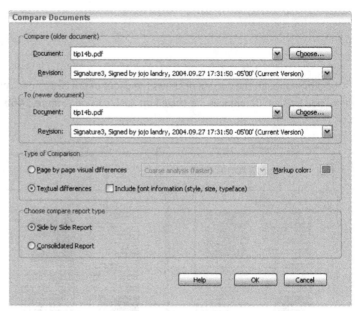

Figure 146c Choose options to use to compare documents. You can choose different documents, or different versions of the same document.

- Choose the report type. The default is shown in Figure 146b, showing the pages side by side. A consolidated report, on the other hand, shows the comparison information on one copy in a note (**Figure 146d**).

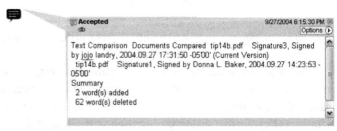

Figure 146d A consolidated report shows you basic analysis results in a note comment.

Click OK to close the dialog and compare the documents. The next time you want to make a comparison, the previous options remain selected in the dialog.

TIP 147 Creating Security Policies

Does your workflow require you to add security to documents using the same settings over and over? Tiring, isn't it? Acrobat 7 Professional has combined all your security management needs into dialogs that you use to create a policy and then apply it as often as you need. Security policies work in a very similar way to building and using styles for text, and you can create policies for passwords and certificates. If you work in an enterprise environment, you may have Adobe Policy Server, a separate Adobe Server product that manages security policies.

Click the Secure task button and choose Manage Security Policies or choose Document > Security > Manage Security Policies to open the Managing Security Policies dialog. Click New [New] to open the New Security Policy dialog. The steps involved in creating each of three types of policy are listed at the left of the dialog.

Each of the three types has different requirements and customizations. All types use the same initial pane for choosing a security type, all use a General settings pane, and all have a Summary pane at the end of the dialog:

- For password security, click the Use passwords radio button at the right of the dialog; the customization pane is used to set document restrictions.

- For public key encryption, click the Use public key certificates radio button; the steps include one pane you use to select recipients.

- For policy server encryption, click the Use the Adobe Policy Server radio button; the steps include a pane to choose recipient permissions.

For each type of security, click the appropriate radio button to choose a type of security on the first pane of the dialog. Follow through the wizard-like dialogs to complete the policy. Click Cancel at the bottom of the dialog at any time to close the dialog.

(Continued)

Naming Names

When you are creating certificate policies, decide in advance if you want to generate policies for a specific group of people on a regular basis, or if you need to send documents to different people at different times. You can save a lot of time by planning in advance. In the General settings pane for writing a Public Key certificate policy, shown in Figure 147b, once you name and describe the policy, check the option to Ask for recipients when applying this policy if you want to generate a different list of recipients each time you apply the policy; deselect the option if you plan to use the policy to circulate material to the same group of people on a regular basis.

Policy Servers

There are three types of policy server you can use with Acrobat. All are available by choosing Advanced > Security Settings to open the Security Settings dialog. Settings and access to these servers is controlled by your systems administrator:

- Directory server—The VeriSign Internet Directory server is a system used for third-party signatures and encryption. Rather than exchanging certificates with individuals, your content is managed by the server.

- Time Stamp server—If your network or system allows for a time stamp server, you use the server's capabilities to authenticate time displayed in your documents' signatures.

- Adobe Policy server—This Adobe-hosted server controls access to your document using named users, and can track document access, versions, set dates on documents, and apply watermarks and expiration dates.

Here are some tips to keep in mind as you construct and work with policies:

- Regardless of the type of policy you are creating, make sure to add information on the General settings pane of the dialog (**Figure 147a**) as it is used to display the policy in the list of policies.

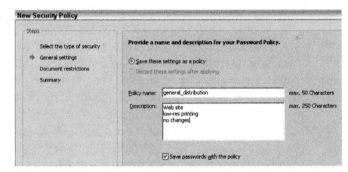

Figure 147a When the name and description of the policies you create are meaningful to you, it's simpler to work with security settings.

- When you are creating password policies, be aware of the password inclusion option on the General settings pane. Deselect Save passwords with the policy, shown in Figure 147a, if you want to specify a password and restrictions whenever you use the policy; leave the option selected if you want to store the passwords within the policy's information.

- Choose an encryption method in keeping both with your users and what you need to secure. For example, unless your users have Acrobat 7 or Adobe Reader 7, they can't use the AES-encryption option that lets you secure only attachments; unless your users have Acrobat 6 or Adobe Reader 6 or newer, you can't exclude metadata from the secure document components (**Figure 147b**).

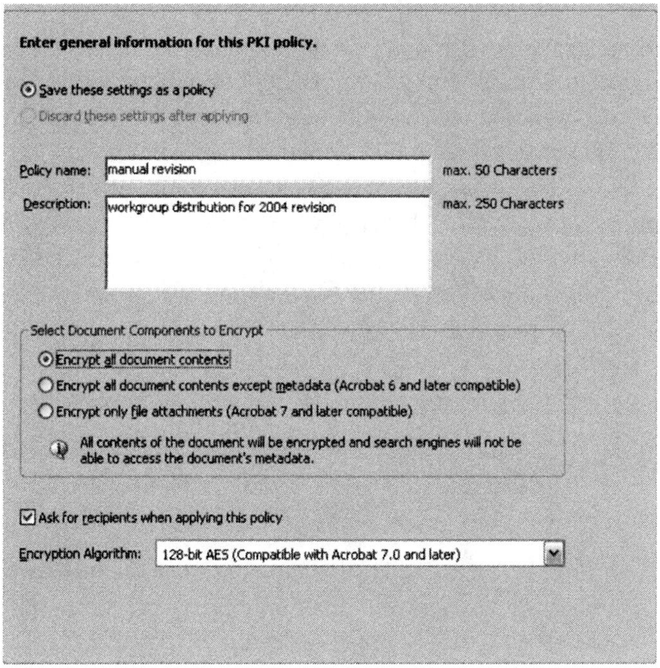

Enter general information for this PKI policy.

⦿ Save these settings as a policy

◯ Discard these settings after applying

Policy name: manual revision   max. 50 Characters

Description: workgroup distribution for 2004 revision   max. 250 Characters

┌ Select Document Components to Encrypt ─────────────────────────────────┐
⦿ Encrypt all document contents
◯ Encrypt all document contents except metadata (Acrobat 6 and later compatible)
◯ Encrypt only file attachments (Acrobat 7 and later compatible)

   ⓘ All contents of the document will be encrypted and search engines will not be
      able to access the document's metadata.
└──┘

☑ Ask for recipients when applying this policy

Encryption Algorithm: 128-bit AES (Compatible with Acrobat 7.0 and later) ▼

Figure 147b Make sure the encryption level you choose for your documents corresponds with your users' capabilities for reading them.

TIP 147: Creating Security Policies

TIP 148 Using and Managing Security Policies

Acrobat 7 Professional provides one interface to manage all the security in your documents. If you want to add security to a document, choose Document > Security > Secure This Document or click the Secure task button and choose the command from the pull-down menu. The Select a Policy to Apply dialog opens, listing the policies available to use. Here, you can create new policies [New], copy an existing policy [Copy], view its contents [View], or refresh policies [Refresh] that are stored on the Adobe Policy Server.

If you have a large number of policies, you can filter the list for ease of use. Click the Show pull-down menu, shown in **Figure 148a**, and select to display only organizational or user policies. Click a policy from the list at the top of the dialog to view its details at the bottom of the dialog. Click Apply and follow the sequence of dialogs and prompts to secure the document.

Figure 148a Select a filter to modify your list of policies.

When you want to work with your policies, such as changing the permissions or passwords within an existing policy, use the Managing Security Policies dialog instead to access additional options. Choose Document > Security > Manage Security Policies, click the Secure task button, and choose the command from the pull-down menu to open the dialog (**Figure 148b**).

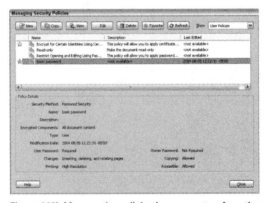

Figure 148b Manage the policies in your system from the Managing Security Policies dialog.

Both security policy dialogs are quite similar; in the Managing Security Policies dialog you can also edit an existing policy. Click the policy in the list and then click Edit on the dialog's toolbar. A sequence of dialogs appears; their content depends on the type of policy you select. Click Delete to remove an existing policy from your system; read about using Favorites in the sidebar.

Regardless of the method you use to encrypt or secure a document, you can change or remove the protection from within Acrobat if you have the rights:

1. Choose File > Document Properties > Security.

2. In the Security pane, click the Security Method pull-down arrow and choose No Security (**Figure 148c**). Click OK to close the Document Properties dialog.

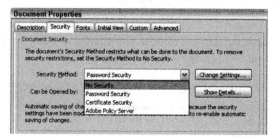

Figure 148c You can remove or change document security in the Document Properties dialog.

3. The confirmation dialog opens. Click OK to confirm that you want to delete the security and remove the passwords from the document.

It's One of My Favorites

In many workflows, you often use the same policy over and over. Rather than opening the dialogs and choosing the policy, save a couple of mouse clicks and define a policy as a favorite. In the Managing Security Policies dialog, click the policy in the listing at the top of the dialog, and then click Favorite ⭐ Favorite on the dialog's toolbar. Any policies you define as Favorites show a star at the left of their listing in the dialog. When you close the policies dialog, the next time you need to secure a document, your favorite is listed on the Secure task button's pull-down menu.

Make It Personal

You can create other templates to use for the eEnvelope. Create and save a document as a PDF. Then store it in this location: Program Files\Adobe\Acrobat\ DocTemplates\ENU. The next time you want to create an eEnvelope, your custom template is included in the list; select it as you work through the wizard.

149 Using Secure ePaper

One of the coolest new features in Acrobat 7 Professional is the ability to "wrap" your document and other files you choose to include, regardless of their file format, in a secure envelope for distributing to others. eEnvelopes even look like envelopes!

Suppose you have a bank loan application and have to include a record or employment or some other personal document with the application. Simply embed the attachments in an eEnvelope, encrypt the eEnvelope using a password or certificate security method, and then email it. Only the person with rights to open the eEnvelope can see the contents.

Encryption using an eEnvelope doesn't modify the file attachments in any way; once your recipients extract the file attachments and save them, the files are no longer encrypted.

You apply an eEnvelope using a wizard:

1. Choose Document > Security > Secure PDF Delivery, or click the Secure task button and choose the command from the pull-down menu to open the wizard (**Figure 149a**).

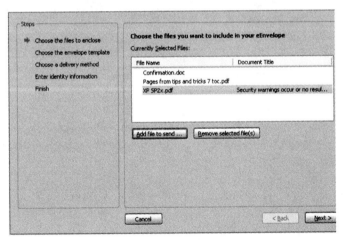

Figure 149a Use an eEnvelope to securely send documents.

2. Step through the wizard:

- Select documents to attach.

- Choose a template—**Figure 149b** shows examples of each of the three available templates.

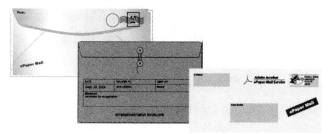

Figure 149b Use one of the available templates or create your own.

- Attach a security policy (Click Show All Policies on this frame of the wizard to display your list).

- Choose either to complete the process manually (see the sidebar, "Do It Yourself"), or complete the eEnvelope and email it.

- Add identity information for the eEnvelope; the provided templates include fields for adding names, dates, or text messages.

- Click Finished to close the dialog.

3. Enter your recipient's email address in the email dialog that opens, and click Send to send it on its way.

Once your recipient receives the email, the eEnvelope is shown as an attachment. The recipient can't open the attachment without the proper permissions, such as entering the password used to encrypt the eEnvelope.

(Continued)

Which Is Which?

If you intend to use the program's templates, take a minute and rename the files. Open the document folder (the path is shown in the "Make it Personal" sidebar), and then open the three template PDF files. Rename them using names you recognize, and save them with the new name in the same folder. The next time you want to secure a document, it's simpler to choose the right template using your custom names.

TIP 149: Using Secure ePaper

If you are working with the Adobe Policy Server, you can apply the eEnvelope process directly through your email program. In Outlook, open an email message window, and click Attach as Secured PDF 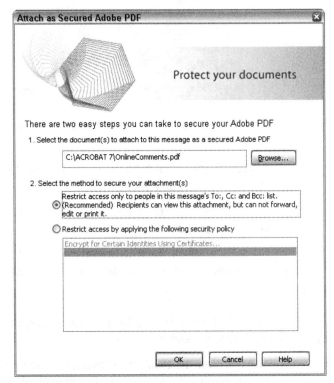 on the Standard toolbar. In the Attach as Secured PDF dialog, choose the file you want to send, and then select a security option (**Figure 149c**). You can either restrict opening to the names listed in the To and CC fields of the email, or select a policy and click OK. The document attachment to the email displays as usual, but (Secure) appears in the attachment's name. Repeat to add documents, and then send the email.

Figure 149c Attach a secured document to an email if you are working with Adobe Policy Server.

TIP 150 Troubleshooting Security

Working with security policies can be confusing at first. It gets easier the more you work with them. To help you along the way, here are some troubleshooting tips:

- Make sure the members of a review group all have the same sets of certificates; a missing certificate results in an unknown signature. You can get certificate information directly from a signature to use to validate that signature. Verify that the reason the signature isn't validating is not simply that the certificate is missing. Right-click/Control-click the signature appearance on the document and choose Validate Signature. The Signature Validation Unknown dialog opens, describing why the signature can't be validated. Click Signature Properties to open the Signature Properties dialog (**Figure 150a**). At the right of the Summary tab, shown by default when the dialog opens, click Show Certificate. When the Certificate Viewer dialog opens, click the Trust tab, and then click Add to Trusted Identities (**Figure 150b**). Follow the prompts to add the certificate to your list and verify the signature.

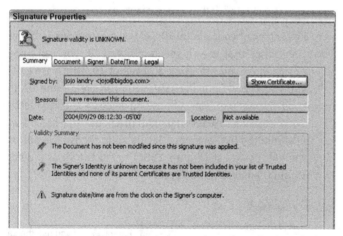

Figure 150a If a certificate is missing, or you haven't received one from a colleague, you see an unknown status for a signature.

(Continued)

Who Are You Today?

When you create a policy you specify which of your digital IDs can access the document. Be careful with your selection. If you choose one digital ID and a method of application when building a policy, you have to use the same settings to open the document to which you applied the encryption; otherwise you can't open your own document!

Select a Digital ID from the listing at the top of the Document Security - Digital ID Selection dialog, included in the wizard-like sequence of dialogs used to create an encryption policy. Check the options at the bottom of the dialog. In the Digital ID Selection Persistence section of the dialog, choose an option:

- Ask me which Digital ID to use next time, which is the default. When you choose this option, each time you click a signature field the Apply Digital Signature dialog opens.

- Use this Digital ID until I close the application is a useful option if you are in a workflow where you are reviewing, commenting, modifying, and signing documents.

- Choose Always use this Digital ID if you work with one signature all the time.

TIP 150: Troubleshooting Security

Saving Signed Files in a Browser

You can sign a document in a browser, but it is stored differently than a signed document on your hard drive. Click Sign to sign a document in your browser; only the portion of the document that changed from the previous signature until you signed it is automatically saved to your hard drive. If you want the entire document, sign the document, and then click Save a Copy on the Acrobat toolbar.

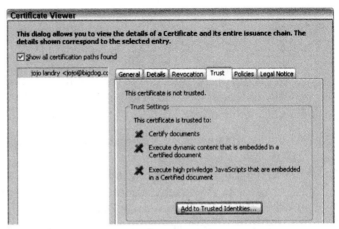

Figure 150b Add a Trusted Identity to your system using a signature's certificate.

- Don't make a habit of using the certificates from signatures. If you have to use one, such as when you are offline, ask the person to send you a certificate file as soon as it is convenient or practical.

- If you plan to use a signature field for users working with Adobe Reader, you have to add a blank signature field to the document. Choose Sign > Sign This Document or click the signature field and follow the prompts.

- Keep track of your Digital IDs. If you create a public key encryption policy that uses a specific Digital ID, you can't open the document if you are using a different ID, which isn't good for your workflow! In many cases, you can create one ID and use it on an ongoing basis. Choose Advanced > Security Settings to open the Security Settings dialog. Choose the ID you want to use from the list, and click Set Default; choose the option from the pull-down list (**Figure 150c**) to set the ID as a default for signing, encrypting, or both.

Figure 150c If you use the same signature all the time, make it your default.

APPENDIX A

Other Sources of Information

This appendix contains a list of URLs referenced in this book, as well as other sources of information you may find useful in your work.

Adobe Sites

These URLs link to information/resource sites at Adobe:

- **Adobe Studio (requires login and ID):**
  http://studio.adobe.com/expertcenter/acrobat/main.html

- **Acrobat Support Knowledgebase:**
  www.adobe.com/support/products/acrobat.html

- **User-to-User Forum/Macintosh:**
  www.adobeforums.com/cgi-bin/webx?14@@.ee6b2ed
  (You must create a user account and login to access the site).

- **User-to-User Forum/Windows:**
  www.adobeforums.com/cgi-bin/webx?14@@.ee6b2f2
  (You must create a user account and login to access the site).

- **Downloads for Windows and Macintosh:**
  www.adobe.com/support/downloads/main.html

Information Sites

These sites offer valuable information on the PDF file format:

- **Planet PDF:** Information on all things PDF; offers a very active user-to-user forum. www.planetpdf.com.

- **PDFzone:** Another large PDF and document management site. www.pdfzone.com.

- **Creativepro.com:** Offers articles, reviews, and other information for designers. www.creativepro.com.

System Requirements and Installation

Make sure your computer meets the minimum system requirements for operating Acrobat 7.0 Professional. There are several issues to consider when using Acrobat 7.0 Professional.

Installation Requirements

Windows

The minimum and recommended system requirements for using Acrobat 7.0 Professional and Adobe Reader 7.0 on Windows systems are:

- Intel Pentium processor

- Microsoft Windows 2000 with Service Pack 2, Windows XP Professional or Home Edition, or Windows XP Tablet PC Edition

- Internet Explorer 5.5 or greater

- 128 MB of RAM (256 MB or greater recommended)

- 510 MB of available hard disk space. Optional installation file cache requires additional 510 MB of hard disk space. Adobe Reader requires 35 MB of hard disk space

- 1,024x768 minimum screen resolution Adobe Reader requires 800x600 minimum screen resolution)

- CD-ROM drive

- Support for Internet Explorer 5.5, 6.0, 6.0 SP1 and Netscape 7.1 browsers

Macintosh

The minimum and recommended system requirements for using Acrobat 7.0 Professional and Adobe Reader 7.0 on Macintosh systems:

- PowerPC G3, G4, G5 processor

- Mac OS X v.10.2.8 or 10.3

- 128 MB of RAM (256 MB or greater recommended)

- 495 MB of available hard disk space; Adobe Reader 7.0 requires 35 MB of available hard disk space

- 1,024x768 minimum screen resolution; Adobe Reader 7.0 requires 800x600 screen resolution monitor

- CD-ROM drive

- Support for Safari 1.2.2 browser

Activation and Maintenance (Windows)

Acrobat 7.0 for Windows includes an activation process that is required in order to use the program. When you install the program, you are prompted to activate the software. The activation process can be done by Internet or by telephone. You can defer installation for up to 30 days after installing the program, which you can install on two computers.

If necessary, you can transfer the activation information. Choose Help > Transfer Activation and follow the steps in the dialog. You deactivate a copy of the program in order to install it elsewhere, such as when you transfer programs to a new computer.

Tools are available that you can use to help Acrobat integrate with other programs on your computer and to keep it running in top fashion:

- When installing Acrobat 7.0 Professional on Windows, the installation program asks if you would like to cache the program. Choose Yes to store a copy of the program on your hard drive, which comes in handy for repairing or updating your system; choose No if you don't want to use the hard-drive space for storage. The cache requires 510 MB of hard-drive space.

- If you install an application after installing Acrobat that can use a PDFMaker, choose Help > Detect and Repair from the Acrobat program menu; the PDFMaker is installed into the program automatically.

Index